Black Leadership

Black Leadership

Manning Marable

Columbia University Press

NEW YORK

Columbia University Press
Publishers Since 1893
New York   Chichester, West Sussex

Copyright © 1998 Columbia University Press

Library of Congress Cataloging-in-Publication Data
Marable, Manning
    Black leadership / Manning Marable.
        p.   cm.
    Includes bibliographical references and index.
    ISBN 0-231-10746-3 — ISBN 0-231-10747-1 (pbk.)
    1. Afro-American leadership. I. Title.
E185.615.M2783   1998
323.1'196073—dc21
                                                    97-32969

Casebound editions of Columbia University Press books are printed on
permanent and durable acid-free paper.
Printed in the United States of America
c 10 9 8 7 6 5 4 3 2 1
p 10 9 8 7 6 5 4 3 2 1

CONTENTS

ACKNOWLEDGMENTS

BLACK LEADERSHIP is the product of an intellectual and political journey toward an understanding of the political culture of black America. The articles presented here were written over a period of fifteen years. Most of them were originally published in academic journals or edited volumes. Several were prepared specifically for this volume. And a few were drafted in an essayist's style, without the usual documentation of footnotes or bibliography. I decided after some reflection to keep these last largely as they were, because the content and point of view expressed in them were closely connected to their style and language of presentation. Of course, the manuscript as a whole underwent extensive editing and revision.

The central concern of this book is an analysis of black leadership in the twentieth century. Three topics are of primary interest: ideology, culture, and politics. The intersection of these areas provides the foundation for exploration into some of the personalities that have given shape and substance to contemporary black America. The articles in this volume were never intended to represent a comprehensive overview of all major black American political figures. The omission of such prominent leaders and activists as Marcus Garvey, A. Philip Randolph, Ida B. Wells, Martin Luther King Jr., Ella Baker, Malcolm X, Fannie Lou Hamer, and Jesse Jackson in no way suggests their lack of significance. Similarly, a central theme that runs throughout the entire fabric of black politics and culture is the thought and leadership of African American women. One cannot and should not ignore or underestimate their powerful and poetic voices or their many contributions to the struggles for black freedom. Any detailed analysis of the Civil Rights Movement as it was actually organized at a community level illustrates that the effort was based largely on the work of African American women activists. The Montgomery bus boycott, to cite only one example, was sparked by the bold actions of Rosa Parks and was organized largely by Jo Ann Robinson. Martin Luther King Jr. was only the national spokesperson for this mobilization made possible by black women. Leith Mullings and I are currently at work on an anthology that explores in some detail the speeches, writings, and related political documents of many African American women leaders.

My limited objective here was to profile the ideas and leadership of four significant figures in the social and political history of black America: Booker T. Washington, W. E. B. Du Bois, Harold Washington, and Louis Farrakhan. These four leaders symbolically represented very distinct approaches to the problem of black empowerment in a predominantly white society. All of them operated within the contradictory context of a liberal democratic state and a market economy. Each took a different path in moving toward leadership for an oppressed community within this racialized social formation. The remaining essays examine other dimensions of the problem of leadership in American society, from the debates and compromises over slavery and race that were part of the adoption of the U.S. Constitution in 1787 to the current search for new directions by black Americans inside organized labor.

Every book is a product of many different contributions. I owe a special debt to my editor at Columbia University Press, Kate Wittenberg, who from the beginning of our early conversations several years ago about this book has provided strong support and constructive criticism. To Jan McInroy, I am indebted for her extraordinary ability in copyediting and for suggesting several important changes in the manuscript. A friend of many years, Linda Rocawich, was gracious enough to review the original drafts of the essays, especially those that had been previously published several years ago. As former editor of *Southern Exposure* and former managing editor of the *Progressive*, she possesses a clear understanding of the politics behind each of the essays. Her skillful editorial revisions and suggestions for the entire manuscript greatly improved its readability.

This book is also the most recent product of a research project supported by the Institute for Research in African-American Studies at Columbia University. Johanna Fernandez, a doctoral student in the Department of History, collected hundreds of articles and other reference materials that were essential to the development of the most recent essays. Angela Zivkovíc, my secretary at the institute during the academic year 1996–1997, typed and proofread the entire manuscript with care. Special thanks are also due Daria Oliver, my executive assistant at the institute, who gave me the space and time to complete this book, and Theresa Wilcox, who provided secretarial support during the final stages of copyediting and last-minute revisions.

Finally, and most important, I owe my greatest debt of thanks to Leith Mullings. Three years ago, most of the articles in this book were part of a much larger collection of my historical, cultural, and political writings. Leith suggested that I divide the essays thematically and topically into two very different works. The first volume, *Beyond Black and White*, was published in 1995. This second volume is dedicated to her. As my intellectual partner and political companion, she continues to open new doors to my mind and spirit.

Leadership in Black America

SEPARATED BY ALMOST EXACTLY one century, two significant public events captured the essential problematic of black leadership in white America. The first was Booker T. Washington's Atlanta Compromise address of September 1895, which endorsed the "separate but equal" doctrine, spelling the end of the brief experiment in biracial democracy throughout the South. The second was Louis Farrakhan's Million Man March of October 1995, which called upon African American men to "atone" and to assume greater leadership within their communities. To most historians and political scientists, these two prominent figures in twentieth-century black America appear to represent two fundamentally different visions about the politics of race. At the time of Washington's address, he was widely praised for his conciliatory remarks and accommodation to racial segregation. As the founder of the Tuskegee Institute, one of the nation's largest agricultural and vocational training schools for Negroes, Washington symbolically reassured white America that blacks would not challenge its institutions. In contrast, in 1995 most white observers were perplexed and unsure of how to respond to the mass spectacle of a million black men who had been summoned to Washington, D.C., by the head of the Nation of Islam. For many, Farrakhan remained a racial demagogue, an advocate of hate.

Superficially, Washington and Farrakhan seem at opposite ends of the political spectrum. But beneath their rhetoric, similar basic principles and goals characterized their worldviews. Both individuals came into public prominence at times when racial liberalism was declining and when policies designed to safeguard civil rights and economic opportunities for blacks were being dismantled. Both preached the doctrine of black self-help, relying on resources found within black communities for group development, rather than government handouts. Both were convinced that African American entrepreneurship and property ownership held the keys to black economic advancement. Washington and Farrakhan both, to varying degrees, favored the conservative economic and social policies of the Republican Party. These parallels don't make Booker T. Washington a black nationalist separatist or Louis Farrakhan an accommodationist. They do, however, illustrate that the underlying dynamics of blacks' collective efforts to achieve empowerment have been remarkably consistent for a century. The striking similarities of the two leaders' public positions have little to do with their personalities, which were extremely different. Rather, both men recognized and tried to address through their respective organizations and political alliances the structural problems of inequality and marginalization that every oppressed people suffers within a racialized state and society.

Simply stated, the central political dilemma that has confronted black America for several centuries now is whether and how the principles and practices of liberal democracy can be extended and guaranteed to black people. This question actually centers around two concepts: freedom and equality. Both were effectively denied to African Americans within the U.S. Constitution as well as within the institution of slavery. During Reconstruction, the promise of freedom finally existed. Black men won the right to vote and became active in public affairs. Black Reconstruction established schools and social and economic programs that benefited both racial groups. Nevertheless, it would still take another century, filled with suffering and struggle, to achieve the basic freedoms and democratic rights that most white Americans took for granted. And then, after that Second Reconstruction, black people still questioned whether their newly won political rights could lead to greater socioeconomic parity. Freedom without genuine equality of material conditions seemed empty, devoid of real meaning. Could African Americans devise a plan to utilize their collective resources, to more effectively address the structural crises that manifested themselves in the hundreds of social and economic problems that plagued their communities? Or was it possible to persuade a significant segment of the white population—workers, intellectuals, liberals, and others—that the black community's historical struggle to enrich and expand the meaning of democracy, the egalitarian quest for social justice, was also in its interests? These and other unresolved questions have been the terrain upon which nearly all black leaders and social movements have sought practical solutions.

The leaders who have come from a series of black political and social movements in the twentieth century represent very different personalities, organizational affiliations, and political ideologies. There is, however, one powerful model or tradition of leadership that has evolved within black political culture. To some extent, this tradition has been characterized by a charismatic or dominating political style. A number of black personalities have possessed a powerful, magnetic presence and the ability to articulate deeply held grievances and hopes among their people. Often these figures have had considerable organizational skills and have inspired groups that then promoted their ideas. Styles of charismatic leadership are amply represented in black political life: Frederick Douglass, Booker T. Washington, A. Philip Randolph, Marcus Garvey, Elijah Muhammad, Malcolm X, Martin Luther King Jr., Jesse Jackson. Some years ago, in my book *Black American Politics*, I characterized this approach to leadership as the "black messianic" style. The political culture of black America since slavery was heavily influenced by the Bible, particularly the Old Testament saga of Moses and Joshua as "deliverers" of an oppressed, enslaved people who found themselves in a foreign land. The harsh material circumstances of black survival and struggle contributed to a merger of the secular and the spiritual: messianic leadership expressed itself as the ability to communicate effectively programs that in some measure represented the interests of most blacks, while also constructing bonds of collective intimacy through appeals to the spirituality and religiosity among many African American people.

The political culture of the segregated South after slavery reinforced the messianic and autocratic leadership tendencies within the black community. The principal social institution within every black community was the church. Ministers occupied both spiritual and secular roles. As religious leaders they inspired and motivated the faithful by their examples. The churches were often social service and economic institutions, providing goods and services to a wide constituency, and successful ministers had to develop practical organizational skills. But as political leaders, the black clergy were usually the primary spokespersons for the entire black community, especially during periods of crisis. As the political system became more democratic and as more blacks were permitted to participate in voting, it was only a small shift from running a large church to running for public office. With hundreds and sometimes thousands of devout church members, black ministers could employ their religious constituency like a

secular political organization. Almost inevitably, black political organizations modeled themselves along the lines of African American churches:
rigid, patriarchal hierarchies with women largely confined to lower-level
organizational tasks; mass meetings designed to galvanize support and enthusiasm for the leadership's objectives; public recognition ceremonies for
individual members, which helped to cement the intimate personal and
political bonds with the leadership; strict sanctions, such as isolation and
expulsion, for members who challenged or questioned the group's public
positions and stated ideology; and the cultural and social construction of
the benevolent, committed leader who operated almost above the masses,
a visionary who sought to bend history toward his objectives.

Turning again to Booker T. Washington and Louis Farrakhan, we find
striking similarities between these two men. Washington was the most
powerful black leader of his era and arguably the most influential black
politician within the context of state power in the twentieth century. His
authority came not just from the philanthropic, corporate, and political
elites, which approved of his accommodationist policies and acquiescence
to Jim Crow. He also won considerable popular support among black
farmers and entrepreneurs through organizations like the National Negro
Business League. The league's annual meetings had something of the
character of evangelical revivals, as individuals were presented with rib-
bons and rewards for their personal achievements. Washington used his
resources to advance the careers of his supporters among the masses
through the ownership or control of black newspapers. Farrakhan's immediate constituency is the Nation of Islam, a core of dedicated believers who
have faith in the organization's doctrines and have been trained to obey di-
rectives. For Farrakhan's larger constituency, his charismatic image and
popularity among many youth and an increasingly nationalistic segment of
the black middle class are aggressively promoted by a flood of publications, video- and audiotapes, and other consumer items. Farrakhan consciously packages himself for black audiences as "one of their own," as a
powerful and uncompromising leader who operates solely in the interests
of African Americans. The charismatic, autocratic style of these leaders
permitted both to make assorted deals and compromises with powerful
white Republicans and conservative interests, while keeping their core
constituencies safely in check.

An excellent insight toward an understanding of black leadership is provided by civil rights activist Ella Baker. As a former field secretary of the
NAACP and the director of the Southern Christian Leadership Conference's
national office during the Second Reconstruction, Baker worked closely

with Martin Luther King Jr., Ralph David Abernathy, Andrew Young, Walter Fauntroy, and other leaders. From her practical experiences she concluded that it was preferable to promote the development of "group-centered leaders" rather than "leader-centered groups." For that reason, Baker was critical of King's charismatic style and the patriarchal, hierarchical politics of the SCLC. She recommended to the idealistic young activists who were forming the Student Nonviolent Coordinating Committee (SNCC) in 1960 that they should cultivate a more egalitarian, participatory approach to politics. As historian Clayborne Carson observed in a 1994 article in *Black Scholar*: "The most successful SNCC projects unleashed the power of communities, allowing residents to become confident of their collective ability to overcome oppression. . . . The most effective organizers of the 1960s realized that their job was to work themselves out of a job. They avoided replacing old dependencies with new ones."

The politics of a Harold Washington can be placed somewhere in the middle of the continuum, between the charismatic paternalism of Booker T. Washington and Louis Farrakhan and the transformationist, egalitarian politics of SNCC. Throughout much of his public career, Harold Washington was a member of one of the most corrupt political machines in American history, the Cook County Democratic Party organization. He thought of politics largely in pragmatic terms, as the art of the possible. Yet he became the spokesperson for a strong social movement for political reform and democratic empowerment, based in the black and brown urban communities of Chicago. Washington's 1983 and 1987 campaigns for mayor were not politics-as-usual but an outgrowth of grassroots mobilization with the goal of utilizing elections to achieve social change. As I later argue in this book, Washington's victories came to symbolize for millions of blacks and other progressive people throughout the country the possibility of expanding and redefining electoral politics for the empowerment of working-class and poor people.

But despite the strengths of this urban movement, it also exhibited major contradictions. Washington had been trained in a paternalistic, autocratic style of leadership, which profoundly affected his political behavior and decision making. Instead of harnessing the tremendous energy and activism generated by the electoral defeat of the local Democratic machine by training and advancing new "group-centered leaders," he retained his primary commitment to practical politics. In Chicago, as elsewhere, that meant taking positions and enforcing policies that sometimes were against his constituents' best interests. His charismatic, dominating public personality became the cultural epoxy that bound together constituencies divided by racialized ethnicity, gender, sexual orientation, language, nationality, and class. When Washington died suddenly in late 1987 his movement immediately stalled, then died.

W. E. B. Du Bois represents a very different kind of leadership model. Unlike Booker T. Washington and Louis Farrakhan, he never commanded political or religious organizations. He was never personally comfortable with the informalities and public conversations that effective politics requires. Unlike Harold Washington's, Du Bois's venture into electoral politics, at the height of McCarthyism and the Cold War, was unsuccessful. To those who did not know him well, he seemed aloof and arrogant. Even his closest friends, such as educator John Hope, had difficulty understanding him. Du Bois worked for twenty-four years to build a national organization, the NAACP, but he lacked the skill and ability to save his position or to rally his supporters when the leadership behind Walter White pressured him to resign in 1934.

What Du Bois did accomplish, more than any other black leader, was to remake and define how his people would interpret and understand the world and themselves. Du Bois was a leader of ideas, not of organizations and institutions. He first thought that social change would be possible if scholars simply investigated social problems and came up with solutions. Racism was largely a product of ignorance, and the remedy was to be found in education and legal reforms. Gradually, Du Bois came to the conclusion that beneath the color line of phenotypic and social differences lay a greater structure of class and economic interests. As he researched *Black Reconstruction*, he came to understand that it was the masses of oppressed human beings, not a privileged "Talented Tenth," who through their struggles could make new history. Du Bois also knew that black social thought should not be defined or restricted by the rigid criteria of traditional academic disciplines. He had been trained at Harvard and Berlin as a historian, but he also continued to produce sociological studies, political essays, journalistic commentaries, plays, and poetry. For Du Bois, intellectual leadership was profoundly cultural, in the broadest sense of the term: to encourage and suggest new patterns of thought and life.

Leaders are essentially individuals who have the ability to understand their own times, who express or articulate programs or policies that reflect the perceived interests and desires of particular groups, and who devise instruments or political vehicles that enhance the capacity to achieve effective change. In very limited ways, leaders imprint their personal characteristics or individual stamp on a given moment in time. Leaders do make history, but never by themselves, and never in ways that they fully recognize or anticipate. The social forces that define all historical conjunctures create the opportunities or spaces for talented individuals to make themselves heard above others. For relatively brief moments, they may create an illusion that it is they, and not the vast majority, who determine the possibilities of the future. Black leaders have given their own particular style and language to various phases and moments of American history, and they will continue to do so. But it may be the measurement of our ability to achieve a full redefinition of America's democratic project if over time black Americans are able to move away from the charismatic, authoritarian leadership style and paternalistic organizations toward the goal of "group-centered leaders" and grassroots empowerment. In short, instead of leadership from above, democracy from below. The time for all voices to be heard is long overdue.

Black Leadership

PART ONE

Foundations of Inequality

1

The Racial Contours of the Constitution

THE AMERICAN REVOLUTION spawned a political and moral movement to eliminate the slave trade to the colonies. By 1780, consistent with the democratic ideology of the Revolution, several states began to move toward the general emancipation of all slaves. However, most political leaders, drawn largely from the planter and merchant classes, were unwilling to extend democratic rights to blacks and preferred to maintain a hierarchy based on race, class, and economics. The sentiments of these leaders were reflected as they drafted the United States Constitution. Thus the Constitution halted the promise of democracy to all Americans and directly promoted the Jim Crow codes subsequently passed by states and cities.

Paradoxically, the American Constitution represented an affirmation of representative government and democracy as well as a confirmation of the slave trade and human enslavement. This paradox can be explained only by a survey of the racial and political relations between black and white Americans during the mid- to late eighteenth century.

I

Before the American Revolution, laws throughout the colonies were designed to perpetuate the supremacy of the merchant and planter classes.[1] The underlying purposes of discriminatory legislation in the colonial period were the general suppression of all lower-class working people and

3

small farmers, black and white alike, and the maintenance of a planter-merchant elite that exercised nominal local authority.[2] The American colonial frontier was no land of political democracy or economic opportunity for the majority of whites. Most were disfranchised by property requirements.[3] In the Southern colonies, the slaveholding planter aristocracy rigidly controlled all public decision making. Even in the Northern colonies (many of them founded to preserve religious freedom), democracy was virtually nonexistent.[4]

Consequently, blacks and poor whites sometimes cooperated with each other to challenge the conservative political status quo.[5] The American Revolution deeply divided the white colonial elite and immediately unleashed a democratic and popular movement among the lower classes. About a third of all whites remained loyal to the British Crown. But in the ranks of those who favored independence, the powerless and enslaved suddenly seized the political initiative. Black Americans had an impact upon national political culture and independent ideology that was stronger than that of any other Americans. They expanded the democratic principles underlying the white colonialists' disagreements with British authorities, and they carried these radical ideas to their logical conclusions.

Poet Phillis Wheatley and many other blacks likened British "tyranny" to the enslavement of black Americans.[6] Similarly, a group of African Americans living in Boston in 1773 petitioned the Massachusetts assembly to abolish slavery and to permit the resettlement of blacks back to Africa. Their petition declared: "On behalf of our fellow slaves in this province, . . . the divine spirit of freedom seems to fire every humane breast on this continent. . . . As the people of this province seem to be actuated by the principles of equality and justice, we cannot but expect your house will again take our deplorable case into consideration, and give us that ample relief which, as men, we have a natural right to."[7]

In 1779 Connecticut slaves petitioned their legislature, using the rhetoric of the Enlightenment and Thomas Jefferson's Declaration of Independence: "Reason and Revelation join to declare that we are the creatures of [God] . . . we perceive by our own Reflection, that we are endowed with the same faculties [as] our masters . . . we are convinced of our right . . . to be free . . . and can never be convinced that we were made to be Slaves."[8]

An unprecedented liberalization of race relations was the direct consequence of the Revolution. Thomas Paine, the great democrat, bitterly attacked his fellow white patriots: "If they could carry off and enslave some thousands of us, would we think it just? One would almost wish they could for once; it might convince more than reason, or the Bible."[9]

In 1779 the First Continental Congress, meeting in Philadelphia, declared: "We will neither import nor purchase any slave imported after the first day of December next, after which time we will wholly discontinue the slave trade and will neither be concerned in it ourselves nor will we hire our vessels nor sell our commodities or manufactures to those who are concerned in it."[10] Philadelphia Quakers created the Society for the Relief of Free Negroes Unlawfully Held in Bondage and barred membership in the Society of Friends to all slaveholders. In 1776 Delaware's constitution banned the slave trade, and Vermont's constitution outlawed slavery in 1777.

Even Southern whites who owned hundreds of slaves sought to demonstrate their egalitarian and democratic credentials. When the British army invaded South Carolina, John Laurens called for the enlistment of three thousand slaves, with the promise of emancipation after the conflict. White colonists in Darien, Georgia, issued several public resolutions declaring their "disapprobation and abhorrence of the unnatural practice of Slavery in America." Negro slavery was denounced as "highly dangerous to our liberties (as well as lives), debasing part of our fellow-creatures below men, and corrupting the virtue and morals of the rest."[11] By the end of the American Revolution, a substantial minority of white Americans deeply believed that slavery was morally wrong. As historian Winthrop D. Jordan observed: "It was perfectly clear that the principles for which Americans had fought required the complete abolition of slavery; the question was not *if*, but *when* and *how*."[12]

After formal independence from Great Britain was achieved, African Americans continued to agitate for their democratic rights. State legislatures received petitions from blacks calling for the gradual abolition of slavery. In rural areas, runaway slaves and occasionally poor whites began a series of attacks on plantations. For instance, in August 1782 Edmund Randolph warned Virginia slaveowner James Madison of the "alarming activities of a group of whites and fugitive slaves numbering about fifty men" whose attacks on plantations represented "a serious menace to life and property."[13] A large number of runaway slaves built a stockade north of Savannah, and for several years conducted guerrilla warfare against white planters. In 1786 the militias of Georgia and South Carolina seized the black fortress but suffered "heavy casualties" in the battle.[14] Blacks had attempted to reason with white Americans for justice, and now growing numbers were prepared to resort to violence in their pursuit of freedom.

As the rhetoric for independence subsided, the planter-merchant elite that had been at the head of the patriotic movement began to question its own political ideology. Had the demand for democracy gone too far?

Should slavery be abolished gradually? Could black males with property be permitted to vote? From 1780 to 1787, there was a period of ideological ambiguity. Many prominent politicians continued to identify themselves with the cause of gradual abolition.[15] Several state legislatures moved slowly toward manumission.[16]

There was also, however, a significant trend toward racial retrenchment. In New Hampshire black citizens drafted a petition urging "that the name of slave may not more be heard in a land gloriously contending for the sweets of freedom."[17] Yet the state legislature refused to approve legislation freeing New Hampshire's black population. In 1784 Congress voted down Jefferson's proposal to keep slavery out of the western territories. Antislavery efforts in Delaware were also defeated in 1786, as the state legislature voted against gradual manumission.

II

Several Southern politicians now began to speak out, privately and publicly, against the democratic principle of black freedom. Chief among them was George Washington. The master of Mount Vernon owned more than two hundred blacks, and he constantly complained about their poor work habits and destruction of his property. Blacks who were not in "awe" of their white overseers, he wrote, would "of course do as they please."[18] After his election as president, Washington shipped some of his personal slaves from the capital city of Philadelphia back to Mount Vernon after the Pennsylvania Abolition Society tried to win their freedom. Washington coldly justified their removal, declaring that "the idea of freedom [was simply] too great a temptation for them to resist."[19]

Even liberals began to doubt the democratic justification for black emancipation. In *Notes on Virginia*, published in 1785, Jefferson continued to deplore the existence of slavery. Yet he also openly expressed a deep racial prejudice toward all blacks. Jefferson argued that blacks had "a very strong and disagreeable odour, and appeared to require less sleep" than whites. On matters of sexuality, Jefferson suggested that black males "are more ardent after their female: but love seems with them to be more an eager desire, than a tender mixture of sentiment and sensation."[20] On balance, blacks could never be integrated into white society: "Deeply rooted prejudices entertained by the whites; ten thousand recollections, by the Blacks, of the injuries they have sustained; new provocations; the real distinction which nature has made; and many other circumstances, will divide us into parties and produce convulsions which will probably never end but in the extermination of the one or the other race."[21] Henceforth the Virginia democrat refused to use his political prestige to push for emancipation in the North and was generally silent as slavery rapidly expanded into the western territories.

Some liberal whites began to search for a solution to the "Negro Problem" that would permit them to adhere to their humanistic and democratic principles. One British Quaker friend of Benjamin Franklin, John Fothergill, proposed the colonization of West Africa by newly freed blacks. In 1787 the Sierra Leone Company in Great Britain began to transport free Negroes from Nova Scotia and England to the upper Guinea coast. The concept of black colonization had occurred to Jefferson as early as 1777.[22] James Madison also endorsed the colonization concept, but only as an alternative to the general emancipation of slaves.[23] Madison and Jefferson astutely recognized that emancipation would require the inevitable granting of suffrage to blacks and, later, the full desegregation of civil and social relations between the races. This was the point at which democratic principles collapsed and white supremacy came to the forefront. By shipping blacks out of the country, liberal whites could accomplish two things. They could applaud themselves for their humanistic act of freeing their slaves, which was in keeping with their democratic ideology, and they could eliminate potentially dangerous black rebels and thus better control and exploit those blacks who still remained in bondage.

The fifty-five men who came to Philadelphia for the Constitutional Convention in April 1787 belonged to "two basic groups, northern capitalists and southern plantation owners." Historian Staughton Lynd observed: "The Constitution represented not a victory of one over the other but a compromise between them."[24] Some Northern delegates came prepared to challenge both the slave trade and slavery itself. New York politician Gouverneur Morris, a conservative, condemned the South's "nefarious institution," which damned Negro slaves "to the most cruel bondage." Could such practices be tolerated within a government "instituted for the protection of rights of mankind"? Benjamin Franklin had agreed to present an antislavery charter to the convention—but subsequently changed his mind. At least twenty-five convention delegates owned slaves, and few of them were prepared to part with their profits. South Carolina planter Charles Cotesworth Pinckney warned that he would vigorously oppose the adoption of any Constitution that did not protect slaveholders' interests.[25] Another South Carolina plantation owner, John Rutledge, informed his colleagues that the convention "had no business dealing with religion or morality; the only question was whether mutual interests would allow the southern states to be parties to the Union."[26]

In the end, the desire for compromise outweighed any consideration of religion or morality. Originally, Pinckney had proposed that no ban on the slave trade should be passed until the year 1800. But with the support of some Northern delegates, Pinckney managed to push the date forward to 1808. Article I, Section 9, was deliberately worded ambiguously: "The Migration or Importation of such Persons as any of the States now existing shall think proper to admit, shall not be prohibited by Congress prior to the Year one-thousand-eight-hundred and eight, but a Tax or duty may be imposed on such Importation, not exceeding ten dollars for each person."[27]

Delegates differed sharply over the meaning of the terms *Migration*, such Persons, and *Importation*. Some argued later that Article I, Section 9, included white immigrants as well as Negro slaves; others insisted that the section included both the transatlantic slave trade and the interstate sale and transportation of slaves within the United States. New Jersey delegate Jonathan Dayton would claim that the phrase "such Persons" referred only to African American slaves, and the sole reason that the word *slaves* was not specifically used was "that it would be better not to stain the Constitutional code with such a term."[28] Whatever the justification, this section clearly established the legality of American Negro slavery and illustrated beyond any doubt that the young republic would encourage human bondage.

III

In two additional sections, the Constitution affirmed the economic and political interests of the slaveholding class. In Article I, Section 2, there was the "three-fifths compromise": those "bound to service for a Term of Years" would be counted as "three-fifths of all other Persons" for the purposes of apportioning "Representatives and direct Taxes."[29] Article IV, Section 2, states: "No Person held to Service or Labour in one State, under the Laws thereof, escaping into another, shall in Consequence of any Law or Regulation therein, be discharged from such Service or Labour, but shall be delivered up on Claim of the Party to whom such Service or Labour may be due."[30] This latter provision was designed to overcome the legal legacy of the 1772 *Somerset* decision, in which Lord Chief Justice Mansfield essentially outlawed slavery in England.[31] Article IV, Section 2, was reinforced by Congress several years later with the Fugitive Slave Law of 1793.[32] As John Hope Franklin notes:

> Masters could legally seize a runaway in any state and carry him before any federal or state magistrate in the vicinity, and obtain a certificate warranting his removal to the state from which he had fled.

This law allowed no trial by jury and required conviction only on the oral testimony of the claimant or on an affidavit certified by a magistrate of the state from which the Negro was alleged to have fled.[33]

The national debate over the ratification of the Constitution illustrates the vagueness of the document's clauses on Negro servitude—to the point that they permitted diametrically opposing viewpoints. Liberal Federalist James Wilson of Pennsylvania, speaking before his state legislature, stated that Article I, Section 9, had established "the foundation for banishing slavery out of this country; and though the period is more distant than I could wish, yet it will produce the same kind of gradual change which was pursued in Pennsylvania." Wilson insisted that the new federal government would soon outlaw the expansion of slavery in the west. But in the South Carolina legislature, Federalists "swore that they would never have agreed to confederate without winning agreement on the right to import slaves."[34]

Few politicians were sufficiently principled to oppose the Constitution primarily on the grounds that it perpetuated an evil and oppressive labor system. One of the finest exceptions was Luther Martin of Maryland. A proponent of gradual manumission, he immediately grasped that slavery threatened to destroy the fragile bonds of unity between the North and the South. Dismayed with the compromises over slavery, Martin boycotted the final sessions and refused to sign the Constitution. Urging Maryland's legislature to oppose ratification, Martin declared that the controversial sections "ought to be considered as a solemn mockery of, and insult to that God whose protection we had then implored, and could not fail to hold us up in detestation, and render us contemptible to every true friend of liberty in the world."[35] The Constitution had given "national sanction and encouragement" to the slave trade, Martin stated, and thus had exposed the American people "to the displeasure and vengeance of Him, who is equally Lord of all, and who views with equal eye the poor African slave and his American master."[36]

IV

As subsequent events would illustrate, the passage of the Constitution greatly reinforced the slave trade and slavery itself. Between 1780 and 1820 the African American slave population nearly tripled in size. From 1790 to 1800 Virginia's black population increased by 17.8 percent, and the North Carolina black population grew by 32 percent.[37] The invention of the cotton gin in 1793 increased the amount of cotton planted across the South, as well as the number of blacks demanded by the new frontier plantations.

Between 1803 and 1808, for instance, South Carolina legally imported almost 40,000 slaves.[38]

As the peculiar institution became even more profitable, the vaguely proslavery sentiments expressed by the Constitution contributed to even more racist local and state legislation aimed at destroying any residual rights the Negro people held. In 1792 Kentucky was admitted to the union as a slave state, followed four years later by Tennessee. Northern states established the first legal regulations of Jim Crow. Free blacks were frequently denied the right to purchase public lands. They were refused service in thousands of hotels and restaurants. In New York property and educational qualifications were imposed on free blacks' electoral franchise. Pennsylvania, Indiana, and other states denied all free black males the right to vote. In 1805 Maryland prohibited blacks from selling wheat, corn, or tobacco without a state license. Ohio legislators approved an 1807 law calling for "the registering and bonding, in the sum of five-hundred dollars, of every Negro."[39]

Free blacks acutely sensed that a political reaction against real democracy had occurred, and they used every legal means to fight back. Massachusetts Negroes, led by Methodist minister Prince Hall, demanded equal educational facilities for their children. In 1791 free blacks in Charleston, South Carolina, petitioned their state legislature, deploring the fact that they were "debarred of the Rights of Free Citizens by being subject to a Trial without the benefit of a Jury and subject to Prosecution by Testimony of Slaves without Oath."[40]

What more humanistic alternatives might the drafters have employed? We should not distort the evidence beyond its logical shape or actual historical context in the pursuit of this question. Nevertheless, a close reading of the historical facts suggests that more liberal and less racist possibilities were achievable in the period between 1780 and 1800.[41] For example, economic and political expansion in the western territories was not dependent upon slavery per se, and a free labor market would have been more efficient.

In addition, the Constitution could have provided measures for the gradual elimination of slavery, with federal compensation to the slaveholders, along the pattern of British manumission in the West Indies in the 1830s.[42] The Constitution also could have barred the future importation of slaves, effective immediately, and provided a fund for the voluntary migration of freed Negroes to Africa. Moreover, the Constitution could have defined all free blacks as citizens of the republic and granted them all legal rights and privileges shared by whites in the various states.

Even though these were workable alternatives, an "antiracist" Constitution could have existed only if the crucial provisions of the Fourteenth Amendment had been inserted in the original draft: "No State shall make or enforce any law which shall abridge the privileges or immunities of citizens of the United States; nor shall any State deprive any person of life, liberty, or property, without due process of law; nor deny to any person within its jurisdiction equal protection of the laws."[43] Winthrop D. Jordan suggests:

> In retrospect, the pity of antislavery's failure was that in the decade after the Revolution, success against slavery seemed almost within reach. If the Negro had been freed in the eighteenth century rather than in 1863, if only in Virginia, he would have suffered far less degradation. . . . After the Revolution, the Negro would have been freed more for his fundamental equality and less because slavery nagged the nation's conscience as an anomaly in the civilized world. A general emancipation . . . would have come as a glorious triumph, the capstone of the Revolution; guilt could easily have been foisted onto the British and the whole nation stirred with pride.[44]

Unfortunately for black Americans—and indeed for all American people—the 1787 Constitution marked the end, not the beginning, of a democratic and egalitarian social movement.

2

Black History and the
Vision of Democracy

How do oppressed people come to terms with their exploitation? This is the central theme of African American political history. As slaves, we were aware of the immense contradiction between this nation's democratic ideology and its treatment of peoples of color. In the South we were legally defined as private property, and in the North we faced racial discrimination, disfranchisement, and legal segregation decades before the Civil War. The literature of black abolitionism is filled with the cries of a people who wished to participate in the democratic process yet found the door of opportunity closed to them. "What to the American slave is your Fourth of July?" asked Frederick Douglass in 1852. "In answer, a day that reveals to him more than all other days of the year, the gross injustice and cruelty to which he is the constant victim. To him your celebration is a sham; your boasted liberty an unholy license; your national greatness, swelling vanity."

Morris Marable, my great-grandfather, was not Frederick Douglass, and yet he felt the same yearning to be free. My late grandmother Fannie Marable often told me about Morris's early life. The son of a black household worker and a white planter named Robinson, Morris was sold for five hundred dollars in Rome, Georgia, at the age of nine. I have tried, without success, to learn my great-great-grandmother's name. Family folklore reveals only that Morris's mother wept bitterly when her son was sold from her. She never saw him again. Morris became the property of a white plantation owner named Marable in 1854, and the boy was transported to the Alabama Black Belt. He worked in the fields by day and at dusk was sent to the slave quarters. Morris's new extended family was the field slave population on the Marable plantation. From slave Johnson Adolphus, who became his "elder brother," he learned mechanic skills. From other slaves he gained a sense of community and ritual, hope, and dignity. And from the overseers Morris experienced the sting of the lash.

What did freedom mean to the slave? First, the absence of human exploitation. Blacks engaged in a variety of disruptive activities to retard the production process. Slaves added rocks to the cotton they picked, to wreck the cotton gin; they burned crops and sabotaged farm machinery. Morris assumed the mask of the loyal slave but stole food from the whites' kitchen and passed it out in the slave quarters. Slaves attempted nearly every form of day-to-day resistance, but always short of open rebellion. Still, slaves constantly heard about conspiracies and even small revolts throughout Alabama. In August 1854 a slave murdered his master at Mt. Meigs and, according to white authorities, "boasted of his deed." The black man was burned alive, according to the *Montgomery Journal*, "from an imperative sense of the necessity of an example to check the growing and dangerous insubordination of the slave population."

As the Civil War approached, Alabama slaves exhibited greater tendencies toward rebelliousness. In Talladega County, Alabama, a slave conspiracy was discovered in August 1860. A roving band of "maroons," runaway slaves, was captured and executed. In the same month a white man in Montgomery County was arrested for "holding improper conversations with slaves." And in December several hundred blacks in the central Black Belt were uncovered in a conspiracy with several "poor whites." The would-be rebels had called for the redistribution of "the land, mules, and money." The *Montgomery Advertiser* commented on the conspiracy on December 13, 1860: "We have found out a deep laid plan among the negroes of our neighborhood, and from what we can find out from our negroes, it is general all over the county. . . . They have gone far enough in the plot to divide our estates, mules, lands, and household furniture." About twenty-five blacks and four poor whites were executed.

Alabama white planters reinforced their social controls over the black population. In 1853, the state legislature declared that any slave found with the ability to read would receive a hundred lashes. The number of night patrols was increased. These "patterrollers," as the slaves called them, rode the country lanes at night searching for secret meetings or runaway slaves. Sometime during these years Morris met and fell in love with a household slave named Judy Brooks, who lived about eight miles distant on another farm. Such relationships were difficult to maintain; either Morris or Judy might be sold at any time. But over time Morris had carefully cultivated his master's trust, and he was permitted to close the barn and to repair broken tools after dark. Quietly, he made his way into the pine woods, circling down beyond a creek, and after running for well over an hour arrived at Judy's cabin. An hour before dawn he returned to his plantation. Morris performed this feat with regularity, dodging patterrollers and their dogs. He was never caught, and his master and overseer never knew. But the slaves did, and they relished this small act of freedom. Perhaps they sang to themselves:

> *Run nigger run de patterroller get you,*
> *slip over de fence*
> *slick as a eel*
> *White man catch you be de heel*
> *Run, nigger, run.*

Morris's master permitted his slaves to hold regular religious services on Sunday afternoons, and these gatherings often lasted well into the night. The planter may have reasoned to himself that Christianity was good for labor discipline. The Negro spirituals spoke of freedom only in the after-life, and the Bible taught servants to respect and obey their masters. But for the slaves the religious meetings were an assertion of their cultural autonomy. Their songs of praise to the Lord revealed more than accommodation to temporal suffering:

> *He delivered Daniel from de lion's den,*
> *Jonah from de belly ob de whale,*
> *And de Hebrew children from de fiery furnace,*
> *and why not every man? . . .*
> *O blow your trumpet, Gabriel*
> *Blow your trumpet louder;*
> *And I want dat trumpet to blow me home*
> *To my new Jerusalem.*

To the slaves the Lord was not an impersonal force. He was real, and he sympathized with them. The Bible was viewed not as a set of rigid doctrines but as a living, creative work, a set of parables by which people could lead a moral life. Black prophetic Christianity gave spiritual freedom to the slaves and a sense of humanity that transcended the slavery system.

The Union army did not reach central Alabama until 1864. Some slaves may have left the Marable plantation, making their way to the Union lines. Other slaves in nearby Troy, Alabama, organized a widespread conspiracy, which was discovered in December 1864. Morris, now nineteen years old, waited for his opportunity. His master, an officer in the Confederate army, was severely wounded near West Point, Georgia. Morris was ordered to transport his master from the battle back to his home. Still trusted implicitly, he performed this service. But late one evening he gathered together his personal items, took forty dollars in gold from the house, and somehow escaped. Morris and Judy Brooks made their way into the sparsely populated hills of northeastern Alabama. This was no new Jerusalem, but freedom was theirs.

Like many other black freedmen, Morris understood that the best guarantee of freedom was land ownership. He purchased a small section of property near Wedowee, Alabama, and began to cultivate cotton. Through careful savings and backbreaking labor, Morris was able to purchase more than one hundred acres of farmland in two decades. This was no mean achievement. In the 1880s the average Alabama farm was less than sixty acres, of which about thirty-five acres were cultivated. Black tenant farmers usually occupied less than one-third of that amount. Morris relied on the labor power of his thirteen children to plant and harvest the crop. When Judy Brooks Marable died in the early 1880s, Morris soon remarried. His second wife, who had the curious name Warner Clockster, was a descendant of the Creek Indians, who had lived in the region before the 1830s. Warner and Morris's sixth child was my grandfather, Manning Marable, born in 1894.

Morris's skills as a mechanic, acquired during slavery, may have been responsible for his later interest in business. Sometime during the early 1890s, Morris and his best friend and neighbor, Joshua Heard, raised sufficient capital to start a cotton gin of their own. Most of the nearby towns already had gins—Lafayette and Talladega, Alabama, and West Point, Georgia—but whites owned the ginneries and warehouses. Black producers were usually dependent upon white brokers, who cheated them with regularity. Most of the farmers, black and white, purchased their supplies and farm implements on credit, and according to Roger L. Ransom and Richard Sutch, annual interest rates charged by rural merchants during the 1880s were about 60 percent. Since most farms yielded about 150 pounds of cotton per acre and cotton prices were then eight to nine cents a pound, an average white farmer could expect to gross $250 to $400 annually. Black sharecroppers, however, had to divide their profits with their landlords—and after paying off their debts, they usually found themselves with nothing. Morris was determined to break out of the cycle of poverty and to compete against the white merchants. Black farmers soon supported Morris and his partner, and the ginning enterprise prospered.

During the 1880s, many black and white farmers in Alabama joined the Alliance, a radical agrarian movement against the conservative business and planter elite. Populism, which followed in the early 1890s, drew upon the same small-farmer strata. Morris was attracted to the movement, perhaps because of its racial egalitarianism. Throughout Georgia and Alabama, black and white Populist Party members held joint picnics, rallies, and speeches. Populist candidate Reuben F. Kalb actually won the state's gubernatorial contest in 1894, but the conservatives used extensive voting fraud to swing the election. On the periphery of this activity, in his small rural town, Morris Marable became sheriff with the support of blacks and whites. He was intensely proud of his office and completed his duties with special dispatch. According to family legend, he even carried out two public executions—although the race of the victims is unknown. Morris carried a small Bible in one coat pocket at all times and a revolver under his coat. In either case, he always planned to be prepared.

My great-grandfather's dream of freedom collapsed after the 1890s, with the demise of Populism and the rise of racial segregation. Between 1882 and 1927, 304 lynchings occurred in Alabama. The Sayre Election Law of Alabama made it illegal to assist voters in marking ballots—thus effectively disfranchising thousands of illiterate whites and blacks. Poll taxes and county levies were initiated by 1901, and the vast majority of poor and rural voters was eliminated. The total number of black voters in the state fell to 3,700 in 1908. Many white Populists turned bitterly against blacks at this time, and many rural blacks became the victims of white vigilantes. My grandmother's favorite tale about Morris concerns the harassment of one of her cousins by local whites. For some real or imaginary offense, the young man was being viciously beaten in the public streets. Morris calmly walked into the mob, revolver in hand, and brought the boy home. The whites had too much respect—or perhaps fear—to stop him.

After exercising the right to vote for more than thirty years, finally Morris was turned away from the ballot box. Disgusted, he became a Republican; he even named his last child Roosevelt, in honor of the president, in 1905. If politics could not liberate black people, economic power could. But the next blow came in 1914–1915. The boll weevil, introduced into the United States in 1892, had made its way into southern Alabama by 1910. In the summer of 1914, it reached the northeastern part of the state. Cotton production in infested counties usually fell by 50 percent. That autumn, with the outbreak of World War I, the European markets that had been the largest consumers of Southern cotton were closed. Cotton prices immediately plummeted to five to eight cents per pound, well below the earlier market price of thirteen cents. Large white merchants and planters were able to obtain credit and store their cotton in warehouses, but black entrepreneurs and small farmers were unable to cope with the crisis.

As black farmers defaulted on loans, small black-owned banks and businesses collapsed. The number of black banks in Alabama fell from seven to one between 1911 and 1918; thousands of blacks lost their land, forced to sell it for only a fraction of its real value. Between 1910 and 1920 the total number of farms in Alabama declined from 110,400 to 95,000. The crisis of 1914–1915 was the beginning of a long decline in black land tenure throughout the South. Black farm acreage in the South peaked at more than fifteen million acres in 1910; sixty years later, the total was less than six million acres. Morris had no choice but to sell the cotton gin, and he abandoned business entirely. At his death in 1927, Morris was still in debt, but his spirit remained unbroken.

Each successive generation of African Americans has pursued the goal of freedom, the new Jerusalem, which would make the promise of democracy a reality. Manning Marable's road to freedom was the same as his father's. Manning married Fannie Heard, the soft-spoken but strong-willed daughter of Joshua Heard, in 1916. Together they raised thirteen children, and in the 1930s they started a small lumber company. With a little side income from my grandfather's illegal whiskey still, the lumber firm began to grow. Manning repeatedly told his children that the means of achieving racial independence was through business: "You have to beat the Southern white man at his own game." My father, James Marable, learned this lesson and ultimately became a successful entrepreneur. But always there was this moral commitment, born of the slavery and Reconstruction experience, that united most members of the community in pursuing common goals: respect as human beings, unfettered participation in the economic and political life of this country, full civil liberties, and equal protection under the law.

Four generations removed from slavery, the vision of a just, democratic society remains. Yet the structural barriers to economic equality are more clearly discernible. In Macon County, Alabama, where most of the Marable extended family still resides, black entrepreneurs owned 234 businesses in 1977, according to the Bureau of the Census. About 76 percent of these firms, 178 in all, did not have a single paid employee. The 7 black taxicab firms averaged $12,300 in annual gross receipts. The county's 94 selective services—everything from barbershops to pool halls—recorded an average of $15,400 gross receipts and employed a grand total of 31 people. In a county with 24,000 blacks, minority-owned firms employed only 119 workers. The dream of economic self-sufficiency may have been reasonable to pursue under capitalist conditions in the late nineteenth century, but as a grand strategy for black group advancement in the period of monopoly capitalism, it represents a dead end.

Part of Morris Marable's dream was realized during the Civil Rights Movement. Black working people and the poor challenged the Jim Crow system and won. This effort, like all significant black social movements, was rooted simultaneously in a political and moral critique of institutional racism. Just as the slaves developed a religious outlook that negated their masters' political power, civil rights activists of the 1960s led a crusade for social justice that expressed a moral dimension. The workers in the Student Nonviolent Coordinating Committee (SNCC) sang this in the Albany, Georgia, desegregation campaign of 1962:

> *Ain't gonna let nobody turn me 'round*
> *Turn me 'round, turn me 'round*
> *Ain't gonna let nobody turn me 'round*
> *I'm gonna keep on walkin', keep on a-talkin'*
> *Marching up to freedom land.*

Morris Marable would have understood at once the significance of these words. Jim Crow meant inferior schools and political disfranchisement, low-paying jobs and second-class citizenship. The pursuit of democracy demanded a moral commitment on the part of the oppressed to organize.

> *No more Jim Crow, no more Jim Crow*
> *No more Jim Crow over me*
> *And before I'll be a slave*
> *I'll be buried in my grave*
> *And go home to my Lord and be free.*

A generation has passed since the social upheaval called the Second Reconstruction. There are now more than nine thousand black elected and appointed officials throughout the United States. The highest number of black officials in any state is in Mississippi. The murderer of Medgar Evers has been convicted finally, many years after the crime. Two Southern presidents have been elected to the White House since 1976, both of whom received the overwhelming support of the African American electorate. Despite these gains, there remains across the South the harsh reality of racial bigotry and class inequality.

Is the democratic vision an illusion for African Americans or a dream deferred? The struggle has not been without hardship, but the faith of a people in bondage remains the moral guide for their descendants. The organic history of black Americans is a pattern of suffering and transcendence, of sacrifice and hope for the future. It has its own language, rhythms, and direction. It embraces the customs and collective experiences of those who have known slavery, Jim Crow, and Reaganism. The moral imperatives of the slave community still find their way into the discourse and programs of a Jesse Jackson. An intimate knowledge of this history and rich cultural legacy is essential to our collective struggles for a democratic society in the future.

PART TWO

Ideology and Political Culture:
The Age of Segregation

3

Booker T. Washington and the
Political Economy of Black Accommodation

BOOKER T. WASHINGTON was the most influential black American educator in the early twentieth century. Born as a slave in 1856, he attended Hampton Institute, an industrial and agricultural school for blacks and American Indians. At the age of twenty-five, in 1881, he was appointed principal of Tuskegee Institute, an industrial school that had recently been created by the Alabama state legislature. Washington constructed a comprehensive economic and social program for black development within the capitalist system during the period from 1880 to 1915. His achievements—and those of black educators who accepted his ideas—were substantial. Black schools were largely successful in improving literacy rates and health standards and in promoting black land tenure and capital formation.

The limitations and problems inherent in Washington's political strategy, however, helped to establish a rigid system of racial inequality and segregation—termed *Jim Crow*—across the U.S. South. Many social dilemmas confronting black American universities and educators today, a century later, are rooted in the conceptual and programmatic contradictions of Washington's educational and economic paradigms.

I
The social forces that produced Booker T. Washington and an entire generation of conservative black educators stemmed from the American Civil

War and the collapse of Reconstruction. During the Reconstruction period following the Civil War, from 1865 to 1877, the nation extended the electoral franchise to black males and abolished slavery, and the newly freed black laborers articulated two political demands above all others—the right to universal education, including access to black colleges and vocational institutes, which would have to be created, and "the acquisition of the land they had tilled and developed and learned to think of as their own."[1] These central concerns were closely linked: capital accumulation and a higher standard of living in a rural society were not possible without land tenure, and an educated black community could develop its own resources to extend credit and finance economic and social institutions.

The black college, as Benjamin E. Mays, former president of Morehouse College, has written, was the social product of an "era of change."[2] Only twenty-eight African Americans earned baccalaureate degrees at white colleges before 1860.[3] As the "social forces" that "precipitated the Civil War" emerged, as Mays noted, Lincoln University was founded in Pennsylvania in 1854.[4] Seventeen black colleges were established between 1854 and 1890, including Morehouse College, Howard University, Hampton Institute, Atlanta University, and Tuskegee Institute. Most were private training schools for teachers or focused primarily on industrial and agricultural education. The growth of black institutions was retarded by the U.S. government's exclusion of blacks from funding under the Morrill Act of 1862, which created land-grant colleges with direct federal subsidies. In the 1890s, however, this policy was reversed, and a second group of state-supported but racially segregated institutions was created in most Southern states.

It is frequently and conveniently forgotten today that millions of white Southerners vehemently opposed the creation of institutions of higher education for blacks, even behind the barriers of Jim Crow. As Daniel C. Thompson notes:

> Almost everything was done to discourage the founding of Black schools. State legislatures and local school boards tended to ignore Blacks' efforts to establish schools. The white masses often took drastic steps to squash the school movement sponsored by the Federal government, missionary groups, and a few private philanthropists; teachers were beaten, schools were burned, the Black students and their parents were frequently intimidated.

Such opposition was usually expressed in explicitly racist terms; at its core, however, was the white South's determination to suppress the entire labor force and to maintain blacks as a subordinate stratum beneath white workers. As Thompson explains, "Underneath these apologies was the white employers' perennial belief that educated Blacks are largely unfit for the dirty, menial, low-paying jobs traditionally assigned to them."[5]

By 1899 a total of eighty-one Negro colleges and institutions for agricultural and vocational training had been established, seventy-five of them in the South. The severe limitations of these schools can be understood only against the harsh environment of black Southern economic and social life immediately after Reconstruction. More than 90 percent of the black population lived in the South, and 80 percent of all blacks in the region lived in rural areas. The vast majority of black farmers rented their homes and property—in 1890, 82 percent of black farmers were tenants, compared with only 47 percent of whites. By the end of Reconstruction, fewer than three million acres of land had been purchased by or redistributed to black freedmen.

The rural black peasantry was caught in an almost impossible cycle of penury. In 1890, 65 percent of them were illiterate. They had scant knowledge of such modern agricultural techniques as crop rotation and soil conservation or the use of complex farm machinery. Barely one-fifth of them could even afford fertilizers. As sharecroppers, they were forced to give half of their annual crop to their landlords. Most had little capital left over after selling their cotton and corn crops. Black farmers needed credit for canned goods, farm equipment, seeds, and other supplies from rural merchants. And according to economists Roger L. Ransom and Richard Sutch, white merchants extended credit in the 1880s at an average annual interest rate of 35 to 60 percent, and they usually refused credit to farmers who were not producing cotton or corn. Consequently, only 3.7 percent of all black farms produced any other cash crops. This economic dependence on credit and the cotton market had several social effects. The per capita production of sheep and swine dropped, and families suffered as a result. Although the data are not conclusive, there is even some evidence that black life expectancy at birth actually fell slightly from its level under slavery, from an average of thirty-five years in 1850 to less than thirty-four years in 1900. During the same period, white life expectancy increased from forty to about fifty years.[6]

Black oppression in the South was an essential component of class exploitation throughout the region. The dominant Southern classes of the period may be roughly subdivided into two major groups. The older elites were located in the South's "Black Belt," an agricultural region noted for its fertile black soil and high percentage of rural black workers, stretching nearly a thousand miles from eastern North Carolina to Texas. About fifty thousand white planters, only 2.5 percent of all Southern farmers, constituted this rural elite. These planters usually owned farms varying in size from three hundred to three thousand acres and hired poor black and white tenants, sharecroppers, or wage laborers to do their work.[7] A second group, which emerged only after the Civil War, consisted of the new industrialists—owners and managers of the South's growing textile mills, railroads, iron, coal, and timber resources.

These two factions of the South's capitalist class were frequently in conflict over matters of electoral politics and regional economic policies, but they shared common objectives regarding the black worker. Both required a steady supply of workers and used state governments and the courts to procure their labor quotas. The most infamous method was the "convict-leasing" system, wherein prisoners were leased by state and local authorities to private contractors for a fee. As the demand for labor increased, states complied by enacting increasingly repressive legislation: in Mississippi, for example, the theft of a pig was defined as "grand larceny," punishable by up to five years' imprisonment. Many white politicians grew wealthy from the bonuses they received by leasing convicts. The state of Georgia alone netted more than $350,000 in 1906.[8]

Both planters and industrialists vigorously opposed the formation of labor unions and were fearful of any signs of interracial coalitions developing among black and white workers, since such alliances might threaten the status quo. Both groups also generally favored the creation of black agricultural and trade schools in the 1880s and 1890s. As Sterling D. Spero and Abram L. Harris observed in their classic study *The Black Worker*:

> To the proponents of Negro industrial education, an efficient worker
> was one who was reliable, capable of giving the maximum return for
> his wages, and loyal to his employer. Enlightenment on the problems
> peculiar to the wage earner in modern industry had no part in the edu-
> cation which the industrial schools gave to the future Black workers.[9]

This was the socioeconomic background challenging the resources of most black educators in the United States a century ago. Booker T. Washington advanced a strategy of black economic development through the resources of black state-supported and private institutions. Washington understood that growth in per capita income for blacks was possible only under several conditions. Increased productivity was possible if labor were reorganized along more efficient lines. The development and utilization of new technologies and the reeducation of the labor force would also increase productivity. Nevertheless, sustained economic growth could not occur without increased capital investment—that is, growth in the ratio of capital to labor. How could the black colleges augment the process of black savings, reinvestment, and the general formation of capital?

II

The Tuskegee Institute approach to black development rested on four key points.

First, it took the social and cultural transformation of the black Southern labor force to be a major responsibility of black educational institutions. These schools tried to retrain the black peasantry by creating extension programs, establishing rural training centers, and holding colloquia, where farmers learned the importance of agricultural diversification and studied techniques of soil conservation and crop rotation. In a concerted effort to reduce the level of black illiteracy, Tuskegee sent its students to teach at rural primary and secondary schools. The institute also placed great emphasis on personal hygiene, diet, and the improvement of residential quarters.

Tuskegee encouraged black farmers to break away from their dependence on landlords by gradually purchasing their own lands. The problem here was essentially one of credit. So long as black farmers relied on white merchants for working capital at exorbitant interest rates, the growth of black land tenure would be minimal. To provide an alternative credit source, Tuskegee started a savings department, which functioned as a local bank. Tuskegee graduates used these funds to initiate "social settlements" in rural areas; after purchasing former plantation properties, they resold them to black sharecroppers. Other black colleges and churches established similar lending establishments, and by 1911 there were two black-owned banks in Georgia, eleven in Mississippi, and seven in Alabama. These banks and other black-owned lending institutions in the United States did $22 million worth of business by 1910.[10]

Second, Washington and the Tuskegee Institute staff tried to make their school a model for all black educational institutions in the South. The student population, drawn primarily from the rural black peasantry of Alabama, Georgia, and Mississippi, was taught to respect authority without debate. "We are not a college," Washington informed students in an 1896 campus convocation, "and if there are any of you here who expect to get a college training, you will be disappointed." Washington reluctantly permitted courses in sociology and psychology at Tuskegee, but he immediately put a stop to faculty efforts to start classes in Latin and Greek.

Male students scheduled rigorous courses in carpentry, printing, agricultural economics, and other technical training, while females learned the skills of laundry, sewing, and kitchen duties. Male students were even responsible for producing clay bricks in the institute's kiln and constructing all classroom buildings, dormitories, and faculty houses. Every aspect of their work fell under Washington's constant scrutiny. At mandatory religious exercises, all students had to pass by him for inspection. "His keen, piercing eyes were sure to detect any grease-spots that were on the students' clothes or any buttons that by chance were conspicuous by their absence from the students' clothing." Every day, Washington received extensive faculty reports on the smallest aspects of campus life: the "daily poultry report," the "daily swine herd report," the state of the latrines, the "condition of the kitchens."

Faculty who seemed to shirk their duties were strongly censured. Washington checked with the campus librarian to learn which teachers had not checked out books. The campus's assistant principal, Warren Logan, maintained a list of "teachers who were conspicuously irregular in their attendance upon prayers." Louis R. Harlan, Washington's biographer, comments: "Washington was paternalistic and even dictatorial in the manner of the planters and business tycoons for whom he always reserved his highest public flattery." Despite such measures, the institute acquired a notable reputation. By 1901, the school had 109 full-time faculty, 1,095 pupils, and owned property valued at nearly $330,000. Many of black America's leading researchers and scholars found employment at the institute: gifted agricultural chemist George Washington Carver; architect Robert R. Taylor; dramatist Charles Winter Wood; and Monroe N. Work, director of records and research and the editor of the *Negro Year Book*.[11]

The third component of Washington's strategy was the development of a black middle class, and in particular a highly organized black entrepreneurial stratum. According to records of the U.S. Bureau of the Census, there were only 431 black lawyers, 909 black physicians, and 15,000 black college, secondary, and elementary school teachers in 1890, out of a total black population of 7.5 million. Barely 1 percent of the black labor force was employed in clerical, professional, or business-related activities. In 1893 there were only 17,000 black-owned businesses in the United States, and well over 80 percent did not have a single paid employee.

Washington and other black educators (such as W. E. B. Du Bois) believed that Negro college-trained students could form the core of an entrepreneurial class, based on domination of the black consumer market. In 1900 Washington initiated the National Negro Business League, a black version of the Chamber of Commerce, to promote black private enterprise and cooperative activities among black businessmen. The "Tuskegee spirit" was subsequently expressed in the creation of other black professional societies: the National Bar Association in 1903, the National Negro Bankers Association in 1906, the National Association of Funeral Directors in 1907, and the National Negro Retail Merchants Association in 1913. The close cooperation between black educational institutions and the black private sector in providing thousands of young entrepreneurs with business and managerial skills and a modest access to capital was largely responsible for the creation of a new black elite in the early twentieth century. In these years the number of black-owned drugstores rose from 250 to 695; of black undertakers, from 450 to 1,000; of black retail merchants, from 10,000 to 25,000; and of black-owned banks, from 4 to 51.[12]

The fourth aspect of the Tuskegee strategy was the cultivation of white financial support for Negro education. During Reconstruction, several Northern philanthropies had begun to make modest subsidies available to black trade schools and colleges. Tuskegee's first outside grant, amounting to $1,000, was donated by the Peabody Education Fund in 1883. Most of these funding sources were rather small and usually permitted the continuation of existing programs rather than the development of new ones.

Booker T. Washington recognized that the conservative leaders of the newly emerging industrial and commercial enterprises were potentially a much greater funding base for black vocational education than the older liberal philanthropic agencies with ties to the abolitionist tradition of the northeastern United States. Washington's relationships with camera manufacturer George Eastman and steel industrialist Andrew Carnegie are illustrative. After reading Washington's Horatio Alger–style autobiography, *Up from Slavery*, Eastman promptly sent $5,000 to "Tuskegee Institute." From 1910 to 1915, Eastman gave $10,000 annually to Tuskegee, and upon Washington's death, he sent the school $250,000. After Carnegie heard Washington speak at a public forum, he handed the Negro educator ten $1,000 bills as a "secret gift." In the spring of 1903, Carnegie gave Tuskegee Institute $600,000 in U.S. Steel Company bonds, stipulating that one-quarter of that amount was for Washington's personal use. Washington used these funds to build Tuskegee, but he also used much money to subsidize other ventures, such as expansion of the Negro Business League and the purchase of controlling shares in major black newspapers.[13]

The apparent successes achieved by this strategy of educational political economy—the development of black-owned commercial establishments, the initiation of black private firms and small banks, and the dependence upon funding from conservative capitalists—were difficult to refute. In Macon County, Alabama, the home of Tuskegee, the number of black landowners increased from 157 in 1900 to 507 by 1910.[14]

Of course, many other examples of educational institutions' promoting black self-help also existed. In the early 1890s R. L. Smith, a graduate of Atlanta University and principal of the Oakland, Texas, Normal School for Negroes, established the Farmers' Improvement Society of Texas. The society's activities were many: it urged blacks to grow their own food supplies and sell their produce cooperatively and to improve their homes; it taught farmers the latest methods in agricultural production; and it provided insurance to black families. By 1909, the society had twenty-one thousand members in Arkansas, Texas, and Oklahoma and had created a bank and a rural vocational college. Hampton Institute initiated the Negro Organization Society in 1909, which was soon joined by local organizations representing 85 percent of the state's black population. The Virginia Society stressed the Tuskegee and Hampton Institutes' philosophy of capital accumulation, land ownership, and patronage of black-owned businesses, and it sponsored programs in family hygiene, health care, and literacy.[15]

The Tuskegee approach to the political economy of black education was not confined to the United States. During a visit to London in 1899, Washington promoted a Pan-African conference organized by Trinidadian lawyer Henry Sylvester Williams as a "most effective and far reaching event." The product of this 1900 conference was the modern Pan-Africanist movement, which was later led by W. E. B. Du Bois and George Padmore.[16] Henry Sylvester Williams had corresponded with Washington in 1899 and 1900 and asked him to distribute materials on the "proposed conference . . . as widely as is possible."[17]

Washington established an economic partnership with a private German firm that held concessions in Germany's African colonies. In January 1900 three Tuskegee graduates and one faculty member initiated an agricultural project in Togo. Tuskegee graduates were employed in the Sudan, Nigeria, and the Congo Free State. Inspired by Washington, Zulu Congregationalist minister John Langalibalele Dube spoke at Tuskegee's commencement in 1897, and four years later started the Zulu Christian Industrial School in Natal, South Africa.[18] The sage of Pan-Africanism, Edward Wilmot Blyden, also endorsed Washington's leadership. After reading a speech by Tuskegee Institute's principal, Blyden declared that Washington's "words" and "work will tend to free two races with prejudice and false views of life."[19]

III

The political linchpin of the Tuskegee educational and economic agenda was Washington's philosophy of "racial accommodation." His real rise to national attention came in September 1895, when he delivered a speech at Atlanta's Cotton States and International Exposition. Washington observed that one-third of the South's population was black and that an "enterprise seeking the material, civil or moral welfare" of the region could not disregard the Negro. Blacks should remain in the South—"Cast down your bucket where you are"—and participate in the capitalist economic development of that area. During the Reconstruction era, blacks had erred in their priorities. "Ignorant and inexperienced" blacks had tried to start "at the top instead of at the bottom"; a congressional seat "was more sought than real estate or industrial skill."

To the white South, Washington pledged the fidelity of his race, "the most patient, law-abiding, and unresentful people that the world has seen." And on the sensitive issue of racial integration and the protection of blacks' political rights, Washington made a dramatic concession: "In all things that are purely social we can be as separate as the fingers, yet one as the hand in all things essential to mutual progress. . . . The wisest among my race understand that the agitation of questions of social equality is the extremest folly."[20] Washington's social policy "compromise" was this: blacks would disavow open agitation for desegregation and the political franchise; in return, they would be permitted to develop their own parallel economic, educational, and social institutions within the framework of expanding Southern capitalism. Obscured by accommodationist rhetoric, Washington's statement was the expression of the nascent black entrepreneurial elite, many black landholders, and some educators.

White America responded to Washington's address with universal acclaim. President Grover Cleveland remarked that the speech was the foundation for "new hope" for black Americans. More accurate was the editorial of the *Atlanta Constitution*: "The speech stamps Booker T. Washington as a wise counselor and a safe leader."[21] Within several years after the "Atlanta Compromise" address, Washington had become the nation's preeminent black leader. Through his patronage, black and white supporters were able to secure federal government posts, and his influence with white philanthropists largely determined which Negro colleges would receive funds.

The "Tuskegee Machine" never acquiesced in the complete political disfranchisement of blacks; behind the scenes, Washington used his resources to fight for civil rights. In 1900 he requested funds from white philanthropists to lobby against racist election provisions in Louisiana's state constitution. He privately opposed Alabama's racial disfranchisement laws in federal courts and, in 1903–1904, personally spent "at least four thousand dollars in cash" to advance "the rights of the Black man."[22] Nevertheless, Washington's entire public approach to racist policies in the United States implied to whites that blacks were no longer interested in political power or civil rights.

Washington cemented his alliance with white capitalists by making polemical attacks on organized labor. Even before his rise to prominence, Washington professed antilabor opinions. Strikes were caused by "professional labor agitators," he commented critically in his autobiography. Striking workers must spend "all that they have saved" during their protests and must later "return to work in debt at the same wages."[23] Organized opposition to the demands of capital seemed foolish, even criminal, to Washington. He encouraged the Negro to seize the "opportunity to work at his trade" by "taking the place" of striking white workers. "The average Negro does not understand the necessity or advantage of a labor organization which stands between him and his employer and aims apparently to make a monopoly of the opportunity for labor," Washington wrote in 1913. Black laborers were "more accustomed to work for persons than for wages." The capitalist was the best friend of the unemployed Negro, not an enemy. The black worker should "not like an organization which seems to be founded on a sort of impersonal enmity to the man by whom he is employed." The black man's labor is "law-abiding, peaceable, teachable . . . labor that has never been tempted to follow the red flag of anarchy."[24]

The most controversial incident to test Washington's economic strategy occurred in 1908, during the Alabama coal miners' strike. The Alabama United Mineworkers (UMW) had twelve thousand members, six thousand of them black miners. When U.S. Steel refused to renew the workers' contracts and ordered substantial wage cuts, the miners announced a strike. The state government of Alabama assisted the company by sending convicts to work in the mines. The conflict soon escalated: miners dynamited the homes of non-union strikebreakers; police and company security guards shot and physically assaulted UMW leaders; the governor of Alabama ordered the state militia to destroy the tent camps of black and white strikers; and hundreds of labor leaders were imprisoned.

Washington did not hesitate to choose sides in the class struggle. Negroes must not be "given to strikes," he declared. The collective bargaining process of unionism must be avoided as a "form of slavery." As thousands of white miners lost their jobs, non-union black laborers replaced them at lower wages. Following the collapse of the UMW strike, the companies worked with Tuskegee Institute to initiate a form of non-union "welfare capitalism." U.S. Steel hired Tuskegee graduate John W. Oveltree as its "efficiency social agent" to monitor the work habits of fifteen thousand black laborers. The De Bardeleben Coal Company of Alabama employed another Tuskegee alumnus, R. W. Taylor, as its supervisor of black coal miners. In gratitude, each year the company awarded several scholarships to Tuskegee to children of its black employees.

The reaction of white miners to the strikebreaking tactics of Tuskegee was predictable. By 1910 fewer than six hundred blacks were members of the umw, and even those had no access to positions of union leadership. Non-union blacks now constituted 75 percent of all miners in Alabama, but their reduced wages left them only marginally above poverty.[25]

Washington's open alliance with white capitalists and public acceptance of racial segregation could be justified to the small black petite bourgeoisie in economic terms. "No race that has anything to contribute to the markets of the world is long in any degree ostracized," Washington observed.[26] As white firms retreated from the black sections of towns and rural areas, the graduates of Tuskegee Institute and other industrial schools were fully prepared to assume their roles as entrepreneurs in the private-enterprise system. Black consumers were poor, but collectively their market was large enough to maintain a black petit bourgeois stratum. In turn-of-the-century Montgomery, Alabama, for example, black entrepreneurs had established twenty restaurants, twenty-three grocery stores, and three drugstores in a town with only two thousand blacks. Montgomery's black community also included twelve building contractors and five physicians and could patronize fifteen blacksmith shops and two funeral establishments of its own.[27]

By 1913, fifty years after the abolition of slavery, a substantial black entrepreneurial, professional, and landholding elite had developed. Black Americans owned 550,000 homes and had accumulated $700 million in wealth. The number of black-owned businesses had doubled in only thirteen years, from 20,000 to 40,000. African Americans owned 15.7 million acres of land across the South, and 200,000 of the nation's 848,000 black farmers owned their farms. As economic historian Gilbert C. Fite has noted: "When it is considered that Blacks started out without capital or independent business experience and faced severe racial discrimination . . . the record of black ownership by the early twentieth century was remarkable."[28]

IV

African American intellectuals, journalists, and college teachers were largely alarmed by Washington's immense influence. With some exceptions, they did not reject Tuskegee's economic strategy, but they did question its emphasis on rural development at the expense of the urban petite bourgeoisie. Nor were they opposed to industrial and agricultural education for the vast majority of Southern Negroes. Their principal objection was Washington's social policy of accommodation. Abandoning electoral politics and accepting racial segregation in all public accommodations and civic life would, they believed, make black advancement in economic and educational fields extremely difficult, if not impossible.

They also perceived that the "Tuskegee Machine" had developed such influence over national educational policy that nonvocational schools for blacks were in serious jeopardy. The most articulate representative of the anti-Washington tendency in Negro higher education was W. E. B. Du Bois, who in 1910 founded the National Association for the Advancement of Colored People (NAACP). Du Bois thought that only the black liberal arts colleges, not schools based on the Hampton-Tuskegee Institute model, were capable of producing a stable, educated black middle class, or what he termed the "Talented Tenth."

Indeed, Du Bois argued in 1903, "to attempt to establish any sort of a system of common and industrial school training, without first (and I say first advisedly) providing for the higher training of the very best teachers, is simply throwing your money away to the winds." Further, he argued, black America would only be "saved by its exceptional men," those who possessed "intelligence, broad sympathy, knowledge of the world that was and is, and of the relation of men to it." The Talented Tenth must "guide their own and other races."[29] Du Bois believed that industrial and agricultural education was a "splendid thing. But when it is coupled by sneers at Negro colleges whose work made industrial schools possible, when it is accompanied by the exaltation of men's bellies and depreciation of their brains," he declared, "then it becomes a movement you must choke to death or it will choke you."[30]

Washington was totally unscrupulous in his attacks on Du Bois and other black liberal critics. The Negro press aligned with Tuskegee printed personal and political attacks against Du Bois. Black ministers and educators who favored an aggressive approach to civil rights were dismissed or demoted by Washington's surrogates. Spies were planted in civil rights organizations, and black colleges whose faculty or administrators opposed the Tuskegee philosophy were denied funds from white philanthropies and corporations. Even within his own ranks, Washington cautiously looked for signs of insubordination. One Tuskegee Institute instructor expressed misgivings about Washington's authoritarian behavior to his pastor in Boston. Washington's aides managed to steal these personal letters, and the teacher in question was promptly humiliated for actions that "were disloyal to the Institution."[31]

Washington's many efforts to suppress free speech and civil rights reveal his determination to play an aggressive role as "collaborator" with white corporations, the state, and segregationists in controlling the status of the Negro. As sociologist Oliver C. Cox suggested, "the term 'Uncle Tom' does not seem to describe the role of the leadership of Washington. The 'Uncle Tom' is a passive figure; he is so thoroughly inured to the condition of subordination that he has become tame and obsequious." Washington, by contrast, projected himself as a mass leader, but he drew his effective power from the white ruling class. Washington was "an intercessor between his group and the dominant class," Cox noted. He was "given wide publicity as a phenomenal leader" precisely because "he demanded less for the Negro people than that which the ruling class had already conceded."[32]

The contradictions in the Tuskegee approach to black development became apparent only over several years. A public policy of compromise and appeasement to white racism, for example, permitted white legislatures to dismantle much of the black educational system that had been built a generation earlier. In 1900 the state of Georgia spent about one-fourth as much educating the average black child as it spent on a white child attending its public schools; in North Carolina the figure for black children was approximately one-third; in South Carolina, about one-sixth. In Georgia there were 108 black children per teacher compared to 51 students per teacher in white schools; black teachers' salaries were roughly one-half those of white teachers.

By 1915 the educational gap between blacks and whites had widened dramatically. The number of Southern four-year high schools had increased from 123 to 509, but the ratio of white to black students was twenty-nine to one. In 1917, North Carolina had 285 public high schools with a total enrollment of 15,469 students. Its population was then 32 percent black, but the total number of black students enrolled in high school throughout North Carolina was nineteen. The disparity between school expenditures per child for white and black students had also soared. In South Carolina, for example, the average white child received $13.98 annually, and the average black child received $1.13—only about 8.1 percent of the amount received by whites. Student-teacher ratios in Southern black public schools were down slightly, to 95 to one; but in white schools, the figure was 44.6 to one.[33]

This educational underdevelopment was replicated at the university level. Southern whites of most social classes placed little value on higher education generally and allocated marginal resources for the advanced training of their own young adults. As historian C. Vann Woodward notes, white Southern colleges were "pitifully" endowed. In 1901 the combined endowments of all the colleges in eleven Southern states were "less than half of the funds held by the colleges of New York State alone." Harvard University had a larger annual income in 1901 than the combined incomes of "the sixty-six colleges and universities of Virginia, North Carolina, South Carolina, Georgia, Alabama, Mississippi, and Arkansas." Few white technical schools and graduate schools in the South were genuinely capable of doing research, and standards at the bachelor's degree level were barely above those of secondary school levels in the North.[34]

Given the poverty of white higher education, it is not surprising that black colleges and industrial schools fared poorly during the flood of white supremacy. White critics complained that college and technical training had made blacks "uppish" and "bumptious" and prompted them to "despise work."[35] State legislatures sharply cut into the budgets of black state-supported schools. In 1916 the segregated Negro Agricultural and Technical College at Greensboro, North Carolina, received only one-thirteenth of the amount appropriated to white state schools. Also in 1916, the black public colleges in Virginia, Georgia, and the Carolinas "received from their states less than one-eighth of the amount for whites in Virginia alone."[36]

Washington's public position of accommodation to racial inequality prepared the ideological ground for a series of repressive laws governing race relations. Washington had hoped that a conservative social order would respect the civil and political rights of Negro Americans. This was unfortunately not the case. In Alabama, for example, there were 180,000 black adult males of voting age in 1900. After the ratification of Alabama's white supremacist state constitution in 1901, black voters almost disappeared. In 1908, only 3,700 black males in Alabama were registered voters; two decades later, the figure had fallen to 1,500. Other states carried out similar measures. In Louisiana the black electorate declined from 130,000 in 1896 to fewer than 5,000 in less than a decade. In Virginia the number of black voters dropped to 21,000, out of a black adult male population of 150,000. It is important to note that voting restrictions were aimed at poor and working-class whites, as well as blacks. Nearly half of all white male adults in Mississippi were barred from voting by literacy tests and poll taxes.

The demand for white supremacy was extended to public accommodations. Georgia had racially segregated all public streetcars in 1891, and within a decade all other Southern states had followed suit. In 1905 the "Separate Park Law" was approved by the Georgia State Assembly, restricting blacks from public parks. By 1908 Atlanta's major public buildings had racially segregated elevators. In later years Jim Crow restrictions tightened. In 1922 Mississippi adopted a state Jim Crow law for all taxicabs. Texas banned whites and "Africans" from boxing or wrestling together in 1933. Oklahoma barred interracial fishing and boating in 1935. And Birmingham's city council barred blacks and whites from playing dominoes or checkers together in 1930.

Such city ordinances and statewide legislation inevitably gave sanction to racist violence. Alabama had 246 lynchings of Negroes between 1885 and 1918, well behind the national leader, Georgia, which held 381 lynchings. Although the rate of lynchings declined gradually after 1900, these vigilante crimes persisted. In 1915, the year of Washington's death, Alabama recorded 9 lynchings and Georgia had 18, including some in which blacks were burned alive.[37]

The critical weakness of Washington's economic strategy was his failure to comprehend the negative effects of rigid segregation on all sectors of the black labor force. Although the barriers of Jim Crow helped to generate a black consumer market, which was exploited by Negro entrepreneurs and professionals, the reality was that black workers suffered severe income losses in other ways.

First, racial segregation permitted white employers to lower the general rates of wages to all workers. White laborers were protected from higher unemployment rates by the whites-first rule in vocational hirings, yet they also suffered a reduction in wages. White union members frequently accepted poor contracts with companies just to maintain the color line in their industry.[38]

Second, the anti-union philosophy of Tuskegee provided racists inside organized labor with a justification for expelling black members. In the early 1900s there were forty-three national unions with not even one black member. By 1912 thousands of additional black trade unionists had been removed: the national printers' union had only 250 black members, the lithographers' one, the potters' union none, the glass bottle blowers' none, the hatters' union none, and the union of iron, steel, and tin workers had only 2 or 3 blacks.[39]

Third, thousands of black artisans and entrepreneurs who depended solely or primarily upon white clients were displaced with the imposition of Jim Crow. Many positions that had been defined as "Negro jobs" were seized by whites. In 1870, according to Woodward, New Orleans "had list-ed 3,460 Negroes as carpenters, cigar makers, painters, clerks, shoemakers, coopers, tailors, bakers, blacksmiths, and foundry hands, [but] not 10 percent of that number were employed in the same trades in 1904. Yet the Negro population had gained more than 50 percent."[40]

On balance, Washington's policies of accommodation and anti-unionism retarded the accumulation of capital within black working-class households and helped drive thousands of skilled black artisans out of the marketplace.

Tuskegee Institute's curriculum did not adequately respond to the rapidly changing status of black workers in the labor force. Vocational schools continued to train black students as blacksmiths, wheelwrights, masons, plumbers, and for dozens of other trades that no longer offered employment to blacks. Some of these skills became obsolete with the development of new technologies, but many others, such as brickmasonry, eliminated blacks with the expanding racial segregation of organized labor. With the rise in cotton prices during the period 1900–1914, black farmers trained by Tuskegee's methods still had not adequately diversified their crop production. The closure of the European markets during World War I sharply reduced cotton prices, leading to a chain reaction of default. Black rural tenants and landholders were unable to sell their crops at any price, and thousands went bankrupt. By 1918 only one black-owned bank was left in Alabama—the savings firm at Tuskegee Institute. The number of Mississippi black banks declined to only two.

As credit disappeared or became more costly, many black farm families trekked north, where the prospect of higher wages and life without rigid Jim Crow barriers presented a more attractive alternative. The black exodus during 1900–1910 was 170,000; by 1920–1930, it amounted to 749,000. The steady deterioration of the interracial environment, the absence of effective legal rights, and the continuation of vigilante violence combined with economic factors to push many African Americans out of the rural South and into the ghettos of the North.[41]

What was Washington's legacy to the educational and economic development of black America? Writing in 1936, Du Bois suggested a partial answer:

> Washington was an opportunist, slow but keen-witted, with high ideals. . . . He knew that the Negro needed civil and social rights. But he believed that if the Negroes showed that they could advance despite discrimination, that the inherent justice in the nation would gradually extend to deserving Negroes the rights that they merited. . . . He expected that the Black owners of property would thus gain recog-

nition from other property-holders and gradually rise in the scale of society.[42]

Washington was wrong—on his economic policies, on his authoritarian measures of instruction at the institute, on his blind faith in petty-capital accumulation for Negroes, and on his public capitulation to racism. Yet his school still exists in Tuskegee, Alabama; his National Negro Business League provides the leadership for today's black American petty capitalists; and his tactics of political accommodation with white corporations to generate funding for black social institutions are taken as normative behavior among broad sectors of the black educational community. Booker T. Washington's economic and educational insights remain, with their respective strengths and contradictions, a permanent feature of African American social organizations and leaders.

4

W. E. B. Du Bois and the
Politics of Culture

Ranking as he does among the foremost writers of true importance in the country, one wishes sometimes (as a writer oneself) that he could devote all of his time to the accomplishment of that fine and moving prose which distinguishes his books. But at the same time one realizes, self-reproachfully, that with Dr. Du Bois it is a cause—an ideal—that overcomes the personal egoism of the artist.

—EUGENE O'NEILL,
COMMENTING ON W. E. B. DU BOIS

THE MOST PASSIONATE and influential critic of racism in the twentieth century was W. E. B. Du Bois. The African American intellectual is known primarily for three distinct contributions to the political, social, and educational transformation of American society.

I

Du Bois was the first American scholar to undertake the systematic analysis of the African and African American experience. His doctoral dissertation at Harvard University, *The Suppression of the African Slave-Trade to the United States of America, 1638–1870*, published in 1896, established the foundations for scientific studies on the impact on slavery within the Americas.[1] His 1899 sociological survey of black urban life, *The Philadelphia Negro*, was the first empirical critique of social class, educational, economic, and cultural conditions of any black community.[2] Du Bois authored a series of historical works outlining the connections between black Americans and other people of African descent, including *The Negro*, published in 1915, and *Black Folk Then and Now: An Essay in the History and Sociology of the Negro Race*, published in 1939.[3] His most complex and influential work, *Black Reconstruction in America* (1935), was a revisionist interpretation of the role of African Americans after the American Civil War, illustrating the role of race in disrupting the development of democratic institutions.[4] Between 1898 and 1913 he edited a series of sociological studies, the Atlanta University Publications, which examined in exhaustive detail various social, economic, and cultural problems within the African American community.

Second, Du Bois was the central architect for the modern social protest movement for freedom in the United States. Nearly a century ago, in an era marked by widespread lynchings of blacks, political disfranchisement, and the institutionalization of rigid racial segregation, he challenged the black community to defend itself and to struggle for full civil rights. His influential collection of essays, *The Souls of Black Folk*, published in 1903, condemned the growing reality of institutional racism and the tendency of black Americans influenced by educator Booker T. Washington to accommodate to social oppression and inequality.[5] In 1905 Du Bois initiated the Niagara Movement, a group of reform-minded black educators, lawyers, and intellectuals who criticized segregation laws and agitated for civil rights. Within five years, elements of the Niagara Movement merged with white liberals and socialists to create the National Association for the Advancement of Colored People (NAACP). Du Bois left his faculty position at Atlanta University, and for nearly a quarter century served as the editor of the NAACP journal, *Crisis*. His powerful political journalism shaped the protest consciousness of an entire generation of African Americans engaged in the effort to abolish racial segregation.

Third, Du Bois is also remembered widely for his contributions to the political emancipation of Africa. In 1900 he was one of the founders of the first Pan-African Conference, held in London, an attempt to coordinate protest activities across Africa, the Caribbean, and black America. He initiated a series of Pan-African congresses in the United States and Europe, in 1919, 1921, 1923, 1927, and 1945, which helped to spark modern independence and liberation movements across the African Diaspora. For Kwame Nkrumah, Jomo Kenyatta, Eric Williams, and a host of political leaders in the Third World, Du Bois was the "Father of Pan-Africanism." He left the United States as a political exile in late 1961 and died in Nkrumah's Ghana at the age of ninety-five in 1963.

Seldom is Du Bois perceived outside of his immediate political context. Yet the essence of this scholar—who was admittedly egotistic, elitist, aloof from the masses, and arrogant—was the spirit of the artist. Motivating Du Bois's lifelong activities was a uniquely cultural vision of what American and western European societies could become if freed from the shackles of racial dogma and the ideology of economic domination. His cultural quest was to construct a societal order in which the cultures of various social and ethnic groups could function on the basis of social and economic equality, within a political framework of full, participatory democracy. When he considered the basic questions challenging both people of color and white Americans or Europeans to relate to each other as equals, he concluded that they were fundamentally cultural.

For the oppressed, the central and overriding question was one of identity: who are we as a people, what is our cultural heritage, what values or ideals can we share with other groups to enrich society as a whole, and what do we have a right to expect from the state and civil society? Within explorations of culture resides the kernel of an oppressed group's consciousness. So for Du Bois, the challenge was both to negate the existing political, socioeconomic reality and to project a cultural construct that would inform the evolution and development of people of African descent, in a manner that reaffirmed their collective memory and their unique aesthetic sensibility.

Early in his writings Du Bois developed an approach toward the study of cultural issues and group consciousness that would influence his subsequent research and scholarship. Throughout the nineteenth century, two fundamental racial ideologies emerged among African American intellectuals—integration and black nationalism. The integrationists saw themselves not as people of African descent but as American citizens who happened to be black. They opposed any form of institutional separation based on racial categories and agitated for full civil and political rights within the existing system of capitalist democracy. Black nationalists, conversely, identified themselves culturally and politically with other people of African descent in the Americas and emphasized their connections with sub-Saharan Africa. They were critical of alliances with white Americans and distrustful of the government, and they stressed the necessity for blacks to develop their own schools, as well as their own economic and cultural institutions. Between these two racial ideologies stood Du Bois, who attempted to construct a synthesis based on his cultural understanding of black identity.

His cultural formation was the "double consciousness" theory, expressed in *The Souls of Black Folk*. He argued that the core consciousness of the black American people was found within the unity of opposites, the dual reality of their blackness and their American identity. The Negro American, Du Bois insisted, was both "an American, a Negro; two souls, two thoughts, two unreconciled strivings; two warring ideals in one dark body, whose dogged strength alone keeps it from being torn asunder." The entire history of the black American was that of cultural and group psychological conflict, "this longing to attain self-conscious manhood, to merge his double self into a better and truer self." Within his cultural metamorphosis, Du Bois wished to maintain the critical elements of each original source:

> He would not Africanize America, for America has too much to teach the world and Africa. He would not bleach his Negro soul in a flood of white Americanism, for he knows that Negro blood has a message for the world. He simply wished to make it possible for a man to be both a Negro and an American, without being cursed and spit upon by his fellows, without having the doors of Opportunity closed roughly in his face. This, then, is the end of his striving: to be a co-worker in the kingdom of culture, to escape both death and isolation, to husband and use his best powers and his latent genius.[6]

The double consciousness theory helps to explain Du Bois's entire political and academic career; he was constantly at odds with both the integrationist and the black nationalist leaders and organizations. From his position within the NAACP, he championed struggles against all forms of oppression, including sexism and anti-Semitism. He advocated the expansion of full democratic rights to all American citizens. But unlike most of his NAACP colleagues who were integrationists, he also fully identified with the cultures, heritage, and political resistance of people of color throughout the Third World, particularly in the Caribbean and sub-Saharan Africa. His academic research focused largely on the cultural and political role of Africa in world civilization. Politically, he led the fight to achieve independence and full self-determination for nonwhite nations. Domestically, he also favored the continuation of all-black educational institutions, and during the Great Depression he called for the development of all-black consumer and producer cooperatives. Similarly, this existential duality or double consciousness established the matrix for the construction of cultural forms of resistance and self-realization.

The development of an antiracist culture and society, for Du Bois, meant the development of a cultural critique of the reality and foundations of racism. What was racial inequality culturally, and how was it manifested within civil society? He consistently argued that racism was not derived from the real or imputed biological or genetic differences between Europeans and people of color. In 1914 he observed that "race antipathy is not instinctive, but a matter of careful education." Racism is socially constructed and is reinforced by the system of unequal power and privilege exercised by white people.[7]

Several years later, in *Darkwater: Voices from Within the Veil*, Du Bois deconstructed what he termed "the Souls of White Folk." Whiteness as a cultural identity was based upon a historical and hypocritical fraud. "The discovery of personal whiteness among the world's peoples is a very modern thing,—a nineteenth and twentieth century matter, indeed," he observed critically. "The ancient world would have laughed at such a distinction. . . . This assumption that of all the hues of God whiteness alone is inherently and obviously better than brownness or tan leads to curious acts" of oppression. The basis of racial privilege and white superiority is rooted within the dynamics of capitalism, colonialism, and domination:

> This theory of human culture and its aims has worked itself through warp and woof of our daily thought with a thoroughness that few realize. Everything great, good, efficient, fair, and honorable is "white"; everything mean, bad, blundering, cheating and dishonorable is "yellow"; a bad taste is "brown"; and the devil is "black." The changes of this theme are continually rung in picture and story, in newspaper heading and moving-picture, in sermon and school book, until, of course, the King can do no wrong,—a White Man is always right and a Black Man has no rights which a white man is bound to respect. There must come the necessary despising and hatreds of these savage half-men, this unclean *canaille* of the world—these dogs of men. All through the world this gospel is preaching. It has its literature, it has its priests, it has its secret propaganda and above all— it pays![8]

Central to the process of perpetuating white racial identity was the cultural apparatus of western societies. White America's newspapers, radio networks, and other communications systems perpetuated racial stereotypes. The cultural institutions that produced popular music, theater, films, professional athletics, and public amusements of all types reinforced white superiority and black inferiority. White Americans as a group were so heavily bombarded with racial stereotypes that their relations with blacks as individuals and as a group were largely predetermined, structured on a basis of antagonistic conflicts, competition, and hatred rather than within the premises of the search for common human characteristics and mutual respect. Any arguments contradicting the legitimacy of racial domination were dismissed or ruthlessly oppressed. As Du Bois commented in *Crisis* in 1930:

> [Many Americans] have no conception of the meaning of the freedom of speech. They apparently assume that this is the right to express any opinion with which they agree, but that opinions with which they disagree or which they regard as unsound or dangerous, must be

suppressed. Back of this willingness to silence those to whom men do not wish to listen, lies stupidity, cruelty, oppression and disaster.[9]

More devastating was the impact of white racial superiority upon non-whites, fostering a sense of embitterment and self-hatred. For five hundred years, "men had hated and despised and abused black folk. . . . We are instinctively and almost unconsciously ashamed of the caricatures done of our darker shades," Du Bois noted in 1920. The deconstruction of race required the articulation of the validity and integrity of African-derived aesthetics and culture. "Off with these thought-chains and inchoate soul-shrinkings," he urged other African Americans, "and let us train ourselves to see beauty in black."[10]

II

For African Americans to think of themselves in a new way, transcending the imposed blinders of inferiority and self-doubt, Du Bois believed, culture must be seized as a creative, reconstructive tool. The clearest expression of Du Bois's objectives in promoting a permanent, cultural revolution among African Americans was his seminal 1926 essay, "Criteria of Negro Art." He challenged first those who insisted that former slaves had no right to speak of art or aesthetics and that the pressing economic, social, and political problems confronting black Americans were so severe that cultural issues were secondary or superfluous. "What do we want? We want to be Americans, full-fledged Americans, with all the rights of other American citizens. But is that all?" he asked. "We who are dark can see America in a way that white Americans can not. And seeing our country thus, are we satisfied with its present goals and ideals?"

The struggle against racism was at its core a two-sided cultural conflict, an attempt to undermine racist stereotypes and beliefs among whites and to restore a sense of identity and pride among nonwhites. "The white public today demands from its artists, literary and pictorial, racial pre-judgment. The white public deliberately distorts truth and justice, as far as colored races are concerned, and it will pay for no other." Such prejudicial stereotypes had to be challenged at every opportunity. The greatest burden was not against the external oppressor, Du Bois cautioned, but rather within the Negro group itself. Black Americans' search for true self-consciousness was a quest of culture:

> Thus it is the bounden duty of black America to begin this great work of the creation of beauty, of the preservation of beauty, of the realization of beauty, and we must use in this work all the methods that men

have used before. And what have been the tools of the artist in times gone by? First of all, he has used the truth—not for the sake of truth, not as a scientist seeking truth, but as one upon whom truth eternally thrusts itself as the highest handmaid of imagination, as the one great vehicle of universal understanding. . . . The apostle of beauty thus becomes the apostle of truth and right not by choice but by inner and outer compulsion. Free he is but his freedom is ever bounded by truth and justice; and slavery only dogs him when he is denied the right to tell the truth or recognize an ideal or justice. Thus all art is propaganda and ever must be, despite the wailing of the purists. . . . I do not care a damn for any art that is not used for propaganda.[11]

In the field of music, Du Bois repeatedly emphasized the unique genius of the African American spiritual and secular songs, illustrating that much of white American music was based on rhythms and patterns derived from Africa. In 1903 he produced *A Bibliography of Negro Folk Songs* at Atlanta University, one of the first scholarly efforts to document African American music.[12] That same year, in *The Souls of Black Folk*, he wrote of the religious music generated by slaves: "The Negro folk-song—the rhythmic cry of the slave—stands to-day not simply as the sole American music, but as the most beautiful expression of human experience born this side of the seas. . . . It still remains as the singular spiritual heritage of the nation and the greatest gift of the Negro people."[13] In *Crisis*, he periodically reported on developments in black music. In May 1926, for example, he noted the pioneering contributions of John Wesley Work, the artist who helped to "resurrect and make eternal the Negro spiritual."[14] In the black newspaper of Harlem, the *Amsterdam News*, he urged readers to develop a personal "Negro music library," obtaining such works as James Weldon Johnson and J. Rosamond Johnson's *Book of American Negro Spirituals*, W. C. Handy's *Blues*, and W. A. Fisher's *Seventy Negro Spirituals*.[15] Du Bois was one of the first critics to highlight the activities of black artists Bert Williams, Carl Diton, and Will Marion Cook.

Consistent with the double consciousness theory, however, Du Bois always stressed that African Americans were profoundly American and had the democratic right to perform music drawn from the European experience. In 1933, when a *New York Times* reviewer urged Negroes to sing "old-time" darky songs from the plantation era, because they were not capable of the finer expressions of art, he took prompt exception. African American people have the right to sing spirituals, blues, and other expressions from their own cultural and aesthetic background, but this by no means should exclude their creative impulses from other areas. "It is to be trusted that our leaders in music, holding on to the beautiful heritage of the past, will not on that account, either be coerced or frightened from taking all music for their province and showing the world how to sing," he insisted.[16] According to historian Gerald Horne, Du Bois practiced what he preached aesthetically. He was a "patron" of the Harlem Opera Society. He loved Negro spirituals, but as his second wife, Shirley Graham, observed, "his favorite recording [was] the Ninth Symphony by Beethoven."[17]

Du Bois was similarly involved in other creative arts. *Crisis* informed readers of the work of sculptor Elizabeth Prophet, a black American who had studied at L'école Nationale Supérieure des Beaux-Arts in Paris. "Almost without money, without friends, and frail of physique," Du Bois commented, Prophet had produced sculpture that displayed a "fine artistic sense and mastery in her field." He used Prophet to chide the African American community for its failure to provide adequate material resources to creative artists. "Prophet has sacrificed both health and strength to her art. She has starved herself and gone without proper clothing. . . . Grim and determined, she is still working on, without assistance, almost unknown in America."[18] In 1903 Du Bois wrote a short essay on black painter Henry O. Tanner, noting that such artists and creative intellectuals were part of "the advance guard of the race."[19] Two decades later in *Crisis*, its editor complained that only two African Americans had ever purchased a Tanner painting. Du Bois urged every black church and cultural institution to purchase the works of Tanner and other painters.[20] Curiously, he seldom wrote about black dance; in 1940, however, in the pages of Atlanta University's *Phylon* magazine, he noted with approval the successes of "Katherine Dunham and her dance group" in the development of acclaimed "exhibitions of the Negro dance."[21]

III

Du Bois's greatest aesthetic passion was for the theater. Always something of a thespian in both public and private life, he was consistently attracted by the lure of the stage. *Crisis* was frequently a forum for discussions of innovations in Negro theater. "The Negro is essentially dramatic," Du Bois confirmed in 1916. "His greatest gift to the world has been and will be a gift of art, of appreciation and realization of beauty." To create theater, playwrights and performers, individually and collectively, had to cultivate an awareness of their political obligations to the masses of black people. Once transcending the ghetto of "Negro minstrelsy," with "the growth of a considerable number of colored theaters and moving picture places, a new and inner demand for Negro drama has arisen."

Du Bois argued that the obligation of the Negro drama was, in part, to instruct blacks in "the meaning of their history and their rich, emotional life through a new theater" while simultaneously revealing "the Negro to the white world as a human, feeling thing." Again, the duality of the artistic objectives was rooted in Du Bois's cultural matrix of the double consciousness.[22] He expanded on this theme in 1924 in his brief essay "The Negro and the American Stage." The cultural struggle against racist ideology had to be waged on the dramatic stage. Throughout America's artistic history, the African American role in performances "has been a lay figure whose business it was usually to be funny and sometimes pathetic. He has never, with very few exceptions, been human or credible. This, of course, cannot last." He observed yet again, "The most dramatic group of people in the history of the United States is the American Negro":

> Any mention of Negro blood or Negro life in America for a century has been occasion for an ugly picture, a dirty allusion, a nasty comment or a pessimistic forecast. The result is that the Negro today fears any attempt of the artist to paint Negroes. He is not satisfied unless everything is perfect and proper and beautiful and joyful and hopeful. . . . Happy is the artist that breaks through any of these shells for his is the kingdom of eternal beauty. He will come through scarred and perhaps a little embittered, certainly astonished at the almost universal misinterpretation of his motives and aims. . . . But it is work that must be done. No greater mine of dramatic material ever lay ready for the great artist's hands than the situation of men of Negro blood in modern America.[23]

Du Bois's enthusiasm for the theater began quite early in life. As a youth in Great Barrington, Massachusetts, he participated in a high school folk play, *Old John Brown Had a Little Indian*. At Harvard University six years later, now more sophisticated, he helped organize a version of Aristophanes' *The Birds* in an all-black Boston church. At the age of ninety, looking backward in warmth and affection, he wrote: "The rendition was good, but not outstanding; not quite appreciated by the colored audience, but well worth doing. Even though it worked me near to death, I was proud of it."[24] Within months of becoming editor of *Crisis*, he sensed that the theater could serve his larger political objectives. After 1904 Du Bois considered himself a socialist, and in 1911–1912 he briefly joined the Socialist Party. In 1913 he became a contributor to the socialist-oriented *New Review*, along with fellow NAACP leaders William English Walling and young (then radical) journalist Walter Lippmann. Many of these bohemian leftists in New York were promoting theatrical pageants during these years, to dramatize the plight of the oppressed working classes. Inspired partially by his radical white colleagues, Du Bois in 1911 wrote his own dramatic pageant, *The Star of Ethiopia*.[25]

With a projected cast of 350 actors and participants, he single-handedly raised sufficient funds for the pageant's production. The premiere was held in New York in 1913, at the Emancipation Exposition. Popular acclaim led him to restage the pageant in Washington, D.C., with 1,200 participants. The event was well received, but Du Bois, who raised two thousand dollars for the production, was still forced to spend five hundred dollars of his own money. In 1916 in Philadelphia, *The Star of Ethiopia* was performed by more than 1,000 participants at the one-hundredth anniversary conference of the African Methodist Episcopal Church. Nearly ten years later, on June 15 and 18, 1925, *The Star* was performed at the Hollywood Bowl in Los Angeles, with the proceeds going to the welfare bureau of the Los Angeles branch of the NAACP. Thousands of black Americans witnessed these extravaganzas and were profoundly moved. Twelve thousand people, including the daughter of the president of the United States, attended the Washington pageant. Still, there were disappointments. The project attracted little interest from the white public. Du Bois admitted, "There have been within my own race the usual petty but hurting insinuations of personal greed and selfishness as the real incentives behind my efforts." Nevertheless, he reaffirmed, "The great fact has been demonstrated that pageantry among colored people is not only possible, but in many ways of unsurpassed beauty and can be made a means of uplift and education and the beginning of a folk drama."[26]

After World War I, Du Bois's interest and involvement in black theater was revived. In his 1923 essay "Can the Negro Serve the Drama?" he reiterated that the African American had the capacity to produce black Ibsens and Molières.[27] He applauded the organization of the Ethiopian Art Theater, under the direction of Raymond O'Neil, and its performance of *Salomé* on New York's Broadway. Although the play did not succeed financially, Du Bois observed in Crisis, "dramatically and spiritually it was one of the great successes that the country has seen."[28] Following O'Neil, Du Bois decided to become directly engaged with a black theatrical company. In 1925 he participated in the establishment of the Krigwa Players in Harlem, which functioned for two years before disbanding. This direct experience made him more aware of the inherent difficulties in organizing and financing theatrical productions that had larger political functions and goals.[29]

In a 1931 address, Du Bois observed that theater was potentially the most politically and aesthetically liberating of all art forms. "Behind the footlights one is permitted to examine and discuss truth," he argued. But this environment of potential freedom of expression was fundamentally compromised and flawed. The spirit of art was not only "threatened . . . by the well recognized fatty degeneration of musical comedy, but by that secret, internal and devastating malady which attacks an art which is free to treat the truth, and yet afraid to look it in the face." Most playwrights refused to confront the harsh realities of racism, preferring instead to "turn the piteous tragedy of the Negro into cheap pornographic pathos." The Negro artist's fellow actors "persistently [denied] him full recognition" for any perceived talents or creativity. But the problem of cultural freedom was directly linked to the issue of democracy, not simply for the Negro but for all Americans. "A freedom unused is perverted or lost," Du Bois warned. "If the stage dare not frankly portray the Negro problem because of fear and snobbery," the American theater would eventually suppress the discussion of other controversial issues.[30]

IV

Although aristocratic in temperament, Du Bois recognized the importance of popular culture in the social and political development of most working-class African Americans. Occasionally he commented on recent developments in filmmaking, popular humor, professional athletics, and popular music. In 1943 he drafted a short essay called "The Humor of Negroes," which illustrated the political edge of black laughter. The "dry mockery of the pretensions of white folk" embedded within black humor provided both a critique of racial segregation and a confirmation of the human value and self-worth of blacks against the weight of oppression.[31]

Du Bois followed the careers of black athletes for his readers, illustrating the disruptive role that racism played, frequently negating their achievements. For example, in 1914, commenting on controversial heavyweight champion Jack Johnson, he observed that the recent expressions of white public criticism concerning boxing "brutality" were based on racial antipathy to domination by black athletes. In 1923 he commented that boxing was indeed a brutal business, but it was preferable to armed warfare; besides, the racist treatment of black athletes such as Jack Johnson was "beneath contempt."[32] In *Phylon*, Du Bois noted the pugilistic accomplishments of heavyweight champion Joe Louis and welterweight champion Henry Armstrong and the growing white hostility toward black athletic excellence. "It is clear with every successive battle that Louis wins," he wrote in late 1941, "that the attitude of the spectators is worse and worse. His victory receives slight applause and even minor advantages on the part of his opponents are greeted with hysteria."

The root cause of racial partisanship was the Jim Crow structure of collegiate and professional athletics. "Negroes have made brilliant records in football but they are not allowed to compete in any major football leagues," Du Bois complained. "They have always been excluded from professional baseball despite well-known cases of ability. In tennis no Negro can compete except in his own racial organizations."[33] When Jackie Robinson finally broke the color bar in professional baseball in 1947, Du Bois felt that a significant political and cultural landmark had been achieved. He attended the fifth game of the 1947 World Series, in order to see Robinson in the Brooklyn Dodgers' lineup. But he constantly reminded African Americans not to place excessive emphasis on athletic achievements at the expense of the pursuits of knowledge and the creative arts. In May 1947 Du Bois noted in his newspaper column for the *Chicago Defender* that the graduation of John Howard as "the first Negro college graduate of Princeton University" superseded Robinson's accomplishment.[34]

In the struggle to develop a vibrant cultural environment, special emphasis had to be placed on the nurturing and training of black children. Du Bois dearly loved children, seeing in them all of the fullness of human hope and possibility, the transcendence of hate and conflict. In one of his earliest essays, "The Problem of Amusement," published in 1897, he encouraged black parents to create healthy and loving conditions for the raising of their children.[35] Returning to this theme constantly in *Crisis*, Du Bois argued that cultural transformation required a special place for children: "Because to childhood we look for the salvation of the world. To childhood we look for the triumph of justice, mercy, and truth. As the children of this generation are trained, so will the hope of all men in the next generation blossom to fruition."[36]

In subsequent essays, Du Bois's advice to black parents was more prescriptive. In 1912 he analyzed the impact of racial prejudice upon children, discussing whether it was black parents' obligation to shield their children from hardship and discomfort. Some parents mistakenly endeavor to "shield [their] children absolutely," fearful of the knowledge that "cruelty waits on each corner to shadow the joy of our children." At the opposite extreme, some "leave their children to sink or swim in this sea of race prejudice. . . . Out of this may come strength, poise, self-dependence, and out of it too, may come bewilderment, cringing deception, and self-distrust." Both methods were to be avoided, Du Bois suggested. Children must not be thrust into a racist society prematurely, without the proper foundation of self-respect, of knowledge and pride in their heritage. "The day will dawn when mothers must explain but clearly why the little girls next door do not want to play with 'niggers'; what the real cause of the teachers' unsympathetic attitude is, and how people may ride on the backs of street cars and the smoker end of trains, and still be people, honest high-minded people." The deadly power of segregation attempted to negate even a child's perceptions of his or her own humanity, and for Du Bois, the sacrifices of the parents in creating a new cultural and political environment were absolutely essential for the future survival of African American people. "If the great battle of human right against poverty, against disease, against color prejudice is to be won, it must be won not in our day, but in the day of our children's children."[37]

Crisis initiated an annual "children's issue" to offer feature stories designed specifically for children and to assist black parents in matters of family instruction. In January 1920 Du Bois founded the *Brownies' Book*, a monthly publication dedicated to "the children of the sun—designed for all children, but especially OURS. It aims to be a thing of joy and beauty, dealing in happiness, laughter and emulation, and designed especially for the kiddies from six to sixteen." The parables and poetry of the *Brownies' Book* attempted to present black children in human terms, beyond the sterile stereotypes of the racist literature of the day. They acquainted black children with heroes from the African American past and with the cultural, political, and social contributions of blacks to American society. Beneath the magazine's training in racial history and culture lay an ethical purpose: the *Brownies' Book* sought to provide black children with "a code of honor and action in their relations with white children." Looking over the publication's various issues, one sees a mixture of children's literature and a political discourse that seems a bit beyond the capacity of juveniles to assimilate. In August 1920, for example, Du Bois commented on the wave of proletarian uprisings against capital: "There is a new general in the world who is doing great things and you must know about him. His name is 'General Strike.'" More effectively, in February 1921 Du Bois's character "the Crow" became for children the basis of a progressive political critique of racism, poverty, and capitalism: "There are things I do not understand as I fly among men. There is food—they eat not; there are clothes—they freeze; there is joy—they cry. Why—why—why?" The magazine was too expensive to produce, however, and with considerable regret Du Bois published the final issue in December 1921. Despite the cost, he was proud of his effort to enrich the culture and education of black children.[38] In *Dusk of Dawn*, published in 1940, he recalled with "infinite satisfaction" the "beautiful publication" for black children.[39] Critics and educators agreed. One reviewer described the *Brownies' Book* as a "magnificent publication . . . an effort to restore a sense of self-esteem to the black child, our child of the sun. It brought satisfaction to the thousands of children who knew it."[40]

V

Perhaps Du Bois's greatest influence in reshaping African American culture was his writing in the areas of poetry, the novel, and literary criticism. His appreciation for literature began as a child, as he was growing up in New England's Berkshire Mountains. As a teenager submitting a letter to the black publication the *New York Globe*, he questioned the "absence of literary societies" among Negro communities.[41] In late 1884 he reported that a black "literary and social improvement" society, calling itself the Sons of Freedom, had been formed in Great Barrington. Du Bois was elected secretary-treasurer of the society.[42]

During his first tenure as a professor at Atlanta University, he initiated *Moon*, a journal of political and cultural commentary that included notes on Negro literature. The March 1906 issue, for example, contained a brief essay on African American literature and a bibliography of the poetry and other works of Paul Laurence Dunbar.[43] *Crisis* published the works of young black writers and encouraged their careers. Du Bois was one of the first intellectuals in the post–World War I period to recognize the talent of a younger generation of black writers who had begun to cluster in Harlem. In April 1920 he applauded the latest writings of black literary artists and declared: "A renaissance of American Negro literature is due."[44] In June 1922 *Crisis* called for the establishment of "an Institute of Negro Literature and Art," which would encourage the development of black cultural creativity.[45] In April 1931 Du Bois announced the creation of a "literary prize" competition for the sum of one thousand dollars. The award, named for himself, was designed to foster "a more human and truthful portraiture of the American Negro in the twentieth century."[46]

Throughout his professional life, Du Bois expressed his political and social ideals in the form of protest poetry and in a series of novels. His first novel, *The Quest of the Silver Fleece*, published in 1911, was probably his best. Through his two central characters, Blessed Alwyn and Zora, he attempted to depict the social tragedy and political conflict of African Americans against the white ruling class in the South.[47] *Dark Princess*, published in 1928, was a product of the late Harlem Renaissance period. Although the plot focuses on the romantic relationship between a black man, Matthew

Towns, and an Indian princess, Kautilya, the central issue is the political conflict between oppressed people of color in the Third World and white colonialism. For Du Bois, the novel was an effort to use fiction to project his own vision of an international, nonwhite alliance, forming the basis for democratic empowerment and cultural emancipation. The critics were divided. Some viewed the novel as mechanical and melodramatic; others, such as George S. Schuyler, praised the work as "a masterful . . . portrayal of the soul of our people."[48]

A quarter century later, at the end of his life, Du Bois returned to the novel form to express his political ideology. In a series of works titled *The Black Flame*, he presented the fictional life of Manuel Mansart, relating the character's interaction with a host of important figures throughout African American cultural and social history.[49] Taken as a group, Du Bois's novels do not represent great literature, but what they lack in artistry and technique, they compensate for in political and moral passion. The goal of cultural intervention was to advance the boundaries of politics.

As creative works and as political broadsides, Du Bois's collected poetry was more effective than his novels. Two of his most influential works are "The Song of the Smoke" and "A Litany at Atlanta." "The Song of the Smoke" was published in *Horizon*, a small political and cultural journal edited by Du Bois after the termination of *Moon*. The poem captures his double consciousness theme by inspiring pride in one's racial heritage as well as the determination to achieve full rights. It prefigures the militant protest literature of both the Harlem Renaissance and the Negritude movement decades later:

> *I am the smoke king,*
> *I am black.*
> *I am swinging in the sky,*
> *I am ringing worlds on high;*
> *I am the thought of the throbbing mills,*
> *I am the soul of the Soul toils kills,*
> *Up I'm curling from the sod,*
> *I am whirling home to God.*
> *I am the smoke king,*
> *I am black.*
> *. . .*
>
> *I am the smoke king,*
> *I am black.*
> *I am darkening with song,*
> *I am hearkening to wrong;*

I will be black as blackness can,
The blacker the mantle the mightier the man.[50]

"A Litany at Atlanta" was written in the aftermath of the bloody race riot in Atlanta in 1906. Characteristically, Du Bois wrote a political essay about the riot in the journal *World Today*, emphasizing that institutional racism, political indifference, and police brutality had combined to create white vigilante mobs that were terrorizing the African American community.[51] But his call of anguish was expressed artistically in "Litany," published in *The Independent*:

O Silent God, Thou whose voice afar in mist and mystery hath
*   left our ears an-hungered in these fearful days—*
Hear us, good Lord. . . .
A city lay in travail, God our Lord, and from her loins sprang
*   twin Murder and Black Hate. Red was the midnight: clang,*
*   crack, and cry of death and fury filled the air and trembled*
*   underneath the stars where church spires pointed silently to*
*   Thee. And all this was to sate the greed of greedy men who hide*
*   behind the veil of vengeance.*
Bend us Thine ear, O Lord! . . .
Sit no longer blind, Lord God, deaf to our prayer and dumb to our
*   dumb suffering.*
Surely Thou, too, art not white, O Lord, a pale, bloodless, heartless
*   thing!*
Ah, Christ of all the Pities![52]

VI

Du Bois's centrality as a creative force in shaping the contours of African American literature and culture can best be measured during the period of the 1950s, under the political repression of McCarthyism and the Cold War. Because of Du Bois's political identification with socialism and the international Left, his books were barred from libraries; he was denied the right to speak in public venues; for seven years the American government illegally blocked his right to travel outside the United States. One critic, Lenneal Henderson, correctly characterized Du Bois as "the most discredited and maligned black scholar of the twentieth century." Yet during this period of political persecution, black cultural workers continued to be inspired by his example. Playwright Lorraine Hansberry studied with Du Bois in the 1950s at New York's Jefferson School; novelist Alice Childress was described by historian Gerald Horne as being "under Du Bois's spell" as well. Du Bois inspired the Committee for the Negro in the Arts, whose members included artist/activist Paul Robeson, Hansberry, Childress, singer Harry Belafonte, and actor Sidney Poitier. Many white artists shared those opinions. Henry Miller described Du Bois as "one of the truly deep influences of my life." Novelist Truman Capote consulted Du Bois in 1959 when he attempted to gain access to the People's Republic of China.[53]

Such testimony indicates the profound influence of Du Bois among a wide spectrum of artists, writers, and cultural critics. But he never managed to translate his political and cultural accomplishments into a coherent critical intellectual tradition that would be expressed in the literature and essays of later generations of African Americans. There were several reasons for this curious lacuna, this gap between the prolific writer and his admirers. The first and surely the most vexing difficulty concerned Du Bois's double consciousness formulation, which occupied the center of his intellectual constellation. Friends and foes alike tended to bifurcate his intellectual and political legacy, focusing on various aspects of his writings or public engagements without synthesizing the divergent elements of his theory and practice.

Over all was a grand design, but it eluded them. Reform-minded politicians dedicated to the abolition of racial segregation debated Du Bois's writings on public policy; historians wrestled with his *Black Reconstruction* and other social science texts; sociologists focused on his social research on the urban Negro population; artists read his poetry, novels, and other literary works. An essayist rather than a system-builder, Du Bois left literally thousands of newspaper pieces, articles in academic journals, and occasional essays covering politics, folk religion, music, cultural history, and sociology. By not ever writing a central theoretical statement clearly articulating his worldview and its meaning, Du Bois left his disciples to interpret the master in a variety of ways.

Temperamentally, Du Bois was not inclined to establish a coherent school of cultural and political criticism. His political battles with black American educator Booker T. Washington throughout the period 1903–1915 and his subsequent ideological conflicts with Jamaican black nationalist leader Marcus Mosiah Garvey during the 1920s set the terms of debate for much of African American social and political theory. But Du Bois fought more frequently with his political friends than with his political opponents. Inside the NAACP, he took on virtually every other leader at one time or another. In 1934, in a dispute over policy, he resigned from the organization he had founded. Accepting a faculty position at Atlanta University, he accused that institution's president, Rufus E. Clement, of conspiring against him. When Du Bois was retired involuntarily from the university in 1944, Clement characterized him as "uncooperative" and "antagonistic."[54] Returning to the NAACP as director of research, Du Bois was summarily fired four years later when he openly opposed the decisions of the association's national secretary.

This combativeness was a problem, but his inability to explain his complex ideas clearly, in a useful way, compounded it. "I was no natural leader of men," Du Bois once observed. "I could not slap people on the back and make friends of strangers. I could not easily break down an inherited reserve; or at all times curb a biting, critical tongue."[55]

Despite these and other personal contradictions, W. E. B. Du Bois dedicated himself for nearly a century to the struggle to end racial discrimination, the exploitation of nonwhite people across the globe, and other manifestations of social and political oppression. His vision of the nature of this conflict was at once cultural and political. As he explained in his conclusion to *Black Reconstruction*: "This the American black man knows: His fight here is a fight to the finish. Either he dies or wins. . . . He will enter modern civilization here in America as a black man on terms of perfect and unlimited equality with any white man, or he will enter not at all. . . . This is the last great battle of the West."[56]

For both the artist and the scholar, the politician and the dreamer, the cultural vision of W. E. B. Du Bois was an essential component of the politics of human equality.

5

The Black Faith of
W. E. B. Du Bois

W. E. B. Du Bois—founder of the National Association for the Advancement of Colored People and editor of its journal, *Crisis*, sociologist, civil rights leader, and Father of Pan-Africanism—is seldom viewed as a Christian. His biographers note that he frequently attacked all Christian denominations for their support of racial segregation. In published articles, Du Bois described himself as an "agnostic" and questioned the "immortality" of man.[1] As a college student and in later life, he affirmed that "work, systematic and tireless," was his only true faith.[2] In December 1940 he announced that he worshiped "Truth and Truth only. . . . I will face each sunrise with one prayer: There is no God but Love and Work is his Prophet."[3] At the end of his public career, Du Bois declared, "I believe in communism," renouncing American "free enterprise [as] leading the world to disaster," and he died an exile in Ghana.[4]

I

This image of Du Bois reveals only one aspect of his multifaceted character, however. For he also wrote extensively, throughout his life, on the black church. His earliest published essays focus on black religious life in his hometown, Great Barrington, Massachusetts.[5] One of his latest articles, written in 1962, was an introduction to a photographic study of storefront churches in the ghetto of Buffalo, New York.[6] In the intervening years he wrote several hundred articles on religion, the black church, and the social and political function of religious institutions. Du Bois was simultaneously an agnostic and an Anglican, a staunch critic of religious dogma and a passionate convert to the black version of Christianity. His belief in his people was expressed in his own black faith for the world.

Du Bois's religious sensibility was formed early in life. His grandfather, Alexander Du Bois, was senior warden of the black Episcopal Parish of St. Luke, founded by black residents of New Haven, Connecticut, in 1847.[7] His mother, Mary Burghardt, was deeply religious and frequently but softly urged her high-spirited son to attend church services regularly and "never to go into a liquor saloon or even near it." Life in Great Barrington during the Gilded Age was largely defined by the church and its strict moral code. Du Bois and his mother attended two churches: a small Negro Methodist Zion church, formed by a small colony of "'contrabands,' freed Negroes from the South," and Great Barrington's Congregational church, which was patronized by the leading merchants, farmers, and "professional men" of the community.[8] Even as a teenager, Du Bois noticed the class divisions within his small community, as manifested in the existence of various denominations. The local Catholic church "was perched across the river beyond the mills, and thither the [Irish] girl servants trudged faithfully early mornings to mass. This and other traits of the Irish became the basis of jokes and ridicule in town." Colored people, by contrast, despite their lower-class status, were cordially welcomed in white middle-class congregations. The Episcopal church catered to "older families and the more well-to-do," and most of Du Bois's extended family in the region belonged to this congregation. In the northern section of the town, near the mill, was an unpretentious "small white wooden Methodist church," attended by "the less well-known inhabitants" of Great Barrington.[9]

Du Bois graduated from high school in June 1884, and his mother died several months later. His subsequent academic career would have been in doubt had it not been for the timely intervention of three leading citizens: the Reverend Mr. Scudder, pastor of the Congregational church; Edward Van Lennep, superintendent of the Congregational church's Sunday school and principal of a local private school; and the Reverend C. C. Painter, a retired Federal Indian Agent and former pastor of several Congregational churches in Connecticut. The church in Great Barrington and Painter's churches agreed to donate one hundred dollars a year for Du Bois's college education. The black youth wished to attend Harvard, but Painter insisted that "the reconstructed South . . . was the place for me to be educated."

Over the objections of "my family and colored friends," Du Bois was sent to Fisk University in Nashville in September 1885.[10]

Painter's decision to send Du Bois to the South fundamentally shaped the young man's life. Growing up in New England, Du Bois had known little racial prejudice, and his contacts with other blacks had been few and brief. In Nashville, a world of color was revealed, and the young Puritan was sorely out of place at first. "I was thrilled to be for the first time among so many people of my own color. . . . Never before had I seen young men so self-assured and who gave themselves such airs, and colored men at that; and above all for the first time I saw beautiful girls." Years of sexual repression and conservative training put him at odds with his contemporaries, who had "loose sexual morals." Years later Du Bois admitted frankly, "I actually did not know the physical difference between men and women. At first my fellows jeered in disbelief and then became sorry and made many offers to guide my abysmal ignorance. This built for me inexcusable and startling temptations."[11] Regarded as a "liar" or "freak" when he revealed his virginity, he sought familiar refuge in the arms of the church. He dutifully attended church services, revivals, and morning prayers at the beginning of each school day, in a desperate search for inner tranquillity. Writing to Reverend Scudder in February 1886, the young college freshman observed that he had "united with the Church and hope that the prayers of my Sunday School may help guide me in the path of Christian duty." Du Bois faithfully continued to correspond with members of the Great Barrington Sunday school class until at least 1892.[12]

But in Nashville he encountered controversy in his faith from "fundamentalist" quarters. One of Du Bois's classmates, "Pop" Miller, brought him before the congregation and accused him of "a particularly heinous form of sin"—public "dancing." Du Bois protested in vain that he had "never attended public dance halls" and had only engaged in the "innocent pastime . . . at the homes of colored friends in the city." Fisk University teachers supported Miller, warning the young sinner "that my dancing might well be quite innocent, but . . . my example might lead others astray." Du Bois deeply resented their intervention and much later concluded that this little tempest "led to my eventual refusal to join a religious organization." But for the moment, he still "never questioned [his] religious upbringing. Its theory had presented no particular difficulties: God ruled the world, Christ loved it, and men did right, or tried to; otherwise they were rightly punished."[13]

Another aspect of the black social and religious experience became part of Du Bois's development in the summers of 1886 and 1887. In east Tennessee, he obtained a minor position as a rural schoolteacher at twenty-eight dollars per month. At last he encountered "the real seat of slavery . . . I touched intimately the lives of the commonest of mankind—people who ranged from barefooted dwellers on dirt floors, with patched rags for clothes, to rough hard-working farmers, with plain, clean plenty." His schoolhouse was nothing but a log hut with no door, "a massive rickety fireplace," and little furniture. "I was haunted by a New England vision of neat little desks and chairs, but alas the reality was rough plank benches without backs, and at times without legs," Du Bois noted. "They had the one virtue of making naps dangerous, possibly fatal, for the floor was not to be trusted."[14]

Among his class of nearly thirty youths, many older than himself, was "a thin, homely girl of twenty," Josie—later to be described as an unforgettable figure in *The Souls of Black Folk*.[15] The heart of Southern black life and labor was opened to Du Bois. Here he found warmth and unpretentious friendship that he had not thought possible. Frequently after classes were finished, he visited the families of his pupils: sitting on the porch eating fresh peaches with Josie and her talkative mother; visiting Doc Burke's farm, helping himself to fried chicken, wheat biscuits, string beans, and plump berries. Here he also discovered the mystery of sex, sleeping with an "unhappy wife who was my landlady." Time for these folk seemingly stood still. To be sure, life "was dull and humdrum," Du Bois wrote in his *Autobiography*: "I have called my community a world, and so its isolation made it. There was among us but a half-awakened common consciousness, sprung from common joy and grief, at burial, birth or wedding; from a common hardship in poverty, poor land and low wages; and, above all, from the sight of the Veil that hung between us and Opportunity."[16]

But the essence of black life was to be found on Sunday mornings, as the dawn broke above the rural countryside. In the center of the colored district of Alexandria, Tennessee, were "the twin temples of the hamlet, the Methodist and Hard-Shell Baptist churches." In these unadorned wooden halls, the black folk made "the weekly sacrifice with frenzied priest at the altar of the 'old-time religion.'" It was here that the families of his students sang in "soft melody and mighty cadences" the black spirituals of slavery. At first Du Bois was baffled by this experience. "We in Berkshire . . . were very quiet and subdued, and I know not what would have happened those clear Sabbath mornings had someone punctuated the sermon with a scream, or interrupted the long prayer with a loud Amen!" Sensitive about his strict background, and yet alienated from the Congregational church in Nashville, Du Bois was "determined to know something of the Negro in the country districts." Their deep expressions of spirituality were utterly new to him. As a budding scholar and, more important, as a black man, he was determined to understand their religion and to integrate it into his own embryonic worldview.[17]

II

The basic anatomy of the black religious experience was expressed in three factors: "the Preacher, the Music, and the Frenzy." The black minister, Du Bois later suggested, "is the most unique personality developed by the Negro on American soil." The black minister emerged during slavery as a powerful force in community life. "He early appeared on the plantation and found his function as the healer of the sick, the interpreter of the Unknown, the comforter of the sorrowing, the supernatural avenger of wrong, and the one who rudely but picturesquely expressed the longing, disappointment, and resentment of a stolen and oppressed people." Thus the social dynamics that produced white clergy and religious institutions differed radically from the organic evolution of the black church and its preachers. The transition from traditional African social systems to the plantation South was nothing less than "a terrific social revolution, and yet some traces were retained of the former group life, and the chief remaining institution was the Priest or Medicineman." This charismatic representative of the *nommo* or essence of his people, a synthesis of "bard, physician, judge, and priest," became within the American South "the Negro preacher." During Reconstruction and after, other basic characteristics were added to his social profile: he was at once "a leader, a politician, an orator, a 'boss,' an intriguer, an idealist. . . . The combination of a certain adroitness with deep-seated earnestness, of tact with consummate ability, gave him his preeminence," Du Bois noted, "and helps him maintain it."[18]

The music of black faith "is that plaintive rhythmic melody," Du Bois wrote in *The Souls of Black Folk*, "which, despite caricature and defilement, still remains the most original and beautiful expression of human life and longing yet born on American soil." Even when he was a small boy, Du Bois reflected, "these songs . . . stirred me strangely. They came out of the South unknown to me, one by one, and yet at once I knew them as of me and mine." The spirituals and the "Sorrow Songs" revealed the anguish and hope of a people in bondage, a mass of illiterate slaves whose spiritual strivings brought together an aspiration of secular emancipation and religious freedom. In such songs, "the slave spoke to the world" in an Aesopian language, partially "veiled and half articulate." "Steal away to Jesus" could mean different things to the masters and the slaves. There was the "cradle-song of death which all men know—'Swing low, sweet chariot'"; "songs of the fugitive like that which opens 'The Wings of Atlanta'"; and songs that revealed the full glory of the end of life's oppression—"'My Lord, what a mourning! when the stars begin to fall.'" In the Carolina swamplands, the slaves sang:

> Michael, haul the boat ashore,
> Then you'll hear the horn they blow,
> Then you'll hear the trumpet sound,
> Trumpet sound the world around,
> Trumpet sound for rich and poor,
> Trumpet sound the Jubilee,
> Trumpet sound for you and me.

The spirituals were simultaneously sorrowful and yet filled with hope, or as Du Bois expressed it, "a faith in the ultimate justice of things. The minor cadences of despair change often to triumph and calm confidence." In the face of oppression, the music provides a "faith in life"; it offers "sometimes assurance of boundless justice in some fair world beyond." The transition to Jim Crow and lynching was the secular political reality that created the living aesthetic space for such songs to continue to capture "the tragic soul-life" of black people. They express the hope "that sometime, somewhere, men will judge men by their souls and not by their skins."[19]

The "Frenzy or 'Shouting,' when the Spirit of the Lord passed by, and, seizing the devotee, made him mad with supernatural joy, was the last essential of Negro religion," Du Bois wrote, adding for emphasis, "and the one more devoutly believed in than all the rest." The shout was at once a purgation of the believers' anxieties, fears, and doubts created under slavery and segregation; it was a catharsis, the expression of transcendence, a cry of faith and hope, a physical and collective explosion that was necessary for a people trapped in the permanent vise of social anxiety and frustration. "It varied in expression from the silent rapt countenance or low murmur and moan to the mad abandon of physical fervor—the stamping, shrieking and laughing, the vision and trance." The common rapture was expressed by man but was not of man: the frenzy, for the black Christian, was the "visible manifestation of God." Blacks believed that, without this catharsis, "there could be no true communion with the Invisible."[20]

III

The soul-searching experiences in the Tennessee countryside placed Du Bois increasingly at odds with established Christian theology, and with himself. When assigned a text on Christian logic at Fisk, he commented that it now "affronted my logic. It was to my mind, then and since, a cheap piece of special pleading." University president Erastus Cravath secured a scholarship for Du Bois's postgraduate work at Hartford Theological Seminary. But Du Bois could not accept it. "I believed too little in Christian dogma to become a minister. I was not without faith: I never stole material or spiritual things; I not only never lied, but blurted out my conception of truth on the most untoward occasions; I drank no alcohol and knew nothing of women, physically or psychically, to the incredulous amusement of my more experienced fellows."[21]

Du Bois chose Harvard University instead. His graduate training there, under the direction of philosophers William James and George Santayana, pushed the black scholar far from "the sterilities of scholastic philosophy to realistic pragmatism."[22] While he was in Boston, however, he pursued his relationship with the black church. On Thanksgiving night, 1891, Du Bois organized and participated in Aristophanes' play *The Birds* at the black community's Charles Street Church. Nevertheless, he expressed blunt criticisms of the black church in an 1891 paper prepared for the National Colored League of Boston: "A religion that won't stand the application of reason and common sense is not fit for an intelligent dog." But his hostility toward the white Christian church was far more profound. In his diary, Du Bois attacked the Anglo-Saxon's "high Episcopal Nicene creed" as a rationale for white supremacy. Musing on the biblical image of "Ethiopia [stretching] forth her hands to God," the young Harvard man fumed, "The spectacle [of] the venerable colored dame in this rather unbalanced position in regard to the Anglo-Saxon god has become somewhat nauseating to the average young Negro of today." For the white West, with the possible exception of the "self-forgetful Quakers," God was dead, Du Bois decided.[23]

If racial oppression and segregation had compromised and destroyed the reality of God among most American whites, Du Bois thought, then he would refuse to participate in the charade. In his first teaching post, at Wilberforce University, a small black Methodist institution, he "wandered casually" into a local black prayer gathering. "Suddenly and without warning, a student leader of the meeting announced that 'Professor Du Bois will lead us in prayer.' I simply answered, 'No, he won't,' and as a result nearly lost my new job." An outraged president forced Du Bois before the school's governing board of bishops, and "it took a great deal of explaining" to convince its members "why a professor in Wilberforce should not be able at all times and sundry to address God in extemporaneous prayer. I was saved only by the fact that my coming to Wilberforce had been widely advertised and I was willing to do endless work."[24]

He quickly acquired a reputation as a troublemaker, cynic, and "agnostic" by refusing "to attend the annual 'revivals' of religion which interrupted school work every year at Christmas time." In May 1896 he threatened the college treasurer in order to receive back payment for his salary.[25] Such irreverent behavior did not go unnoticed beyond Wilberforce. After a fifteen-month stint at the University of Pennsylvania, where he compiled the first major sociological survey of African American urban life, *The Philadelphia Negro*, Du Bois applied for a position at Atlanta University. The college's president, Horace Bumstead, was by nature and political training a cautious man. Several trustees and prominent friends of Atlanta University expressed "objections and misgivings" to him when learning of Du Bois's possible appointment. Bumstead later wrote that "Atlanta University has always had a pronounced religious, though undenominational life" and that its teachers were expected "to help to maintain it." But on that point, such assurances "were not very easy to get" from Du Bois. When asked of his religious affiliation, Bumstead wrote, Du Bois curtly replied, "'None to speak of.' But though reluctant to speak of his religion or to say what he would do at Atlanta," and despite grave "objections and misgivings," he was permitted to join the faculty.[26]

Yet Du Bois's spiritual commitment to his people, which deepened and enlarged his analytic critique of the total society, could not be expressed as a complete rejection of black Christianity. Repeatedly his sociological research focused on the centrality of religion within black life, not only in *The Philadelphia Negro* but also in his 1897 study of black life in Farmville, Virginia, completed for the U.S. Department of Labor, and in his 1898 study of Atlanta, Georgia.[27] The black "First Baptist" church in Farmville is described by Du Bois in intimate detail as "a roomy brick edifice seating five hundred or more persons, tastefully finished in Georgia pine, with a carpet, a small organ, and stained-glass windows":

> Underneath is a large assembly room with benches. This building is
> the central club-house of a community of a thousand or more
> Negroes. Various organizations meet here,— the church proper, the
> Sunday-school, two or three insurance societies, women's societies,
> secret societies, and mass meetings of various kinds. Entertainment,
> suppers, and lectures are held beside the five or six regular weekly religious services. Considerable sums of money are collected and expended here, employment is found for the idle, strangers are introduced,
> news is disseminated and charity distributed. At the same time this
> social, intellectual, and economic centre is a religious centre of great
> power. Depravity, Sin, Redemption, Heaven, Hell, and Damnation

are preached with much fervor, and revivals take place every year after the crops are laid by; and few indeed of the community have the hardihood to withstand conversion. Back of this more formal religion, the Church often stands as a real conserver of morals, a strengthener of family life, and the final authority on what is Good and Right.[28]

Du Bois the agnostic confronted the vibrant reality of black spiritual and social life and could not stand apart from it. As a Pan-Africanist and as a sociologist he came to political terms with the black church in these words: "The Negro church of to-day is the social centre of Negro life in the United States, and the most characteristic expression of African character."[29] The uneven and contradictory synthesis of his religious doubts and faith was expressed, at last, in his famous theory of "double consciousness." If the Negro was at once "an American, a Negro; two souls, two thoughts, two unreconciled strivings; two warring ideals in one dark body,"[30] then the soul of Du Bois would be expressed for the white world in agnosticism or, at best, only in the most critical and formal guise. The soul of Du Bois confronting the black world had no choice but to embrace black Christianity.

IV

As a mature scholar and leader of the NAACP, Du Bois maintained his contradictory position on religion. Before the white world, he made few concessions. Reverting to the denomination of his paternal grandfather, he was nominally an Episcopalian for a time.[31] But inside the color line, he gave poetic expression to his love of God in his "Credo," first printed in October 1904:

I believe in God, who made of one blood all nations that on earth do dwell. I believe that all men, black and brown and white, are brothers . . . knowing that men may be brothers in Christ, even though they be not brothers-in-law. . . . I believe in the Devil and his angels, who wantonly work to narrow the opportunity of struggling human beings especially if they be black; who spit in the faces of the fallen, strike them that cannot strike again, believe the worst and work to prove it, hating the image which their Maker stamped on a brother's soul. I believe in the Prince of Peace. I believe that War is Murder. . . . Finally, I believe in Patience—patience with the weakness of the Weak and the strength of the Strong, the prejudice of the Ignorant and the ignorance of the Blind; patience with the tardy triumph of Joy and the mad chastening of Sorrow;— patience with God![32]

If the Christian ideal retained its meaning, the Christian church as a whole had not. White Christianity, "together with the wisest and richest of the people in the United States, defended [slavery] for 250 years," he declared in 1927.[33] Now white Christians supported the institutional racism, lynchings, and political disfranchisement of blacks. Regretfully, "I have little faith that Christianity can settle the race problem, but I have abiding faith in men."[34] In a biting editorial, "The Negro and the Church," published in the NAACP journal *Crisis* in October 1913, Du Bois denounced Christian "hypocrisy" and charged that the church ruthlessly denied "power" to blacks. "The Negro problem is the test of the church."[35]

A brief review of Du Bois's published writings indicates that the church filled him with revulsion at the same time that it commanded his curious attention to its activities and internal debates, especially as they affected the African American. In private correspondence with the Reverend Samuel H. Bishop, general agent of the American Church Institute for Negroes, and in a published essay in June 1907, Du Bois criticized the Episcopal church for its "hypocrisy." Despite his nominal membership, "I have no particular affection for the Church," he informed Bishop. "I think its record on the Negro problem has been shameful. . . . So far as the Negro problem is concerned the southern branch of the Church is a moral dead weight and the northern branch of the Church never has had the moral courage to stand against it." The Episcopalian leadership was woefully "behind other churches in recognizing human manhood and Christian equality."[36]

In August 1920, in *Crisis*, he heartily congratulated the Methodist Episcopal church for elevating two black men, Robert E. Jones and Matthew W. Clair, to the posts of bishop after "a fight of 25 years," adding, "There are still white Christians in Zion."[37] But when the same Northern Methodists attempted to merge with the Southern Methodists, breaking off relations with the all-black African Methodist Episcopal (AME) church, the *Crisis* editor was filled with scorn. Unity among white Methodists was taking place at the sacrifice of racial equality, he declared. Somewhat sarcastically, he inquired if Northern white Methodists still had "the present address of Jesus of Nazareth."[38]

Du Bois plotted the erratic racial progress of the Baptist World Alliance and praised the organization for holding an interracial convention in segregated Atlanta in 1939.[39] His disputes with the Catholic church symbolize his strained relations with other churches. In 1924, the Knights of Columbus published his book *The Gift of Black Folk*; Du Bois praised "Catholic priests and sisters teaching the colored South . . . for their unselfish work"; he "admired much" of the church's "mighty history." But in March 1925, in his private correspondence with Joseph B. Glenn, Du Bois charged that "the Catholic Church in America stands for color separation and discrimination to a degree equaled by no other church in America, and that is saying a very great deal." In hundreds of years, it had "ordained less than a half dozen black Catholic priests either because they have sent us poor teachers or because American Catholics do not want to work beside black priests and sisters or because they think Negroes have neither brains nor morals." Catholic parochial schools rarely accepted black applicants, and "the Catholic University in Washington invites them elsewhere." In short, the "'nigger' haters clothed in its Episcopal robes" were promoting racism every degree as vicious as "the Ku Klux Klan."[40] The Catholic and Protestant churches failed generally on the race issue, Du Bois perceived, because they had forgotten the living meaning of the teachings of "Jesus, the Jew." The ordeal of the Christ who perished for all humanity was obscured by the coarse blinders of "race hatred."[41]

The black American church, in contrast, served a fundamentally different function: it was the organizational and spiritual center of black life and as such touched every minute aspect of the segregated community's endeavors. It was a race-conscious organization—it could hardly have been otherwise during the Jim Crow era—yet its strength served to preserve and to defend the basic humanity of African American people, and its true vision of itself was one without color or class barriers. Even as a senior at Fisk University, Du Bois recognized that being a Christian meant that "we should not forget the practical side" of Christianity—that is, good works that uplifted the most oppressed groups of society.[42]

A decade later, speaking before a Fisk University graduate audience, he merged the ideals of black faith with the political struggle to transform the material conditions of African Americans. "The German works for Germany, the Englishman serves England, and it is the duty of the Negro to serve his blood and lineage, and so working, each for each, and all for each, we realize the goal of each for all." As the collective expression of all blacks, the church and its clergy were crucial in this process of self-achievement. African American ministers must and "will transform the mysticism of Negro religion into the righteousness of Christianity." Only by "cherish[ing] unwavering faith in the blood of your fathers" could this spiritually moved mass of black humanity achieve political freedom.[43]

In late 1900 Du Bois contributed to the Boston publication *New World* a brief essay, "The Religion of the Negro," which expanded upon these themes. "The Negro church antedates the Negro home," he noted, a historical fact that created "the expression of the inner ethical life of a people in a sense seldom true elsewhere." The church is a haven in a heartless world, as blacks search for meaning in a segregated and politically oppressive society. "Conscious of his impotence, and pessimistic," the Negro "often becomes bitter and vindictive; and his religion, instead of a worship, is a complaint and a curse, a wail rather than a hope, a sneer rather than a faith." At these moments, "one type of Negro stands almost ready to curse God and die." Yet he finds salvation within the Veil, and a spiritual deliverance from earthly suffering. Silently as ever broods "the deep religious feeling of the real Negro heart, the stirring, unguided might of powerful human souls who have lost the guiding star of the past and seek in the great night a new religious ideal. Some day the Awakening will come," Du Bois predicted, "when the pent-up vigor of ten million souls shall sweep irresistibly toward the Goal, out of the Valley of the Shadow of Death . . . [toward] Liberty, Justice, and Right."[44]

Du Bois's faith in the historic goal of black religion did not exempt specific denominations from his criticism. The black church found "greatness" only as it linked the spiritual striving of the masses with a social commitment to challenge Jim Crow laws, political disfranchisement, and all forms of bigotry and economic deprivation.[45] In his edited volume *The Negro Church*, published in 1903 as part of the Atlanta University series, and in subsequent periodical articles, Du Bois carefully scrutinized the progress of the black church.[46] He reminded the black clergy who were more conservative that black religion demanded uncompromising political protest, in the antebellum tradition of slave preacher and rebel Nat Turner. Occasionally in *Crisis* he commended the work of young black ministers who had come "forward to preserve and rescue the good that is in the Negro Church."[47]

In his organizational work Du Bois cooperated with many black ministers who shared his politically liberal views. In the Niagara Movement, formed by Du Bois and radical journalist William Monroe Trotter in 1905 to oppose the accommodationist program of Booker T. Washington, black religious leaders were especially prominent: Reverdy C. Ransom of Boston, J. Milton Waldron of Jacksonville (and later of Washington, D.C.), Bryon Gunner of Newport, George Freeman Bragg of Baltimore, and Sutton E. Griggs of Nashville. The vast majority of black clergy "enunciated a gradualist philosophy of self-help, racial solidarity, and economic progress," thus clearly aligning themselves with Washington's "Tuskegee Machine." Gradually, though, many Northern-based bishops and black religious leaders began to reflect Du Bois's militant political beliefs. Waldron had been a supporter of the Tuskegee philosophy while located in Jacksonville; after relocating to Washington, he rapidly fell into the Du Bois faction and became local president of the NAACP.[48]

One of Du Bois's closest associates was Alexander Walters, a bishop of the African Methodist Episcopal Zion church and presiding chairman of the first Pan-African Conference, held in London in 1900, at which Du Bois served as secretary. Bishop Walters, a founder of the militant National Negro American Political League in June 1908 and the nation's leading black Democrat, frequently advised Du Bois—and sometimes with disastrous consequences.[49] Du Bois was particularly harsh with the AME church. In January 1929 he criticized it for failing to provide sufficient financial support for South African missionary work led by his former Wilberforce student Charlotte Manye.[50] Repeatedly he denounced the many "fakers" and "frauds" among the AME church's leadership.[51]

What was the cultural purpose of the black church beyond its necessary engagement in political life on behalf of African Americans? Du Bois constantly returned to the central themes provided by his experience in eastern Tennessee and, later, his sociological research conducted in Philadelphia, Farmville, and Atlanta. The church was the cradle for the African American gift of song, that rare element of Negro culture that had to be constantly nourished. In 1903, Du Bois published a short *Bibliography of Negro Folk Songs* to encourage scholarly research into African American popular and spiritual music.[52] He praised the musical "labors" of John Wesley Work and his wife, Alice Work, music professors at Fisk University, who had "resurrect[ed]" and made "eternal the Negro spiritual." In *Crisis* he applauded black musical directors in both the churches and the segregated public schools for instructing a new generation of black pupils in the spirituals.

This did not mean that Du Bois did not appreciate other, more popular forms of black music. He noted with grudging approval the development of "ragtime" melodies and in an early issue of *Crisis* congratulated popular black composer J. Rosamond Johnson for the creation of "a new and distinct school of Negro music."[53] In 1925, at the height of the Harlem Renaissance, Du Bois penned a brief essay, "The Black Man Brings His Gifts," which praised the work of William Christopher Handy, the "father of the blues."[54] But his polished New England upbringing seldom failed to assert itself: Du Bois always held a special affection for those among his race who mastered European classical music.[55] He was a friend of the great black concert tenor Roland Hayes and frequently attended his performances.[56] In March 1918 he was the first to bring to national attention a new and gifted "baritone soloist," a nineteen-year-old student at Rutgers University named Paul Robeson.[57]

The songs of black religious praise were the basis for the Negro's special ability in all music. In response to one *New York Times* critic who urged blacks to croon only "old-time" plantation melodies, Du Bois tartly declared, "It is to be trusted that our leaders in music, holding on to the beautiful heritage of the past, will not on that account, either be coerced or frightened from taking all music for their province and showing the world how to sing."[58]

V

The greatest gift of black faith, however, went to the heart of the Christian tradition: its radical reinterpretation of Christ as a historical and spiritual figure for early twentieth-century American society. As a sociologist, Du Bois condemned not merely the profit motive of monopoly capital and its exploitation of labor but also found its espousal of Christian rhetoric empty of social content. In December 1913, for example, his *Crisis* editorial again blasted the racism of the Episcopal church, declaring that any acceptance of bigotry is an abrogation of the teaching of the Son of God. "The church of John Pierpont Morgan [is] not the church of Jesus Christ," he concluded. For the special Christmas issue of *Crisis* in December 1925, Jesus returns to earth and is immediately disillusioned with the gross spectacle of wealth and public avarice that is held in his name. Defiantly he speaks from the heights of the Woolworth Building in Manhattan to condemn the modern mob—"and the people were dumbfounded." In *Darkwater: Voices from Within the Veil,* Jesus returns to earth in Waco, Texas, and teaches white racists to "love" oppressed blacks. When an escaped black convict is unjustly burned alive, a voice comes to him "out of the winds of the night, saying: 'This day thou shalt be with me in Paradise!'"[59]

During the Great Depression, Du Bois suggested that Christmas should be abolished, since "Jesus Christ is not usually invited to his birthday celebration." The living legacy of Christ, Du Bois suggested, could be realized only in a rededication to his historic example as a spiritual rebel against the established dogma and prejudice of the social order. In December 1909 Du Bois declared that white abolitionist John Brown was a nineteenth-century martyr in the true tradition of Jesus Christ. Christ was undoubtedly "the greatest of religious rebels," he wrote in 1928.[60]

Later in his political life, as Du Bois moved closer to Marxism-Leninism, he viewed Christ in a more radical context. In February 1948 he suggested that opponents of South African apartheid were truly Christians in the great tradition of Christ himself. The revolutionary heroes in the emancipation of the world's colored and exploited masses were Mohandas K. Gandhi, V. I. Lenin, and Jesus: their principles could promote an international "fight for freedom" and economic justice. The political purposes of the black church merged with the figure of Jesus to create a secular "freedom fighter" in the battle to uproot racism and capitalism. In the consciousness of the oppressed, in "the Second Coming" Jesus would be born black.[61]

Du Bois was ideologically consistent in politics. As his literary executor Herbert Aptheker writes, "All his life Du Bois was a radical prophet. He tore at the Veil; at the same time, he had a particular perspective from which he saw this country and world, past, present, and future."[62] Before the sterile walls of segregation, he denounced intolerance; and in the Jim Crowed houses of prayer, he defied hypocrisy. Yet his "paradoxical behavior" in religion is no paradox at all.[63] Du Bois saw himself as a legitimate child of the Renaissance and Western culture, but the "Veil" of race permitted him to question the ethical directions of the hegemonic social order. For him, the stoic figure of Saint Francis of Assisi could be transformed into a radical who sought "to satisfy the world's great wants."[64]

White Christianity had failed only because it did not comprehend its inherently radical commitment to serve humanity. Black Christianity, in contrast, had fulfilled that mission for African Americans and served as an example for the larger world. Thus Du Bois the "prophet," or "religious radical," could find peace within this faith. His God was the God of black liberation.

6

The Pan-Africanism of
W. E. B. Du Bois

WILLIAM EDWARD BURGHARDT DU BOIS is generally accorded by black scholars and political leaders alike the title "Father of Pan-Africanism." Trinidadian historian and Marxist activist C. L. R. James writes that "more than any other citizen of Western civilization (or of Africa itself) [Du Bois] struggled over many years and succeeded in making the world aware that Africa and Africans had to be freed from the thralldom which Western civilization had imposed on them." Du Bois was "from start to finish . . . the moving spirit and active organizer" of five Pan-African congresses.[1] Kwame Nkrumah, leader of the Gold Coast independence movement in the late 1940s and 1950s and subsequently prime minister of Ghana, referred to Du Bois as a "treasured part of Africa's history" and recounted his unique contributions to the evolution of Pan-Africanism in several works.[2]

I

Even social scientists who are openly hostile to Du Bois recognize, in a distorted manner, the rich Pan-Africanist legacy of the black scholar. Harold R. Isaacs criticized Du Bois as never having been "a successful leader or organizer or even a popular public figure." His Pan-Africanism was simply a type of "romantic racism" that "got nowhere." Nevertheless, Isaacs acknowledged grudgingly that modern black leaders recognize Du Bois as the

"Father of Pan-Africanism" and that his militant words on Africa now "ring in the air all around us."[3]

In his biography of Du Bois, Francis S. Broderick declared that none of his subject's books "except *The Philadelphia Negro* is first-class." Du Bois's voluminous studies on African culture, history, and politics, which include *The Negro and The World and Africa,* "all possess some information, but nothing which indicates the mind or hand of an original scholar." The Pan-African congresses of the 1920s, Broderick adds, accomplished, if anything, less than the failed Niagara Movement of 1905–1909. Yet even Broderick, blinded by racism, must stand in awe of Du Bois's prophecy of African and Asian nationalism, which swept the Third World in the 1950s and afterward. "After the Asian-African conference at Bandung in 1955," Broderick admits, "who had the last laugh, Du Bois or his critics? Du Bois was a generation ahead of his time. The leaders of at least two [African nations] have publicly made explicit acknowledgment of their debt to Du Bois's inspiration."[4]

This essay is not a comprehensive analysis of Du Bois's Pan-Africanism but rather an examination of his role in the evolution of the Pan-Africanist political movement from 1900 to 1945. Special emphasis is given to the relationship between Du Bois's sponsorship and the development of political programs at the Pan-African congresses during these years and to his overall political life and activities within the United States.

Perhaps the clearest point of departure in the study of Du Bois's Pan-Africanist thought is provided by his literary executor, Marxist historian Herbert Aptheker. In a 1968 essay, Aptheker suggests two basic factors that oriented Du Bois's intellectual endeavors. Aptheker rejects the nearly universal thesis that Du Bois's central conception of black liberation varied from decade to decade. Indeed, his philosophical orientation or method of analysis reveals a startling consistency. "Du Bois's extraordinary career manifests a remarkable continuity," Aptheker states. First, "all his life Du Bois was a radical democrat; this was true even with his 'Talented Tenth' concept which held that mass advance depended upon leadership and service from a trained minority." Certainly the black scholar's "political affiliations or affinities varied as times changed, as programs altered." At various historical moments Du Bois was a reformed Republican, a Democrat, a Socialist, a Communist, and a supporter of the Progressive Party of Henry Wallace. "These were, however, political choices and not defining marks of philosophical approaches." At the root of his politics was a commitment to a democracy defined by the realization of racial equality and social justice for all social groups and classes within the society. Second, as Aptheker notes:

[Du Bois's] penetrating observation, first offered in 1900 and twice repeated in a significant article published the next year—"The problem of the twentieth century is the problem of the color line"—was fundamental to his vision of the unity of all African people (to grow, as Du Bois advanced in years, to the idea that this itself was preliminary, to the unity of all the darker peoples of the earth and that was part of the process of the worldwide unification of all who labor) and was, indeed, first enunciated as the Call of the original Pan-African Conference. This insight forms the inspiration for and thesis of his *The Negro* (London: Home Library, 1915), *Black Folk, Then and Now* (New York: Holt, 1939), *Color and Democracy: Colonies and Peace* (New York: Harcourt, Brace, 1945), [and] *The World and Africa* (New York: Viking, 1947).[5]

Throughout his adult life, Du Bois never identified racism as a purely American phenomenon. He understood that a resolution of the color line could occur only within the international political context and that racism was tied directly to economic exploitation and domination by the white West of peoples of color all across the globe. Pan-Africanism, then, was merely the concrete political expression of Du Bois's intellectual commitment to eradicate racism, colonialism, and all structures of exploitation.

II

What shaped Du Bois's evolving philosophy of Pan-Africanism? In *Dusk of Dawn*, he repeats Countee Cullen's memorable lines:

> *What is Africa to me:*
> *Copper sun or scarlet sea,*
> *Jungle star or jungle track*
> *Strong bronzed men, or regal black*
> *Women from whose loins I sprang*
> *When the birds of Eden sang?*
> *One three centuries removed*
> *From the scenes his fathers loved,*
> *Spicy grove, cinnamon tree,*
> *What is Africa to me?*[6]

"What is Africa to me?" Du Bois pondered. "Neither my father nor my father's father ever saw Africa or knew its meaning or cared much for it. My mother's folk were closer and yet their direct connection, in culture and race, became tenuous; still, my tie to Africa is strong."[7] As a child, Du Bois heard an African melody that his great-grandmother Violet Du Bois had brought from the continent, which over generations had become a "tradition in his family."[8] There were no books on Africa in Great Barrington's modest library. Yet even as a child he had become annoyed with the crude racial stereotypes depicted in his classroom textbooks. In his 1959 interview with Isaacs, Du Bois reflected that he encountered pictures of the races of man in his earliest texts, "a white man, a Chinese mandarin, and a savage Negro. That was what the class got, and it made me especially sensitive. I did not recognize those pictures in the book as being my people."[9]

It was his undergraduate experience at Fisk University that first awakened Du Bois's lifelong identification with African culture. Fisk had the beginnings of an African museum, and young Will examined the small selection of African carvings and artifacts with fascination. Continuing his undergraduate studies at Harvard University, he encountered the pseudoscience of racial dogma, presented as if it were a consequence of the new theory of evolution. No courses on African, Chinese, or Indian history were offered at Harvard. Returning from a period of study at the University of Berlin, Du Bois applied to the doctoral program in social science at Harvard in the spring of 1980. His topic was "the social and economic rise of the Negro people."[10]

For two years, Du Bois was preoccupied with thousands of hours of research in the *Congressional Record*, colonial and state documents, and secondary literature pertaining to the African slave trade. Simultaneously, he participated in the larger cultural and social life of Boston's black community, taking part in church plays and drafting a comprehensive program to improve and expand local black libraries, lectures, literary societies, and Chauatauqua circles.[11] The final product of his labor was his thesis, *The Suppression of the African Slave-Trade to the United States of America, 1638–1870*, which in 1896 became the initial volume of the Harvard Historical Studies series. The importance of this pioneering study, published during a period of rising racial violence, political disfranchisement, and historiographical revision of the role of the Negro in American democracy, cannot be overemphasized. It provided the first serious examination of the impact of the Haitian revolution upon the domestic slave political economy. "The Final Crisis," the chapter on the South's frenzied political attempts to rescind the 1808 ban on the transatlantic slave trade, was not equaled in historical research for decades.[12]

The white academic establishment offered grudging praise: one review in the *American Historical Review* applauded the work as a "valuable review of an important subject" but added that Du Bois occasionally used phrases that "characterize the advocate rather than the historian."[13] For Du Bois, of course, that was the entire point: scholarship served to advance racial interests. Any antiracist research that emphasized the humanity of African people and denounced the profit motive of white slaveholders contributed to the immediate struggle of destroying the color line and expanding democracy to include the Negro.

As Du Bois pursued an academic career, teaching briefly at Wilberforce University and the University of Pennsylvania before settling at Atlanta University from 1897 to 1910 as a professor of economics and history, other black intellectuals became more preoccupied with the cultural and political image of Africa. One of the most ambitious and visionary of the new generation was a young Trinidadian lawyer, Henry Sylvester Williams. Born in 1869, Williams traveled to the United States in 1891 and two years later went to Canada to attend law school. In 1896 Williams moved to London, and within a year he had organized the Pan-African Association. Gradually, he established the basis for a political formation that would embrace blacks in the West Indies, the United States, and Africa. Its unambiguous goals were "to secure to Africans throughout the world true civil and political rights" and "to ameliorate the conditions of our brothers on the continent of Africa, America and other parts of the world."[14] In this effort, assistance was provided by a curious benefactor, the conservative African American educator, Booker T. Washington. In one of history's little ironies, Washington in 1899 promoted the projected Pan-African Conference as a "most effective and far-reaching" activity during a London visit. The president of Tuskegee Institute "beg[ged] and advise[d] as many of our people as can possibly do so" to take an active role in Williams's conference.[15]

Du Bois and approximately thirty other West Indian and African American intellectuals attended the Pan-African Association's conference in July 1900. The meeting attracted minor attention in the press, and the delegates were welcomed by the Lord Bishop of London. Queen Victoria even forwarded a note through her minister Joseph Chamberlain, promising not to "overlook the interests of the natives." The conference drafted "An Address to the Nations of the World," which urged the democratic treatment of black people in majority white nations and the ultimate emancipation of Africa itself. Du Bois penned the most memorable statement of the assembly: "The problem of the Twentieth Century is the problem of the color line." The net results of this gathering, in the short run, were unfortunately minimal. In his *The World and Africa*, published much later, Du Bois noted that "this meeting had no deep roots in Africa itself, and the movement and the idea died for a generation."[16] Williams soon returned to the Caribbean to establish branches of his Pan-African Association. While visiting Jamaica in March 1901, he won the support of radical journalist Joseph Robert Love.[17] But failing to build a viable organization, Williams returned to Trinidad in 1908 and died there in 1911.

The failure of this early attempt to forge an international forum for Pan-African opinion did not diminish Du Bois's interest in Africa. Throughout the first two decades of the twentieth century, he was one of the few American scholars who encouraged others to take an active interest in the cultural, economic, and political history of African people. In 1903 he wrote a review of Joseph A. Tillinghast's *The Negro in Africa and America* that appeared in *Political Science Quarterly*. The review is noteworthy in that Du Bois emphasized the centrality of African culture in the evolution of black American life and history.[18] Several years later, writing for *The Nation*, Du Bois reviewed seven books on African history, including the notable work of E. D. Morel, *The Black Man's Burden*. Du Bois argued here that the recent history of Africa was essentially that of European exploitation, characterized most clearly by the atrocities committed by King Leopold of Belgium in the Congo Free State.[19]

As editor of *Crisis*, the journal of the newly founded NAACP, from 1910 until his resignation in 1934, Du Bois constantly provided his readers with information on Africa and peoples of African descent outside the United States. From 1903 through 1919, Du Bois's journalistic writings on Africa fall into three distinct categories. First, he tried to popularize the idea of a Pan-Africanist perspective, the then utopian notion that the political demand of "Africa for the Africans" inevitably would become a necessity.[20]

Second, he attempted to distinguish his version of Pan-Africanism from the nineteenth-century African emigrationist views of black entrepreneur Paul Cuffe and AME bishop Henry M. Turner. As Harold R. Isaacs correctly notes, Du Bois never "chose the ultimate option of urging anger nor in his deepest despair was he driven to the notion that there was an answer for Negroes in recrossing the ocean to resettle it . . . the homeland of their ancestors. Du Bois had the imagination and intelligence to see, long before anyone else, that the meaningful slogan for beleaguered American Negroes as far as Africa was concerned was not "Back to Africa" but "Africa for the Africans."[21]

In February 1914, and again in January 1916, Du Bois's editorials in *Crisis* attacked various plans by blacks to organize back-to-Africa efforts. Criticizing the emigrationist movement led by Chief Alfred Sam, Du Bois urged blacks not to become involved in speculative schemes destined for failure. To Oklahoma supporters of Chief Sam, Du Bois declared that there was no need to travel across the Atlantic to combat racism: "Fight out the battle in Oklahoma." He cautioned that there was "no steamship in New York building for the African trade and owned by Negroes."[22]

Finally, Du Bois attempted to advance a general thesis linking the continued political and economic exploitation of Africa with the expansion of European imperialism and war. He consistently used *Crisis* to denounce both British and German colonial policies in Africa.[23] More significant, he drafted an important essay in 1915, "The African Roots of the War," which in some respects paralleled the argument that V. I. Lenin made in his 1916 thesis, *Imperialism*. Both argued that the scramble to control raw materials, labor, and territories in Africa and Asia was the root cause of the world war. Du Bois also predicted that the conflict would bring forward new nationalist leaders in India, China, and Africa and that black Americans would play a more central role in the "awakening" of Africa after the conflict in Europe ended.[24]

During World War I, Du Bois recognized that there was an opportunity to revive his Pan-African program in a more concrete form. In 1917 he advocated the creation of "a new African state formed from German possessions and from the Belgian Congo; the following year, he wanted to include, if possible, Uganda, French Equatorial Africa, Angola, and Mozambique." As the conflict concluded, Du Bois received the NAACP's endorsement for the program of semiautonomous governance for Africans living in former German colonies and for the acceleration of educational, social, and economic development on the continent generally.[25] Writing to President Woodrow Wilson on November 27, 1918, Du Bois proposed that the American government support his plans. J. P. Tumulty, the president's secretary, shared the memo with Wilson but replied that it would be impossible for him to meet with Du Bois.[26]

With the NAACP's approval, Du Bois immediately prepared to travel to Europe, hoping both to investigate "the treatment of Negro soldiers" and to represent the interests of "the Negroes of the world . . . before the [Versailles] Peace Congress."[27] Securing passage abroad was a problem. Du Bois learned, however, that Wilson was sending Tuskegee Institute president Robert Russa Moton to France. Du Bois noted that Moton's duty was to speak to the returning Negro soldiers, pacify them, and forestall any attempt at agitation or open expression of resentment upon their return to the United States. As Du Bois remarked much later, "Under those circumstances, my request also to go could hardly be denied."[28]

Even before he arrived in Paris, Du Bois wrote back to the United States explaining his purposes to both white and black followers. He reiterated that his proposal for a new Pan-African congress was not a call for racial separatism. African emigration for the masses of American blacks was "absurd." However, Du Bois emphasized, "the African movement means to us what the Zionist movement must mean to the Jews, the centralization of race effort and the recognition of a racial fount."[29] Visiting members of the Peace Congress, Du Bois lobbied for his ambitious program without success. Colonel House, Wilson's chief aide, listened patiently to Du Bois but did not promise anything. Leaving nothing to chance, on January 1, 1919, Major F. P. Schoonmaker of the U.S. Army Ninety-second Division ordered intelligence officers to monitor "all of [Du Bois's] moves and actions while at station of any unit."[30]

Secretly watched by his own government, Du Bois spent six fruitless weeks in and around Paris, frustrated by his inability to obtain even French permission to schedule his Pan-Africanist congress. The *Chicago Tribune* correspondent, observing Du Bois's plight, cabled home: "[Du Bois's] memorandum to President Wilson . . . is quite Utopian, and has less than a Chinaman's chance of getting anywhere in the Peace Conference, but it is nevertheless interesting. As self-determination is one of the words to conjure with in Paris nowadays, the Negro leaders are seeking to have it applied, if possible, in a measure to their race in Africa."[31]

As Du Bois later wrote, "My plan to have Africa in some way voice its complaints to the world [was] . . . without political backing and indeed without widespread backing of any kind. Had it not been for one circumstance, it would have utterly failed; and that circumstance was that black Africa had the right to send from Senegal a member to the French Parliament."[32] This deputy, Blaise Diagne, was "the most influential colonial politician in France at the time," according to Pan-Africanist scholar George Padmore, and "a close friend" of the prime minister, Georges Clemenceau.[33] Diagne had been born in Gorée, Senegal, in 1872. Despite his origins in poverty, he rose through education to acquire a position as French colonial customs officer. In 1909 he confirmed his status within local white society by his marriage to a Frenchwoman. Five years later, over the strenuous opposition of both the colored *metis* and local white entrepreneurs, the black man won election to the Parisian Chamber of Deputies.

Despite his radical rhetoric, Diagne was always "a Frenchman before being a Pan-African, and insisted upon praising French colonial rule, while attacking the other European powers' operations in Africa."[34] When the French faced "military disaster" in early 1911, Clemenceau named Diagne *commissaire-général* for French West Africa and charged him "with the responsibility of recruiting African troops for the Western front to help stem the German offensive." Within twelve months, under Diagne's direction,

680,000 soldiers and 238,000 laborers from French West Africa were in France.[35] Clemenceau was "overjoyed" and offered Diagne the French Legion of Honor. Diagne modestly refused, pleading that "he had only done his duty and that was reward enough." Many African militants, suffering under the brutal heel of French imperialism, denounced Diagne as "a traitor for having brought the Africans to fight for France" and termed him "a tool of the rich white colonial interests."[36]

When Du Bois approached Diagne for help in scheduling the Pan-Africanist session, however, he quickly consented. Clemenceau could easily have ignored the unknown African American petitioner. But when Diagne personally requested the French government to allow the congress to meet, the prime minister replied, "Don't advertise it, but go ahead."[37] Arrangements were made to reserve suites at the Grand Hotel in Paris. Madame Calman-Levy, the widow of an influential French publisher, "became enthusiastic over the idea of [Du Bois's] congress and brought together in her salon groups of interested persons" from the French and Belgian governments.[38] Frantically, American officials objected to the Pan-African congress; one state department official told the press that "no such conference would be held" and that should the session take place, "no passports would be issued for American delegates desiring to attend the meeting."[39]

Despite belated American opposition, fifty-seven delegates from fifteen countries met on February 19, 1919, for the first Pan-African congress. Among them were twenty-one West Indians, sixteen delegates from the United States, and twelve from nine different African nations. The *New York Evening Globe* reported on February 22, 1919:

> [The Pan-African congress is] the first assembly of its kind in history, and has for its object the drafting of an appeal to the Peace Conference to give the Negro race of Africa a chance to develop unhindered by other races. Seated at long green tables in the council room today, were Negroes in the trim uniform of American Army officers, other American colored men in frock coats or business suits, polished French Negroes who hold public office, Senegalese who sit in the French Chamber of Deputies.[40]

From the beginning of the assembly, Diagne, who was chosen as the president of the congress, and Du Bois, its secretary, were at odds. Diagne's chief concern was that French territorial interests in Africa should be preserved and expanded; the anticolonial polemics of Pan-Africanism should be levied against all other Europeans, but not the French.[41] Du Bois wrote the principal report of the congress, which requested that the European and American powers turn over the former German colonies of Kamerun, Tanganyika, and Southwest Africa [Namibia] to an "international organization." The Allies were asked to "establish a code of law for the international protection of the natives of Africa, similar to the proposed international code of labor."

Nowhere in the congress's demands were Europeans asked to grant Africans the right to complete self-determination. Rather, the congress, speaking for "the Negroes of the world," resolved that "hereafter the natives of Africa and the peoples of African descent" should be governed according to more humane and democratic rules. Land and other natural resources "should be held in trust for the natives" while they acquired the means to "effective ownership of as much land as they can profitably develop." Capital should be "regulated as to prevent the exploitation of the natives and the exhaustion of the natural wealth of the country." All forms of "slavery and corporal punishment" must be abolished, the resolutions urged. The right of every black "child to learn to read and write his own language" and have access to "higher technical and cultural training" must be guaranteed. In terms of political rights, all Africans should "participate in the government as fast as their development permits." Educated blacks must be given the "higher offices of State," culminating in the future of an "Africa ruled by consent of the Africans."[42]

At best, the resolutions had only a minor impact upon the deliberations of the Versailles Peace Congress. Despite the relative moderation of these demands, for European leaders "the very idea of Pan-Africanism was so strange that it seemed unreal and yet at the same time perhaps potentially dangerous."[43]

III

Optimistic, Du Bois returned to the United States, "from where he hoped to build a real organization capable of stimulating the national aspirations of the natives of Africa, and of securing wider support for the activities of the Congress."[44] Over the next two years, Du Bois attempted to raise financial and political support for the Pan-Africanist movement. Throughout the rest of 1919, he and the NAACP were preoccupied with combating the fierce upsurgence of postwar racist violence. But after "corresponding with Negroes in all parts of Africa and in other parts of the world," he scheduled a second congress, to be held in London, Brussels, and Paris from August 28 to September 6, 1921.[45] One hundred thirteen delegates attended the sessions, seven from the Caribbean, thirty-five blacks from America, forty-one from Africa, and the remainder from Europe.

The London meetings were held in Central Hall, facing Westminster Abbey, on August 28 and 29. Leading members of the British Labour Party and Fabian socialists initiated a discussion on "the relation of white and colored labor." The London session unanimously adopted a statement that criticized Belgium's colonial rule in the Congo and provoked "bitter opposition in Brussels" among government leaders. Once in Belgium, Diagne attempted "to substitute an innocuous statement concerning [the] goodwill" of both the Belgian and the French colonialists, and in his capacity as chair, he declared the resolution "adopted" despite "a clear majority in opposition." The last sessions, in the Palais Mondial, located in Paris's Cinquantenaire Park, reversed Diagne's maneuver by upholding the basic London session drafts. The final document read in part:

> To the World: The absolute equality of races, physical, political and social, is the founding stone of world and human advancements. No one denies great differences of gift, capacity, and attainment among individuals of all races, but the voice of Science, Religion, and practical Politics is one in denying the God-appointed existence of super-races, or of races naturally and inevitably and eternally inferior.... The habit of democracy must be made to encircle the earth.... Local self-government with a minimum of help and oversight can be established tomorrow in Asia, in Africa, America, and the Isles of the sea.... The Negro race, through their thinking intelligentsia, demand:
>
> 1. The recognition of civilized men as civilized, despite their race and color.
> 2. Local self-government for backward groups, deliberately rising as experience and knowledge grow to complete self-government...
> 3. Education in self-knowledge, in scientific truth, and in industrial technique, undivorced from the art of beauty.
> 4. Freedom in their own religion and social customs and with the right to be different and nonconformist.
> 5. Cooperation with the rest of the world in government, industry, and art on the bases of Justice, Freedom and Peace.
> 6. The return to Negroes of their land and its natural fruits, and defense against the unrestrained greed of invested capital.
> 7. The establishment under the League of Nations of an international institution for the study of African problems.
> 8. The establishment of an international section of the Labor Bureau of the League of Nations, charged with the protection of native labor.[46]

A small delegation of conference participants, led by Dantes Bellegarde, Haiti's ambassador to France and representative to the League of

Nations, traveled to the Geneva headquarters of the League of Nations and presented the congress's petition. The League's Mandates Commission studied the congress's proposals and soon published them with favorable commentary:

> Consciously or subconsciously there is in the world today a widespread and growing feeling that it is permissible to treat civilized men as uncivilized if they are colored and more especially of Negro descent. . . . [We] urge that the League of Nations take a firm stand on the absolute equality of races and that it form an International Institute for the study of the Negro problem, and for the evolution and protection of the Negro race.[47]

The success of the second Pan-African congress in attracting a level of international support also generated, for the first time, the criticism of the European press. British Africanist Sir Harry Johnston chided the Pan-Africanist intellectuals, noting curtly that American "colored people . . . know so *little about real* Africa." The British humor magazine *Punch* parodied the "Pan-African Manifesto."[48]

More seriously, *Neptune*, a major Brussels newspaper, levied the accusation that the Pan-Africanist congress was "an agency of Moscow and the cause of native unrest in the Congo." It asserted that the congress's leaders had "received remuneration" from the Bolsheviks and predicted darkly that Pan-Africanist propaganda would "some day [cause] grave difficulties in the Negro village of Kinshasa."[49]

Other European leaders and colonial officials confused Du Bois's Pan-Africanist movement with the alarming growth of the militant black nationalist organization, the Universal Negro Improvement Association (UNIA), led by the charismatic Jamaican Marcus Mosiah Garvey. Du Bois later complained, "News of [Garvey's] astonishing plans reached Europe and the various colonial offices, even before my much more modest proposals. Often the Pan-African congress was confounded with the Garvey movement with consequent suspicion and attack."[50] Even as the 1919 Pan-African congress was meeting in Paris, the UNIA newspaper *Negro World* was banned by the acting governor in British Honduras [Belize] and by the Trinidadian governor "on grounds that it [was] seditious." In May 1919 the British Guianan government seized and destroyed *Negro World*; on August 6, 1919, the acting governor of Jamaica ordered postal agents to seize copies of the newspaper; on August 19, "legislation to ban the *Negro World* in the Windward islands [was] advocated by the governor, G. B. Haddon-Smith."[51] Thus, from Du Bois's perspective, any perceived connection with the threat of Garvey's militant black nationalism compromised his Pan-African objectives.

On the other side of the color line, Garvey and his followers denounced the Pan-Africanism of Du Bois as early as 1918. Always the polemicist, Garvey himself was not above distorting the facts to suit his immediate political objectives. Speaking before the Baltimore UNIA branch on December 18, 1918, for example, Garvey stated erroneously that Du Bois and Moton were sent jointly "to France to prevent Negroes from getting the fruits of their sacrifices on the battlefields." Negroes should enjoy democracy, Garvey declared, but whites had "sent for men like Du Bois and Moton to prevent us from getting it."[52] In retrospect, the famous Du Bois–Garvey debate that characterized so much of the politics of the black world during the 1920s began in the circumstances surrounding the first Pan-African congress.

On November 10 and 11, 1918, the UNIA proposed a series of "Peace Aims" to the Allies. Learning of the pending Versailles Peace Conference, the UNIA appointed three members to go to Paris. Only one, a nineteen-year-old Haitian named Eliézer Cadet, was able to secure a passport for the trip.[53] In Cadet's possession were two addresses, to the "People of England and France," respectively, urging them to grant "fair play and justice on the continents of Africa, America and on the West Indies." Europeans were asked to "help us to abolish the lynching institutions and burning at the stake of men, women, and children of our race in the United States of America, to abolish industrial serfdom, robbery, and exploitation in the West Indies and the new slavery and outrages inflicted on our race in Africa."[54]

Unfortunately, Cadet did not arrive in Paris until March 1, several days after the Pan-African congress had ended, and he did not deliver the UNIA's documents to Clemenceau's offices until March 9. His failure to attract the attention of the French authorities or the press was attributed to the intervention of "adversaries." Garvey incorrectly assumed that Du Bois was somehow responsible for Cadet's problems. At a mass assembly of three thousand UNIA supporters, which included A. Philip Randolph and socialist editor Chandler Owen, Garvey declared that the NAACP leader had placed "obstacles in the way of the elected representative efficiently discharging his already difficult duties on behalf of the Negro race." A resolution that "denounced the reactionary leader, W. E. B. Du Bois, and upheld Eliézer Cadet" passed unanimously "with acclamation."[55] On April 5, 1919, *Negro World* repeated the charges that the U.S. government had asked "Dr. Du Bois to go to France" and that he had sabotaged the UNIA's initiatives. To say that Garvey deliberately libeled Du Bois would be too

generous, for the UNIA leader cynically distorted the facts: "Cadet presented these [UNIA] aims to the French people and to the Peace Conference,
[but] Du Bois . . . who was never elected by anyone except by the capitalist class . . . has come out to attack [our aims] in the French papers."[56]

Other black American activists repeated Garvey's charges. Chandler
Owen asserted that only "good niggers" like Du Bois could get passports
to attend the Pan-African congress. Only "men who positively would not
discuss lynching, peonage, disfranchisement and discrimination" were
allowed to go to Paris.[57] Du Bois at first ignored the slanders, but as he
prepared for the second Pan-African congress he responded to Garvey's
attacks. Throughout his visit to France, he "never saw or heard of [Cadet],
never denied his nor anyone's statements of the wretched American conditions, did everything possible to arouse rather than quiet the French
press, and would have been delighted to welcome and cooperate with any
colored fellow-worker." The entire affair had convinced Du Bois that
Garvey had "very serious defects of temperament and training: he is dictatorial, domineering, inordinately vain, and very suspicious."[58]

This minor conflict shortly grew into an ideological war, as the two
men identified by Pan-Africanist George Padmore as "the two outstanding Negro leaders in the Western hemisphere" debated their respective
Pan-African programs.[59] A full critique of the Du Bois–Garvey debate
transcends the scope of this discussion, but, as Padmore notes, "Where Du
Bois differed from Garvey was in his conception of the Pan-African move-
ment as an aid to the promotion of national self-determination among
Africans under African leadership, for the benefit of Africans themselves.
Garvey, on the other hand, looked upon Africa as a place for colonizing
Western Negroes under his personal domination."[60]

More generous is the assessment of Garvey scholar Theodore G. Vincent, who viewed the most important contrast between Du Bois and Garvey as their radically different social positions. The "famous feud pitted an
introspective scholar" against a "gregarious, virtually self-educated, mass
leader. As a social analyst, Du Bois made critical evaluations of all leading
blacks; most could accept it in good spirit; Garvey could not."[61] Historian
John Henrik Clarke, surveying the debate, notes that Du Bois often addressed advice to Marcus Garvey "as if . . . [he] were a misguided child, and
Garvey spoke of Du Bois as if he were a fraud, and a traitor to his people.
At a critical period, this kind of conduct was a negation of the cause that
had been the life work of both men."[62]

The 1921 Pan-African congress was in many respects the high point of
the Pan-African movement in the 1920s. An international secretariat es-

tablished in Paris to facilitate correspondence soon closed for lack of funds. Diagne postponed the scheduled 1923 congress, and "finally without proper notice or preparation" the sessions were held in London and Lisbon.[63] British author H. G. Wells and socialist Harold Laski attended the London sessions; Labour Party leader Ramsay MacDonald wrote to the congress affirming his support. The Lisbon sessions were more productive, with delegates from eleven nations in attendance. Two former colonial administrators of Portugal "Promised to use their influence in getting their Government to abolish conscript labor and other such overdue reforms in the African colonies." In their manifesto, the delegates repeated their demands of two years before, concluding, "In fine, we ask in all the world, that black folk be treated as men. We can see no other road to peace and progress."[64]

Nkrumah would later write that the 1923 congress "lacked funds and membership was limited. The delegates were idealists rather than men of action. However, a certain amount of publicity was achieved, and Africans and men of African descent for the first time gained valuable experience in working together."[65] After the congress, Du Bois visited Africa for the first time, seeing four African islands and five countries. In Liberia, he represented the U.S. government at the inaugural of President C. D. B. King.[66]

In the mid-1920s, Du Bois recognized that "the Pan-African idea was still American rather than African, but it was growing, and it expressed a real demand for examination of the African situation and a plan of treatment from the native African point of view." His plans for a fourth conference, which was to be held in "Jamaica, Haiti, Cuba, and the French islands" in 1925 failed to materialize. Efforts to charter a ship to carry participants across the region were unsuccessful, and one French firm demanded "the prohibitive price of fifty thousand dollars" to transport the black delegates.[67]

One year later, Addie W. Hunton, a naacp field organizer and leader of a black women's association, the Circle of Peace and Foreign Relations, largely initiated the plans for another Pan-African congress, which was held in New York City in August 1927.[68] The sessions attracted five thousand people, far more than the number of participants at all previous congresses combined. There were 208 paid delegates from twenty-two states and the District of Columbia. Others came from India, China, Egypt, Liberia, Nigeria, Sierra Leone, the Gold Coast, and other nations. Despite the presence of Chief Amoah III of the Gold Coast, Du Bois was disappointed with the small number of African delegates. Nevertheless, largely because of the spirited presence of African American women leaders, the congress was productive. As Padmore wrote, "While these Negro women had no intention of voluntarily going back to Africa, they, like so many of their menfolk, took a lively interest in the land of their ancestors."[69] The delegates emphasized "six points" in their resolutions:

> Negroes everywhere need:
> 1. A voice in their own government.
> 2. Native rights to the land and its natural resources.
> 3. Modern education for all children.
> 4. The development of Africa for the Africans and not merely for the profit of Europeans.
> 5. The reorganization of commerce and industry so as to make the main object of capital and labor the welfare of the many rather than the enriching of the few.
> 6. The treatment of civilized men as civilized despite difference of birth, race or color.[70]

The delegates also ratified resolutions that widened the scope of Pan-Africanism. The Soviet Union was applauded "for its liberal attitude toward the colored races and for the help which it has extended to them from time to time." Echoing Marx's famous observation in *Capital*, the congress told the white working class "to realize that no program of labor uplift can be successfully carried through in Europe and America so long as colored labor is exploited and enslaved and deprived of all political power."[71]

The Great Depression and the rise of fascism contributed decisively to the temporary collapse of Pan-Africanism. In 1929 Du Bois attempted to hold a fifth Pan-African congress in Tunisia. "Elaborate preparations were begun," he noted in *The World and Africa*. "It looked as though at last the movement was going to be geographically in Africa. But two insuperable difficulties intervened: first, the French government very politely, but firmly, informed us that the Congress could take place at Marseilles or any French city, but not in Africa; and second, there came the Great Depression."[72]

Six weeks after the stock market crash of October 1929, Du Bois admitted to his *Crisis* readers that "the importance of these [Pan-African] meetings is not yet realized by educated and thinking Negroes" in the United States. He attributed much of the problem to "the unfortunate words and career of Marcus Garvey," who had dampened the interest of many African Americans in African issues. "Nevertheless, the idea of the Pan-African Congress is sound, and in less than a hundred years, it is going to be realized."[73]

Most of the leadership of the NAACP had never been interested in Du Bois's Pan-Africanist vision, and with the cancellation of plans for the

1929 congress at Tunis, the organization silently retreated from involvement in African affairs. Du Bois's departure from the editorial and political leadership of the NAACP in the summer of 1934 and the elevation of staunch integrationist and anti-Communist Walter White to the post of NAACP secretary ended a distinct phase of Pan-Africanist history.

IV

The focus of the Pan-Africanist movement returned to London during the 1930s, largely because of the dynamic personality of George Padmore, the nephew of Henry Sylvester Williams.[74] Born Malcolm Nurse, the young Trinidadian came to the United States in 1924 to pursue a career in law. He joined the Communist Party in 1927 and helped to direct the party's Harlem newspaper for a time. Padmore advanced quickly: by the early 1930s he had become "the foremost black figure in the Communist International — the Comintern — culminating in his receiving appointment as a colonel in the Red Army." Padmore traveled across colonial Africa, recruiting African militants to revolutionary Marxism, and later "as head of the African Bureau of the Comintern in Germany, he organized an International Conference of black workers in Hamburg."[75]

But in 1934 Padmore abruptly severed his association with the Communists. In his judgment, the Communists had been incorrect to condemn Garvey's UNIA and Du Bois's Pan-African congresses "as manifestations of petit bourgeois nationalism, to be fought and destroyed before Communism could ever hope to make inroads in Africa or win the allegiance of the Negro masses in America to the cause of the 'Proletarian Revolution.' . . . The attitude of most white Communists toward Negro organizations has been one of contempt. If they cannot control them, they seek their destruction by infiltration."[76]

Relocated in London during the Depression, Padmore established an informal headquarters at his home for African and West Indian students and activists. A young Kenyan studying anthropology, Jomo Kenyatta, was a visitor and close disciple. Two other associates consulted frequently with Padmore: C. L. R. James and Paul Robeson. Born in Trinidad in 1901, James was the leading black Trotskyist in Europe and, within Padmore's circle of associates, the most articulate theoretician of Pan-Africanism. Writing in the tradition of Du Bois, he produced during these years several classic texts: *The Case for West Indian Self-Government* (1933), *The Black Jacobins: Toussaint L'Ouverture and the Haitian Revolution* (1938), and *A History of Negro Revolt* (1937).[77] Robeson, the great black Shakespearean actor and vocalist, was profoundly interested in African culture and politics. The African American artist appeared in the title role of *Toussaint L'Ouverture*, a 1936 play written and staged by James. These men represented a new generation of black scholarship and political action, which would create the nucleus of the Pan-Africanist upsurge after World War II.

With the Italian invasion of Ethiopia, this new leadership helped to create the International African Friends of Abyssinia (IAFA). Their immediate goal was "to arouse the sympathy and support of the British public for the victims of Fascist aggression and to assist by all means in their power in the maintenance of the territorial integrity and political independence of Abyssinia."[78] Participants in the IAFA included Amy Ashwood Garvey, the first wife of the leader of the UNIA, who served as honorary treasurer; T. Albert Marryshaw of Grenada; Gold Coast leader J. B. Danquah; Mohammed Said of Somaliland; Jomo Kenyatta, the organization's honorary secretary; and James, who was IAFA chairman. Several years later, the International African Service Bureau was founded at the initiation of T. R. Makonnen. Padmore chaired the bureau, writing much of the correspondence in his kitchen. James edited the bureau's *International African Opinion*; Kenyatta served as assistant secretary, and Makonnen, the treasurer, successfully raised funds for the group's activities. Robeson and Max Yergan, a black YMCA secretary who had worked in South Africa, initiated plans during a 1939 London meeting to establish the Council on African Affairs in the United States. Based in New York City, the new organization attracted the energies of Alphaeus Hunton, a Howard University professor of literature. Robeson, Yergan, and Hunton started a regular monthly meeting, devoted to developments in the continent. The council invited African intellectuals and political leaders to speak at public forums.[79]

Despite these hopeful signs, few others besides this circle of intellectuals and radicals perceived the Pan-Africanist cause as anything but a visionary and quiet abstract discourse. Though Du Bois had returned to Atlanta University in 1934, he was still optimistic about the possibility of reviving the Pan-African congress movement. In a June 1940 newspaper column in the *Amsterdam News*, he suggested holding a "Fifth Pan-African Congress" in Haiti in 1942. In the wake of A. Philip Randolph's March on Washington Movement of 1941, the two leaders suggested the preparation of a "Congress of Black People" to coincide with the end of World War II.[80] In his personal correspondence, Du Bois admitted in February 1941 that Pan-Africanism "is only an idea on paper and in the memory of a considerable number of former [Congress] participants in America, the West Indies and Africa." But he also predicted, "If the world ever settles down to peace again, there will be another meeting of the Congress."[81] In 1944

Du Bois discussed the idea of developing "an African Freedom Charter and the scheduling of another Pan-African Congress with Amy Jacques Garvey, the recent widow of the UNIA leader, Robeson, Yergan, and Harold Moody, chairman of the London Missionary Society."[82]

In the summer of 1944 Du Bois returned to the NAACP as director of special research. One of his immediate objectives was to "revive the Pan-African movement and give general attention to the foreign aspects of the race problem."[83] The actual planning of the October 1945 Pan-African congress was, however, accomplished by Padmore and a young, idealistic Gold Coast student, Francis (later Kwame) Nkrumah. James had traveled during the war to North America, first conducting a series of discussions with exiled Marxist Leon Trotsky in Coyoacan, Mexico, then organizing dissident black and white rural workers.[84] In 1943, quite by accident, James met the young African, who was attending Lincoln University. From 1943 to early 1945 Nkrumah "would come up to New York to spend a day or two" with James and his associates. James comments: "Even in those years, Nkrumah was noted for his acute intelligence, his intellectual energy, the elegance of his person, the charm of his manners, and his ability to establish easy relations with any company in which he found himself." When Nkrumah left for England to study law, James scribbled a note of introduction to Padmore. Within weeks, Nkrumah joined Kenyatta as a regular "student" in the Padmore household.[85]

Padmore's opportunity to revive the Pan-African congress concept came with the February 1945 establishment in London of the World Federation of Trade Unions, which brought dozens of "representatives of black labour from Nigeria, Gold Coast, Sierra Leone, Gambia, Jamaica, Trinidad, Barbados, British Guiana, and other colonial lands." A second World Federation of Trade Unions meeting had been scheduled in Paris from September 25 to October 9, 1945. Padmore successfully persuaded these black trade unionists and other political leaders to come to Manchester following the Paris meeting. In March 1945 a "provisional programme and agenda" were set and a working committee formed, which included Padmore and Nkrumah as "joint political secretaries," South African writer Peter Abrahams as "publicity secretary," Kenyatta as "assistant secretary," Peter Milliard of British Guiana as chairman, and Makonnen working once more as treasurer.[86]

In the United States, Du Bois had established correspondence with J. B. Danquah, who was then the general secretary of the Gold Coast Youth Conference, and with Jamaican attorney Norman W. Manley, who would later serve as his country's prime minister.[87] It is clear that Padmore had issued the call for a Pan-African congress without Du Bois's knowledge. On March 22, 1945, he wrote to Padmore insisting that the meeting "ought to be held in Africa" and that the "meeting should not be set for a definite date as yet," since the war had not ended.[88] Within several weeks, however, Du Bois wrote to Padmore that he was "in complete sympathy" with his plans and that he had "changed my mind as to the time of the Congress as well." During the next six months the two men worked closely in coordinating the congress.[89]

The Manchester Pan-African congress attracted the political and intellectual vanguard of the black world. Participants came from across the African Diaspora and Africa: Wallace Johnson, secretary of the Sierra Leone Youth League; Magnus Williams, of the National Council of Nigeria and the Cameroons: Raphael Armattos, of Togoland; J. S. Annan, secretary of the Gold Coast Railway Civil Servants' and Technical Workers' Union; G. Ashie Nikoi, a leader of the Gold Coast Farmers; Marko Hlubi, Zulu representative of the African National Congress; Jamaica's Norman Manley and Alma LaBardie, of the Jamaica Women's Movement; P. M. Harper, of the British Guiana Trade Union Congress; E. de Lisle Yearwood, of the Barbados Labour Party; and Claude Lushington and John Rojas, of the West Indian Nationalist Party. Certain individuals stood out at the congress. Kenyatta was the leading spokesperson for East African affairs. And Nkrumah, heretofore unknown, quickly emerged as a dominant personality among the West African delegates. Padmore and Milliard were the essential organizers of the forums. Amy Jacques Garvey received the warm applause of all participants. Yet the guiding spirit of the congress, all recognized, was Du Bois. As Padmore wrote:

> These discussions were conducted under the direction of Dr. Du Bois, who at the age of seventy-three, had flown across the Atlantic from New York to preside over the coming of age of his political child. This "Grand Old Man," politically ahead of many much younger in years, was given an enthusiastic welcome by the delegates. For he had done more than any other to inspire and influence by his writings and political philosophy all the young men who had foregathered from far distant corners of the earth. Even among the older delegations, there were many who were meeting the "Father of Pan-Africanism" in the flesh for the first time. Dr. Du Bois was by no means a silent spectator at the Fifth Pan-African Congress. He entered into all the discussions and brought to the deliberations a freshness of outlook that greatly influenced the final decisions; the implementation of which are already shaping the future of the African continent.[90]

The fifth Pan-African congress differed from the earlier sessions in several important respects. Most of the Manchester participants were elected leaders of various mass-constituency organizations or had direct contacts with nascent independence movements. Thus their programs had an immediacy and a comprehensive character that drew strength from actual workers' struggles. Most of the two hundred delegates and observers were proposing "a mass movement intimately identified with the underprivileged sections of the colored colonial populations."[91]

The sessions on West Africa focused on the immediate tasks of the independence movements in that region, especially in Nigeria and the Gold Coast. Resolutions in this area included demands for the creation of "independent trade unions and cooperative movements without official interference." British rule was denounced for tolerating "mass illiteracy, ill-health, malnutrition, prostitution, and many other social evils," and organized Christianity was described as a tool that facilitated "the political and economic exploitation of the West African peoples by alien powers." Significantly, delegates also criticized "the artificial divisions and territorial boundaries created by the imperialist powers," which were viewed as "deliberate steps to obstruct the political unity of the West African peoples."

Congress participants were already proposing the cardinal principle of what would afterward be referred to as Nkrumahism: that only by the political and economic unity of all Africa could the legacy of European colonial rule be uprooted.

> The delegates believe in peace. How could it be otherwise, when for centuries the African peoples have been the victims of violence and slavery? . . . We are determined to be free. We want education. We want the right to earn a decent living; the right to express our thoughts and emotions, to adopt and create forms of beauty. We demand for Black Africa autonomy and independence, so far and not further than it is possible in this One World for groups and peoples to rule themselves subject to inevitable world unity and federation. . . . We condemn the monopoly of capital and rule of private wealth and industry for private profit alone. We welcome economic democracy as the only real democracy.[92]

The aftermath of the Manchester congress is, of course, well known. Nkrumah formed the West African National Secretariat to implement the congress's resolutions. Returning to the Gold Coast in 1947, he built the powerful Convention People's Party, and under his leadership the independent nation of Ghana was born in 1957. Kenyatta became the leader of Kenya's independence movement and emerged as that nation's president.

Du Bois's subsequent intellectual activities on African affairs continued to increase. His two major books after the war focused specifically on the pressing necessity of African liberation. After his dismissal from the NAACP in 1948, he became vice chairman of the Council on African Affairs. From March 1947 through February 1948, Du Bois wrote a total of fifty-three essays on African politics, economic development, and history for the Harlem weekly *People's Voice*, owned by Congressman Adam Clayton Powell.

Du Bois's voluminous early works on Africa and race relations became more widely distributed across the Caribbean and Africa during the 1950s, as another new generation of black activists and intellectuals looked for proper theoretical grounding for their national liberation struggles. They recognized, in Padmore's words, that Du Bois "was the first American Negro leader to realize the significance of the colonial liberation movements as part of the struggle of the darker races of Asia and Africa and the importance of fostering closer cooperation between native-born Americans and peoples of African descent in the Western Hemisphere.[93] For Du Bois himself, the pursuit of the Pan-Africanist ideal was directly linked with his vision of radical democracy, or perhaps more accurately, multicultural democracy. Africa and peoples of the African Diaspora could not be truly free so long as democracy existed only for the few:

> The iron curtain was not invented by Russia; it hung between Europe and Africa half a thousand years. When the producer is so separated from the consumer in time and space that a mutual knowledge and understanding is impossible, then to regard the industrial process as "individual enterprise" or the result as "private enterprise" is stupid. It is a social process, and if not socially controlled sinks to anarchy with every possible crime of irresponsible greed. Such was the African slave trade, and such is the capitalist system it brought to full flower. Men made cotton cloth and sold sugar; but between the two they stole, killed, and raped human beings. . . . If a world of ultimate democracy, reaching across the color line and abolishing race discrimination, can only be accomplished by the method laid down by Karl Marx, then that method deserves to be triumphant no matter what we think or do.[94]

7

Political Intellectuals in
the African Diaspora

Many studies have examined the evolution of African politics or the theoretical contributions of individuals who have played significant roles in the patterns of social protest within Africa, but the attempt to chart the actual social development among black intellectuals generated within the African Diaspora has barely begun. We know a good deal about individual leaders, such as Kwame Nkrumah, Julius Nyerere, and Leopold Senghor, but relatively little—in theoretical terms—about their development as political intellectuals against the background of antiracist and anticolonial struggles in sub-Saharan Africa, the Caribbean, and black America. What was the life of the political mind of the African Diaspora in the late nineteenth and twentieth centuries?

I have begun a research project that aims toward a comprehensive historical and theoretical critique of the contours, commonalities, and divergences of African, Caribbean, and African American political and social protest thought. This essay presents a set of conceptual questions that serve as a theoretical framework for that project.

I

The first question is, "What are political intellectuals and what is their function within society?" The most detailed and comprehensive answer is found in the work of the Italian Marxist intellectual Antonio Gramsci. In his seminal study *The Prison Notebooks*, Gramsci suggested that all intellectuals, whether or not they are personally involved in political organizations and activities, perform a political function. They provide an academic rationale for the dominant set of ideological, cultural, and social relations that exist within the social formation. They explain, justify, and legitimate the intellectual status quo. They constitute the ideological glue that binds together the force that Gramsci termed "hegemony." Each social class, Gramsci observed in *The Prison Notebooks*, "creates together with itself, organically, one or more strata of intellectuals which give it homogeneity and an awareness of its own function not only in economic but also in the social and political fields."[1]

Within a society based on capitalist economic patterns of ownership and production, traditional intellectuals—writers, theologians, philosophers, social critics, novelists, artists, and so forth—are directly involved in the production and reproduction of ideological forms that reinforce domination by the classes that control political and economic power. Part of their responsibility is to socialize successive generations to accept the dominant ideology and power relations with the existing social order. Consequently, intellectuals in this context are less concerned with the transmission of knowledge that accurately relates to the material and social conditions of their students and readers than with the promulgation of perspectives that reaffirm the established order. Education in this context becomes a method of obscuring rather than illuminating social reality. Intellectuals also serve to explain social, political, cultural, and even scientific phenomena in a way that reinforces the power arrangements within the political economy and social structure, thus permitting the process of accumulation within the capitalist economy.

Gramsci emphasized that "traditional intellectuals" may not perceive themselves as ideological appendages to the development of capitalism. Indeed, traditional intellectuals view themselves as existing above social classes, independent of partisanship and class affiliation. They do retain a certain autonomy, or as Gramsci noted, "The relationship between the intellectuals and the world of production is not as direct as it is with the fundamental social groups but is, in varying degrees, 'mediated' by the whole fabric of society and by the complex of superstructures, of which the intellectuals are, precisely, the 'functionaries.'"[2]

Social change within a society dominated by capital occurs fundamentally through social-class conflicts or through protests by dominated groups or constituencies—racial, ethnic, or national minorities—against real grievances generated by the political and economic order. Oppressed social classes or racial groups may try to win liberal or sympathetic intellectuals of the ruling class over to their political perspective, in an attempt to challenge existing beliefs. Certainly this has occurred many times during the history of social protest, throughout the African Diaspora: the development of white abolitionism in the United Kingdom and the United States in the early nineteenth century, for example; or, in the twentieth century, white anticolonialist and antiimperialist agitation against the crimes of Europe in Africa.

But Gramsci suggested that such a dynamic is not enough to transform the dominant hegemony, or "common sense," ideologically reproduced by the vast majority of the society's traditional intellectuals. "One of the most important characteristics of any group that is developing towards dominance is the struggle to assimilate and to conquer 'ideologically' the traditional intellectuals," Gramsci noted, "but this assimilation and conquest is made quicker and more efficacious the more the group in question succeeds in simultaneously elaborating its own organic intellectuals."[3]

In contrast, organic intellectuals emerge from the most oppressed and exploited social classes and groups within society. They generally articulate the consciousness of their classes in politics, in social relations, and within the economy. Because their connections with the elites who control the economy or dominate governmental institutions are tenuous or even nonexistent, their objective class position is implicitly or explicitly in direct conflict with the dominant powers. Gramsci believed that in every successful social revolution, oppressed classes generate their own organic intellectuals, who assume a pivotal ideological role in the process of social change.

Organic intellectuals can reveal gross contradictions within the political process, illustrating the distance between those who govern and those who are governed; they may express the deep grievances percolating up from the masses below regarding educational, social, cultural, economic, or political rights; they may promote a counterhegemonic perspective with civil society that establishes a culture of resistance, glorifying beliefs, rituals, or symbols of struggle against the dominant social classes and political elites; and they may assist in the advancement of educational and cultural awareness at a mass participatory level, through public school intervention, literacy campaigns, and so forth. Organic intellectuals do not attempt merely to interpret the world in various ways; their object is to change it.

For several fundamental reasons, organic intellectuals who emerge from social movements seldom have the influence or authority within society to implement their social theories and political perspectives. On a technical level, they lack the institutional resources and standard academic support to engage in long-term research or intellectual investigation. They may be explicitly excluded from the academy solely on the grounds of race, as in the famous case of W. E. B. Du Bois, who earned a doctorate in history at Harvard University and established a brilliant publication record but was unable, for sixty years, to obtain a tenure-track position at any white American university. They may possess a wealth of critical information about some aspect of their oppressed social group's history or political development but lack the traditional academic credentials of mainstream intellectuals. During the period 1919–1939 in black America, for example, some of the most talented and well-read intellectuals included Hubert H. Harrison, the socialist and black nationalist writer; popular historian J. A. Rogers; and militant journalist John Edward Bruce, who founded the Negro Society for Historical Research in 1911. But with the partial exception of Harrison, who held a nontenured position as a "special lecturer" in contemporary civilization at New York University, neither these intellectuals nor their writings were welcome at white colleges and universities.[4]

Organic intellectuals have theoretical perspectives and ideas not generally replicated in the normal discourse or inquiry of traditional intellectuals within the university and professional organizations. Consequently, any innovations or discoveries that they achieve are usually dismissed without serious examination or analysis by the mainstream. It is not that their work is explicitly rejected; rather, it is simply ignored.

One need not develop a rigorous critique of a theoretical statement if the work is neither widely read nor distributed by traditional scholars. Organic intellectuals suffer from a periodic sense of isolation and even social alienation from their base constituency, class, or national group. Developing a sense of history and critical intellectual tradition within the organic or insurgent milieu is always extremely difficult. The absence of mentors who can provide the socialization as well as the external contacts so crucial for professional and intellectual advancement contributes to the sense of isolation. Moreover, organic intellectuals must frequently pay a public price for their academic heresies. In most countries in the African Diaspora dominated by European colonialism or racial segregation (as in the American South), the price has been imprisonment, political harassment, arrest, censorship, house arrest, unemployment, poverty, and sometimes death.

Political censorship and isolation create yet another problem. Isolation can distort or deform the research or scientific interpretation of organic scholars, because they are denied the most recent data on investigative methods or resources. Their physical isolation from the academy can limit the scope of their work. Finally, the political ideas of organic intellectuals frequently take on the characteristics or orientation of the oppressed social classes in which they live in close proximity. The language and style of organic intellectual discourse are often designed for a mass audience rather than an effete coterie of abstract scholars. Organic intellectuals are engaged in problem solving, not in detached academic inquiry. The demands of the broader social movement that consume their energies and passion largely dictate the theoretical question posed in their work.

An additional set of political and social limitations has plagued organic intellectuals within the black world. During the first half of the twentieth century, serious academic work dealing with people of African descent dwelt in an extremely repressive environment. In Africa, the political and social structures of European colonialism controlled society from above. In the American South, the white establishment dismantled the last vestiges of democratic government in the 1890s and imposed a rigid regime of racial segregation in public accommodations, transportation, and the job market—a regime reinforced by the lynching of at least one hundred black men and women a year.

These two repressive forms of society were comparable in many respects. Both colonialism and Jim Crow severely restricted individual and group civil liberties, often outlawing freedom of the press and freedom of assembly for nonwhites. The political apparatus did not permit blacks to participate directly in elections; in the South, blacks who had won the electoral franchise immediately after the end of slavery were now forcibly removed from overseers' rolls. Organized political groups advocating racial reform or the termination of institutional or vigilante violence against nonwhites encountered severe repression. The state frequently prohibited their work and imprisoned their leaders. The legal apparatus of the racist state dispensed a crude yet effective form of civil order, which regulated the public behavior of blacks and protected the security of whites' private property and power within majority black areas. The social and cultural institutions, especially the schools, reinforced—by design—a negative, subordinate self-image among nonwhite children. The curriculum advanced values that justified the hegemony of the white man as an absolute political and cultural necessity. Negro inferiority and white supremacy were postulates as widely accepted in the academy as Newton's laws of gravity and motion. Science, art, and culture translated the dynamics of lynching and disfranchisement into the discourse of detached scholarship.

II

Within this political environment, successive generations of black political intellectuals became preoccupied with several central questions—questions that transcend geography and the peculiarities of local culture, political institutions, and social structure.

What is racism? How did racial prejudice and discrimination evolve as a central ideological feature of western civilization's encounter with the African world? What is the relationship between institutional racism and the structures of colonialism in the Caribbean and Africa, or the apparatus of Jim Crow in the United States? Is it possible to dismantle the structures of political and economic domination without simultaneously challenging the legitimacy of racist ideology and cultural relations? Black organic intellectuals also questioned the historical and theoretical relationship between racial prejudice and democracy, particularly as it applied to the status of minority populations. Is democracy so grounded in narrow cultural assumptions about the process of decision making within pluralistic societies that its applicability or relevance to the African Diaspora is very limited?

More generally, black intellectuals questioned the relationship between institutional racism and other forms of social and political domination: rooted in social class, nationality, religious intolerance, ethnocentrism. Is it a realistic or realizable political project to take as one's goal a society that is not only antiracist but actually committed to human equality? Can humanity transcend the contradictions of its own history and create a more humane political economy and cultural environment? These questions, and others, have preoccupied the research and critical writings of black organic intellectuals for a century and more.

In pursuing the answers to these questions, organic intellectuals of the African Diaspora established several common responses to the existence of white colonial or capitalist domination. Black intellectuals repeatedly asserted the cultural unity and aesthetic identity of all people of African descent. This response was undoubtedly in part an attempt to counter the impact of the ideology of white supremacy, to project the accomplishments and richness of the cultural heritage of African people in a variety of political and social environments. But another essential element was the concept that common cultural threads bound the people of the Diaspora together and that the art, music, literature, and theater of black people expressed these connections. The integrity of this cultural tradition provided some of the ideological ammunition for a critique of European and American cultural hegemony. In short, the artistic and cultural expressions of African people not only established our claim to the rights of humanity but were also an essential aspect of our political assault against the structures of domination.

During the 1920s in black America, for example, the central cultural and artistic movement was the Harlem Renaissance, a phenomenon that—

when it comes to connections between African Americans and both the image and reality of Africa—can only be described as "contradictory." A goodly number of black artists, particularly those who found white patronage, sought to validate the universality of their work by "transcending" their racial identity. Others insisted that African American art should have little to do with political agitation on the issue of racism.

But those organic intellectuals who identified closely, both personally and politically, with the black masses approached the issue of black art and liberation very differently. William H. Ferris, a former member of W. E. B. Du Bois's Niagara Movement and literary editor during the early 1920s of Marcus Garvey's *Negro World* newspaper, argued against the "false conception of art" that should "appeal exclusively . . . to the bourgeoisie." Largely due to "social pressure," Ferris observed, too many black artists "are forced to produce works that bring out 'the higher aspiration of the Negro,' works that with a brutally sterile puritanism steer clear of the beauty and simplicity of true art."[5]

Some of the most productive and influential black writers of the period agreed with Ferris. Claude McKay's famous poem "If We Must Die" captured the necessity for African Americans to organize against racist violence. Black art had to advance the ideological and political interests of the masses. As McKay insisted in his 1923 book *The Negroes in America*, prepared for the Communist International: "The only literature which merits any attention is that which has the character of national propaganda. Almost any Negro writer, however much he might appear to be minding his own business, is really drawn into active work in the area of propaganda."[6] Similarly, Langston Hughes's "The Negro Artist and the Racial Mountain" emphasized the necessity for African American writers to deepen their political and "spiritual" identification with the black masses. Hughes's "mountain," which stood "in the way of any true Negro art in America," was the tendency "within the race toward whiteness, the desire to pour racial individuality into the mold of American standardization, and to be as little Negro and as much American as possible."[7]

The major black nationalist mass movement of the era, the Universal Negro Improvement Association, was in many respects a Pan-African cultural and artistic movement, developing and attracting writers and artists who were committed to black liberation. "We must encourage our own black authors who have character," Garvey himself wrote in 1928, "who are loyal to their race, who feel proud to be black, and in every way let them feel that we appreciate their efforts to advance our race."[8]

Literary clubs and theatrical companies were established at UNIA branches across the African Diaspora. Chapters held concerts featuring local black artists; they scheduled plays, debating contests, poetry readings, and other cultural events. In 1921, the *Negro World* Christmas literary contest offered thirty-six cash prizes to participants. It was not unusual for poets and writers to join the UNIA and to be elevated to political leadership roles. Poet J. R. Ralph Casimir, for example, was the leader of the UNIA branch in Dominica and contributed dozens of Pan-Africanist–oriented poems to the *Negro World* under the name Civis Africanus. After Garvey's publication was officially banned in West Africa, Casimir forwarded copies to J. E. Casely Hayford, editor of the *Gold Coast Leader*. Charles H. D. Este, a major figure of the UNIA's Montreal branch, achieved prominence as a frequent contributor of poetry on black nationalist themes to *Negro World*. The publication attracted the literary contributions of a variety of black writers and political activists alike. Albert Marryshaw, the political reform leader of Grenada and early advocate of West Indian federation during the 1920s, published poetry in *Negro World*. Gold Coast attorney and African nationalist Kobina Sikyi contributed the political poem "The Sojourner" in 1922, calling upon Africans to reclaim their cultural heritage:

> *Awake thee from thy slumber*
> *And quickly disencumber*
> *Thy manhood of the fetters*
> *That make thine equals betters.*[9]

Another common response to white colonial and capitalist domination within the African Diaspora was the general belief, expressed by many black intellectuals as early as the mid-nineteenth century, that the ultimate liberation of African people in any single country was directly connected to the condition of black people in other countries. Part of this analysis derived from the realities of European colonialism; Britain manifested its domination throughout the nonwhite world between 1890 and 1940, from the Caribbean to sub-Saharan Africa, to the Indian subcontinent, to the Middle East. The shape of colonial regimes might differ in form but not in essence. All were structures designed to facilitate economic exploitation and political domination; all involved some form of cultural imperialism, whether modeled after the French assimilationist pattern or the rigidly segregated institutions characteristic of the British and Americans.

The political protests of one community of black people in one corner of the Diaspora might provide critical insights into the appropriate strategies or tactics of resistance in another geographical region. As a practical matter, organic intellectuals understood the need to learn about other black resistance movements, to avoid the mistakes or errors of those groups in organizing against colonial domination, and to maintain regular lines of communication with other formations engaged in similar protest activities. Implicitly, this pragmatic desire to cultivate political connections presumed a Pan-African problematic, a theoretical perspective linking local, regional, and international struggles. They also understood the need for solidarity movements to provide political and moral support for black communities or nations that were under military attack or were experiencing severe racial and political oppression.

III

The first organic intellectual to achieve a profoundly influential critique of colonialism and European racism and to articulate a truly Pan-African political model for agitation was Edward Wilmot Blyden. Intellectuals within the African Diaspora born in the late nineteenth century and coming to political maturity immediately after World War I were heavily influenced by his massive academic and polemical achievement. In a series of essays appearing in *African Repository* from 1860 to 1890, Blyden had provided an articulate rejection of the ideology of European supremacy and racism. His 1888 seminal work, *Christianity, Islam, and the Negro Race*, projected pride in Africa's cultural heritage.

Perhaps even more influential was Blyden's personal model of academic excellence and political engagement on behalf of African people. A native of St. Thomas, Blyden had become a professor of Greek and Latin at Liberia College in Monrovia in 1861 and was named to the presidency two decades later. At different times in his career he was secretary of state, minister of the interior, ambassador to London and Paris, and commissioner to the descendants of Africa in the United States and the West Indies. Blyden's entire approach to his political and intellectual understanding of race was based on a Pan-African model, a theoretical approach transcending the distortions of local ethnic parochialism.

During the period 1919 to 1939, the most prominent examples of Pan-Africanist political organization initiated by the black intelligentsia were Du Bois's Pan-African congresses. But many other organizational efforts also promoted the vision of Blyden. In 1925 African students living in the United Kingdom founded the West African Students' Union. Among the key organizers were J. B. Danquah, later the leader of the United Gold Coast Convention; H. J. Lightfoot-Boston, later the governor-general of Sierra Leone; and J. W. de Graft Johnson of the Gold Coast. Actually, WASU was neither composed totally of students nor limited to West African membership; its constitution permitted anyone of African descent to participate. Its original goals included the promotion of nationalist and Pan-African pride and consciousness; the cultivation of leadership abilities among its members; service "as a Bureau of Information on African history, customs and institutions"; and "act[ing] as a center for Research on all subjects appertaining to Africa and its development."

By early 1926 WASU had established its own publication, *Wasu*. The quarterly magazine was distributed to black communities throughout Africa, Europe, the United Kingdom, and the United States. It developed branches in Accra, Freetown, Kano, and other West African cities. Its official patrons included Casely Hayford and, in the 1930s, African American artist and activist Paul Robeson. Upon Garvey's arrival in England in 1928 immediately following his expulsion from the United States, WASU began to work closely with Garveyites and for a time placed its headquarters in lodgings owned by supporters. In the late 1920s and early 1930s, additional branches of WASU were established in Lagos, Port Harcourt Jos, Cape Coast, Sekondi, and other cities.[10]

During the Depression, other Pan-African formations developed. In December 1931 the League of Africans was organized in London, with the purpose of promoting "mutual understanding" and "sincere, friendly Egyptians and other Native races of North Africa." Among the initial officers were Jomo Kenyatta, general secretary, and A. J. Koi, of the Gold Coast, who would serve a quarter century later in Kwame Nkrumah's cabinet. The League of Africans appears to have disintegrated within two years.

More successful was the League of Colored Peoples, established by Harold A. Moody, a Jamaican medical doctor and civic leader of London's black community. Moody sought to unify Caribbean and African students living and working in the United Kingdom behind a moderate reformist program. The objectives of the league included the improvement of race relations in England, the promotion of cooperative relations between "organizations sympathetic to Colored Peoples" and "to interest members in the Welfare of Colored Peoples in all parts of the World." Whites were allowed to speak at the league's meetings and conferences, but they were barred from the executive committee. Moody's rigid commitment to Christianity and his bias against Marxism alienated some African and West Indian students. In 1932 George Padmore's *Negro Worker* magazine carried an appeal to nonwhite students to "break with the sycophantic leadership of Dr. Harold Moody, a typical 'Uncle Tom.'" But Moody's efforts helped sustain interest and political engagement in a Pan-Africanism that included both the Caribbean and black America.[11]

African students in Paris at the same time were developing similar organizations. Touvalou Houenou, of Dahomey, initiated the Ligue universelle, calling for African and Caribbean political self-determination and emphasizing the cultural and political unity of all African people. Attacked as subversive by Blaise Diagne, the Ligue disintegrated within a few years. More successful was the Ligue de la defense de la race Negro, established by Tiemoho Kouyate. This second formation existed for about a decade before it was suppressed by government authorities.

But perhaps the most important single Pan-Africanist organization during this period was the International African Friends of Abyssinia, established in August 1935, two months before Italy's brutal invasion of Ethiopia. Its officers and international committee members truly represented a Pan-African united front. The chair was Trinidadian Trotskyist C. L. R. James, who was in the process of writing *The Black Jacobins*; the second vice president was Grenadian Albert Marryshaw; Jomo Kenyatta was honorary secretary; Amy Ashwood Garvey, the first wife of the black nationalist leader and a prominent Pan-Africanist; and committee member J. B. Danquah. Although he did not participate in its founding, former Communist International leader George Padmore quickly emerged as the principal leader and organizer of the group. This formation lasted only a year, but it became the nucleus for the International African Service Bureau, led by Padmore, Kenyatta, and James, which would become the informal general secretariat for Pan-Africanist agitation and the promotion of independence movements for both the Caribbean and Africa after World War II.

Political intellectuals as a social group have been central to the process of political, cultural, and social change within the African Diaspora. Further research should reveal even more extensive connections among black nationalist, labor, socialist, and electoral political organizations and their programs, tactics, and strategies for empowerment. It is here, among these organizational and political connections, that we may discern certain patterns that explain the emergence of organic intellectuals and their general strategies toward social transformation.

PART THREE

The Politics of Peace and Urban Empowerment

8

Peace and Black Liberation:
The Contributions of W. E. B. Du Bois

War? Not so, not war:
Dominion, Lord, and over black, not white
Black, brown and fawn,
And not Thy chosen brood, O God,
We murdered.
To build Thy kingdom,
To drape our wives and little ones,
And set their souls a'glitter—
For this we killed these lesser breeds
And civilized their dead,
Raping red rubber, diamonds, cocoa, gold.
For this, too, once, and in Thy name
I lynched a Nigger.

—W. E B. Du Bois, "A Christmas Poem," December 1914

I

In the early 1980s millions of Americans became part of a modern world peace movement. On June 12, 1982, more than one million of them demonstrated in New York in favor of a bilateral freeze of nuclear weapons production by the United States and the Soviet Union. In November 1982 about eleven million Americans voted to endorse the "freeze." In more than fifty cities, a "Jobs with Peace" referendum passed, calling upon Congress to provide more funds for human needs and vocational programs. Many American businessmen noted with some alarm that expenditures for both conventional and nuclear weapons had produced massive federal deficits that might reach $300 billion per year by 1986. Others argued that an immediate freeze on the production, testing, and deployment of nuclear weapons, missiles, and bombers would save $6 billion in 1983 dollars, and perhaps $200 billion over a ten-year period. Opposing the popular movement for peace and nuclear weapons reductions were the conservative policies of the Reagan administration—intervention in Central America, confrontation with the Soviet Union, and, pending before Congress, an unprecedented request for an appropriation of $1.5 trillion for the military. For much of the world, the direction of American military and foreign policy in the 1980s seemed to foreshadow the very real possibility of a third world war.[1]

The strength of this modern peace movement and the broad-based popularity of a nuclear freeze tend to obscure a number of historical issues of special relevance to black Americans and other national minorities. The legacy of the Cold War and McCarthyism has contributed to a kind of "historical amnesia" for many white Americans. Few political commentators in the national media note that many of the public policy concerns raised today about nuclear arms proliferation echo the slogans and campaigns of millions of other Americans of a generation ago. More than one million voters supported the Progressive Party presidential campaign of Henry Wallace in 1948, and millions of others voted for the Democratic Party incumbent, Harry S. Truman, in the vague hope that he would implement a few of the demands for peaceful coexistence and disarmament raised by the Progressives. Moreover, many contemporary white peace activists fear any relationship between their specific activities and/or disarmament proposals with the broader socioeconomic concerns that attract the immediate interest of working-class and nonwhite people—full employment, decent housing, better schools, welfare, adequate medical care.

Indeed, after I delivered a speech on the necessity of linking the issues of racism, imperialism, and reductions in both nuclear and conventional weapons, one white middle-class woman, a supporter of the freeze campaign, privately rebuked me. "Blacks and Latinos aren't interested in peace, or at least they haven't been in the past," she said in a matter-of-fact manner. "It could be that the prospect of a nuclear war is so terrifying that most blacks just aren't able to worry about it." I was willing, for the moment, to ignore her ethnocentrism. What genuinely perturbed me was this woman's simplistic belief that America's defense policies were completely unrelated to racism or colonialism. Somehow, the idea that one could promote the freeze campaign without speaking to the material conditions of poverty, discrimination, and hunger was, from my vantage point, morally wrong and politically inept.

It seems apparent, in the light of history, that no significant reform movement can succeed in this nation without the participation and the decisive leadership of peoples of color, as well as of the working class. This is not simply a question of "race relations," wherein certain numbers of identifiable black, Asian American, and Latino leaders are politely invited to sit on a dais and offer a few words of support. Nor is it the hasty incorporation of the pressing economic, political, and social agendas of the black and brown working classes into the agendas of groups working for disarmament and arms reduction. It is rather the relearning of American social history, from the bottom up, reconstructing the key components of a practical American program for social transformation. At minimum, this involves an intimate awareness of the dialectical unity between wars for national liberation and the necessity for world peace; the need to destroy racial barriers and the necessity that African people and their New World descendants unite; the occasional use of violence to halt the violence imposed by capitalism within people's daily lives.

Many white peace advocates are completely ignorant of the contributions that blacks have made to white movements. For decades, some of the most articulate people speaking for peace have been African Americans. Melvin B. Tolson's "A Legend of Versailles" provides a poet's insight into the seeds planted at the 1919 peace conference from which Hitler and war grew.[2]

Langston Hughes's "Peace" says more in eight lines than a series of treatises could ever relate:

> *We passed their graves:*
> *The dead men there,*
> *Winners or losers,*
> *Did not care.*
> *In the dark*
> *They could not see*
> *Who had gained*
> *The victory.*[3]

The most charismatic and noted proponent of peace in U.S. history was the gentle giant Paul Robeson. A true Renaissance man, Robeson made his mark in athletics and law, in music and drama, in human rights and in the cause of African liberation. At the height of the Cold War, Robeson did not repudiate his political commitment to the peace movement, and to the cause of human emancipation. As Andrew Young has noted, Robeson "loved justice, freedom, compassion" and "hated injustice, oppression, [and] tyranny. To the young of my generation and to those who have followed after, he was a giant among men."[4]

Yet as monumental as Robeson was as a symbol of peace and freedom, he was not primarily a social theorist. Robeson's actions in the face of McCarthyite persecution are an indelible part of the progressive history of the period, but he did not attempt to develop a specific method of social criticism that would establish the linkages among peace, the struggle against racism, and the cause of socialism.

The one American who devoted more than half a century to the principle of peace—and to many other struggles besides—was yet another black man, W. E. B. Du Bois. In his many works on a wide range of issues, we can find the theoretical basis for a more advanced peace movement for our own time. This discussion is not a comprehensive critique of Du Bois's writings on peace and black liberation—notably *Color and Democracy: Colonies and Peace* (1945) and *In Battle for Peace* (1952). Rather, my aim here is to present the thematic content of Du Bois's essays and, most important, his evolving method of historical materialism in developing a critique linking racism, war, and peace.[5]

II

Du Bois always presents special difficulties for the historian because of the wide variety of his research and political interests over seventy-five years as cofounder of the NAACP (1909), organizer of five Pan-African congresses, author of classic texts in black sociology and history—most prominently *The Souls of Black Folk* (1903) and *Black Reconstruction in America* (1935), editor of the NAACP journal *Crisis* (1910–1934), and director of special research for the NAACP (1944–1948). Du Bois is generally viewed through the prism of black history in three specific frames of reference: his conflict with conservative black educator Booker T. Washington; his debates with Jamaican black nationalist Marcus Garvey; and his role as a leader of the NAACP, up to his resignation in 1934. For many white liberal historians, the story of Du Bois's public life ends here, almost three decades before his death. What is especially striking is the failure of virtually every historian—with the outstanding exception of Herbert Aptheker—to analyze one of the principal themes of his entire life's work: Du Bois's theoretical and programmatic understanding of peace.

A single-minded vision of a world without war is everywhere in Du Bois's speeches, articles, and books over the years. As early as 1904, he declared:

> I believe in the Prince of Peace. I believe that War is Murder. I believe that armies and navies are at bottom the tinsel and braggadocio of oppression and wrong, and I believe that the wicked conquest of

weaker and darker nations by nations whiter and stronger but fore-
shadows the death of that strength.[6]

Throughout a long and controversial career as a leader of the black freedom movement, Du Bois never wavered from this commitment to peace. He
recommended books on pacifism to readers of his journal *Horizon* in 1907.[7]
After World War I, Du Bois used the pages of a black children's monthly,
the *Brownies' Book*, to reinforce antiwar sentiments among youth. In one
Brownies' Book column, he argued that the U.S. government should be prohibited from participating in any foreign conflicts unless a majority of voters
passed a national referendum.[8] Ten years later, speaking at a "peace mass
meeting" sponsored by *World Tomorrow* magazine in New York City, Du
Bois declared that America's impulse toward war was driven by the demand
"for cheap labor and materials."[9] In March 1949 he gave a major address
titled "Peace, Freedom's Road for Oppressed Peoples" before the Cultural
and Scientific Conference for World Peace at Madison Square Garden.[10] In
the May 1955 issue of *New World Review*, he made his assessment of the
strengths and weaknesses of the postwar peace movement and his reasons for
reaffirming his long-held faith in reason and right over human conflict.[11]

Du Bois continued to advocate world peace, along with his other principles of civil rights for black Americans and Third World liberation. But
his understanding of peace, unlike that of most white Americans, was a
detailed, dialectical, and dynamic concept, rooted in the material conditions
of humanity and based upon an absolute commitment to social justice.

Du Bois's first and most essential contribution to a black liberation/
peace analysis was his correlation between war and white capitalist hegemony. In "The African Roots of the War," published in the May 1915 issue
of *Atlantic Monthly*, he argued that the European conflict was based upon
imperialist competition for overseas territories in Africa and Asia. At the
root of the war, he insisted, were white racism and the demand to accumu-
late capital at the expense of darker humanity.[12] That same month in *Crisis*
he also attacked the vicious racism found within all-white peace organizations in both Europe and the United States. He wrote that any peace group
that did not simultaneously oppose colonialism, capitalist exploitation of
peoples of color, and racism would be fundamentally compromised.[13]

And, though Du Bois was not aware of it, yet another socialist was making some of these same points, in a very different political context: V. I.
Lenin. Influenced by the 1902 study of British writer J. A. Hobson, and perhaps more decisively by his brilliant pupil N. I. Bukharin, Lenin shared Du
Bois's conviction that "these imperialist countries form alliances against one

another in order to protect or enlarge their possessions, their interests and their spheres of influence" across Asia and other continents. In 1916 Lenin noted that there was an "inseverable bond" between colonial exploitation in Africa and Asia, "between imperialism and the trusts, and, therefore between imperialism and the foundations of capitalism."[14]

Thus, despite his political distance from revolutionary Marxism, Du Bois developed a quasi-Leninist outlook on the relationship between international war, racism, and world capitalism decades before he actually joined the Communist Party. This radical perspective is sharply revealed in his subsequent writings as well. In a brief note published in the October 1923 issue of *Crisis*, the editor noted that the basis for world war was capitalist expansion and a deep-seated hatred of colored people. War produces profits for corporations; colonial expansion "to 'develop' the tropics" creates international turmoil; "it pays to kill 'niggers.'"[15] In January 1947 Du Bois was invited to speak at the sixth annual dinner of the Nobel Anniversary Committee and was asked to make a comment on the prospects for peace. His sharp reply was, "The emancipation of the black masses of the world is one guarantee of a firm foundation for world peace." In short, peace demanded the destruction of racism.[16]

For Du Bois, peace was not the absence of conflict but the realization of social justice and human equality, which would make war unnecessary. In the March 1926 issue of *Crisis*, he suggested three steps toward the realization of world peace—a universal agreement to "outlaw war," a collective means to monitor disagreements between nations and impose arbitration, and, finally, complete disarmament. Even with such agreements in place, wars would still continue unless institutional racism, capitalist imperialism, and the colonial regimes of England, France, Belgium, and other nations were overthrown, because these factors were "basic sources of war." To win a lasting peace, equality for all societies had to be established as a clear goal.[17]

Du Bois's rejection of "absolute pacifism" in the struggle for peace provoked dissension by liberals of all races and cultures. In 1936 an Indian intellectual, N. S. Subba Rao, criticized his views. Du Bois countered that Rao's pacifism promoted "acquiescence" and "subordination" to British authority among the Indian masses. Genuine peace could not come to the subcontinent until the Indian people rose up to overturn the ruling British elite. Achieving worldwide peace would require a united front of the globe's colored people, not with the goal of oppressing whites but with one of liquidating all forms of political tyranny.[18] Du Bois believed in the principle of peace in regard to human relations but not to the point at which fascism and racism would be unchecked and unresisted. Immediately after Pearl Harbor, he urged blacks to "close ranks" and do battle for the democratic rights "of people of all colors." In May 1942 he declared that if World War II was being waged for human emancipation, "my gun is on my shoulder."[19]

For many critics, therefore, Du Bois was not a pacifist at all, and his selective advocacy of war seemed to contradict his many assertions praising peace. But to himself and, more important, in the light of the material interests of his people, Du Bois's position made complete sense. Poland "had to resist Hitler," he argued in March 1947, just as the brilliant former slave Toussaint L'Ouverture was correct in leading his people to revolt against their French slavemasters in Saint Domingue.[20] When Martin Luther King Jr. used nonviolent direct action to defeat segregation on municipal buses in Montgomery, Alabama, Du Bois cheered—but gently criticized the young black minister's "absolute pacifism" and his failure to relate blacks' real class and political interests within a pacifist framework.[21]

The dialectical unity between his advocacy of "peace" and the necessity for certain "types" of warfare is illustrated by Du Bois's many writings on Africa. First, he consistently criticized American pacifists for turning a blind eye to the European partition of Africa and to the relationship between colonialism and war.[22] In the July 1943 issue of *Foreign Affairs*, he pointed out again, as he had done during World War I, that the European nations fighting Germany maintained their exploitive policies within their own African colonies. To guarantee peace after this conflict, the entire process of underdevelopment had to be halted. Africans should possess their own "land and resources," and the governments of these nations should "reflect" the desires of the black masses.[23] In his Atlanta University journal *Phylon*, Du Bois attacked the Roosevelt administration's policies on Africa and singled out an administrator of the Division of Near Eastern Affairs, Henry Villard—the grandson of abolitionist William Lloyd Garrison—for sharp criticism.[24] In a controversial essay for the *New Leader*, Du Bois argued that African and Asian colonialism had been decisive factors in creating both world wars and declared that European imperialism would inevitably encourage more war in the future. His analysis was so uncompromising that one staff writer on the Communist Party's paper, the *Daily Worker*, condemned his remarks as "ultra-leftist."[25]

Throughout the remainder of his life, Du Bois insisted that "until the question of colonialism" and the European capitalists' "rape of Africa" were ended, "there can be no peace in the world."[26] It is also clear that his ideas on the need for world peace to facilitate the drive toward African self-determination found a receptive audience among militant African leaders. The young Kwame Nkrumah, for example, who in 1946 was serving as secretary-general of the West African National Secretariat in London, praised Du Bois for his role in putting before the United Nations a petition representing the demands of "African organizations and the descendants of Africans in America." Nkrumah informed Du Bois that his group "fully supported" the idea of relating "the important question of the treatment of Africans and people of African descent, racial discrimination and colonial matters generally" to the quest to achieve "world peace."[27]

III

Despite his many earlier writings on the subject, Du Bois's international prominence as an advocate for peace did not really gain recognition until the end of World War II. In June 1945 he attended the founding conference of the United Nations, held in San Francisco. Serving as a consultant representing the NAACP, he perceived for the first time a growing rift between the world's oppressed peoples and the United States, which was now the "major colonial power." He wrote in the *Chicago Defender*, "I seem to see outlined a third World War based on the suppression of Asia and the strangling of Russia. Perhaps I am wrong. God Knows I hope I am."[28] His active participation in the Pan-African congress of 1945, his growing political militancy, his advocacy of peace with the Soviet Union, and his support for the 1948 presidential campaign of Henry Wallace, all contributed to his dismissal, in September 1948, as the NAACP's director of special research.

After this second departure from the NAACP, Paul Robeson asked Du Bois to become vice chairman of the Council on African Affairs, without a salary but with secretarial assistance and an office.[29] "I accepted for two reasons," Du Bois writes in his *Autobiography*. "First, because of my belief in the work which the Council should do for Africa; and secondly, because of my belief that no man or organization should be denied the right to a career because of political or religious beliefs."[30] Simultaneously, he became vigorously involved in public efforts to halt the mounting Cold War with the Soviet Union. In concert with other leading intellectuals—Thomas Mann, Lillian Hellman, Linus Pauling, Albert Einstein—Du Bois used his pen and his voice to protest the drive toward another war. At the Cultural and Scientific Conference for World Peace, held in March 1949 in New York City, he declared:

> We know and the saner nations know that we are not traitors or conspirators; and far from plotting force and violence it is precisely force and violence that we bitterly oppose. This conference was not called to defend communism nor socialism nor the American way of life! It

was called to promote peace! It was called to say and say again that no matter how right or wrong differing systems of beliefs in religion, industry, or government may be, war is not the method by which their differences can successfully be settled for the good of mankind.[31]

At the urging of O. John Rogge, a former special assistant to the U.S. attorney general, Du Bois agreed to attend a conference for world peace in Paris in April 1950 and later spoke at an "all-Soviet peace conference" held in Moscow that August. He addressed more than a thousand delegates, and his speech represented, in retrospect, one of the most cogent overviews relating the questions of racism, class exploitation, and peace ever delivered by any American. Du Bois first observed, "I represent millions of citizens of the United States who are just as opposed to war as you are. But it is not easy for American citizens either to know the truth about the world or to express it." In the United States, the opposition to peace had strong historical foundations, which he described in detail—a legacy of slavery, the exploitation of white and black labor, and the massive concentration of wealth in the hands of a few individuals:

> The power of private corporate wealth in the United States has throttled democracy and this was made possible by the color caste which followed Reconstruction after the Civil War. When the Negro was disfranchised in the South, the white South was and is owned increasingly by the industrial North. Thus, caste, which deprived the mass of Negroes of political and civil rights and compelled them to accept the lowest wage, lay underneath the vast industrial profit of the years 1890 to 1900, when the greatest combinations of capital took place. The fight of Negroes for democracy in these years was the main movement of the kind in the United States. They began to gain the sympathy and cooperation of those liberal whites who succeeded the Abolitionists and who now realized that physical emancipation of a working class must be followed by political and economic emancipation or means nothing. . . . Democracy has no part in industry, save through the violence or threatened violence of the strike. No great American industry admits that it could or should be controlled by those who do its work. But unless democratic methods enter industry, democracy fails to function in other parts of life. . . . Organized wealth owns the press and chief news gathering organs and is exercising increased control over the schools and making public discussion and even free thinking difficult and often impossible.[32]

For these historical reasons, the United States was committed to a foreign policy of confrontation with the Soviets and colonial exploitation of the nonwhite world. Du Bois admitted that many Americans had "succumbed" to the "almost hysterical propaganda that the freedoms which they have are being threatened and that a third world war is the only remedy." But millions of others who opposed racism and economic injustice would join him in the battle for peace.

In the spring of 1950 about three dozen Americans met at Rogge's home in New York City to form the nucleus of what became the Peace Information Center. Du Bois joined the group and was quickly identified as its primary leader in the press. At the urging of the Peace Information Center, 2.5 million Americans signed the "Stockholm Appeal," a document calling for the abolition of atomic weapons. On July 12, 1950, Secretary of State Dean Acheson denounced the center, warning Americans that "the so-called 'world peace appeal' or 'Stockholm resolution'" was simply "a propaganda trick in the spurious 'peace offensive' of the Soviet Union." Du Bois's response was immediate and uncompromising:

> The main burden of your opposition to this Appeal and to our efforts lies in the charge that we are part of a "spurious peace offensive" of the Soviet Union. Is it our strategy that when the Soviet Union asks for peace, we insist on war? Must any proposals for averting atomic catastrophe be sanctioned by the Soviet Union? . . . We have got to live in the world with Russia and China. If we worked together with the Soviet Union against the menace of Hitler, can we not work with them again at a time when only faith can save us from utter atomic disaster? Certainly hundreds of millions of colonial peoples in Asia, Africa, Latin America and elsewhere, conscious of our support of Chiang Kai-shek, Bao Dai and the colonial system, and mindful of the oppressive discrimination against the Negro people in the United States, would feel that our intentions also must be accepted on faith. Today in this country it is becoming standard reaction to call anything "communist" and therefore subversive and unpatriotic. . . . We feel strongly that this tactic has already gone too far; that it is not sufficient today to trace a proposal to a communist source in order to dismiss it with contempt.[33]

Du Bois's public response to President Truman's secretary of state, and the concurrent wave of domestic terrorism and McCarthyite politics that Lillian Hellman named "Scoundrel Time," set into motion a series of events culminating in the "political assassination" of Du Bois. In August 1950, as the work of the Peace Information Center continued, Du Bois agreed to run for the U.S. Senate in New York as a candidate of the leftist American Labor Party. He later admitted that he went into the campaign "knowing from the first that I did not have a ghost of a chance for election, and that my efforts would bring me ridicule at best and jail at worst." But the electoral effort allowed him "to speak for peace which could be voiced in no other way."[34] Giving ten major speeches across the state and seven radio broadcasts, Du Bois did not expect to receive 10,000 votes. To his amazement, he received 224,599—about 4 percent statewide, and 12.6 percent of Harlem's votes.[35]

Only one month after Acheson's attack on the Peace Information Center, the Department of Justice declared that the center was "acting as an agent of a foreign principal without having filed its registration statement" as required by the Foreign Agents Registration Act of 1938. Du Bois protested directly to Attorney General J. Howard McGrath that the center was not a "publicity agent" for a "foreign principal," and that the Justice Department's "arbitrary and capricious refusal to confer with me compels me to infer that either the Department is unaware of the import of the statute which it seeks to enforce, or that it is unwise enough to deal cavalierly with the rights of American citizens."[36]

The Peace Information Center was disbanded in October 1950. On February 9, 1951, however, Du Bois and others formerly associated with the center were indicted as unregistered foreign agents. The American press convicted Du Bois even before he had been arraigned, much less tried. On February 11 an editorial in the *New York Herald Tribune* declared, "The Du Bois outfit was set up to promote a tricky appeal of Soviet origin, poisonous in its surface innocence, which made it appear that a signature against the use of atomic weapons would forthwith insure world peace." The newspaper continued, "It was, in short, an attempt to disarm America and yet ignore every form of Communist aggression."[37] The trial date was set for April 2, 1951, but was postponed several times. Finally, on November 8, 1951, the trial began in Washington, D.C.; ironically, Rogge was the chief government witness against Du Bois. Virtually everyone who "had attended any meetings" of the center "was visited by FBI agents, often two or three times, and many of them subpoenaed. So little was discovered, however, that at the last moment most of these witnesses were never summoned."[38] The prosecution failed to present any incriminating evidence, and a directed verdict of acquittal was given on November 20.

Du Bois was free, but his career and political credibility were virtually ruined. NAACP leader Walter White seized the opportunity to bury his longtime rival. A staunch anticommunist, White told associates that the Justice Department had "definite evidence" of Du Bois's guilt, and the New York office of the NAACP took no action to defend their own founder and intellectual mentor.[39] Most black American leaders in the churches, colleges, and business community were silent; in a few rare cases, one or another joined in the jackals' chorus.

But across the world, the arrest and trial of Du Bois became a major political issue. For George Padmore and other nationalist leaders, the trial was an effort to halt Du Bois's "heroic fight for peace. We consider this attempt to blackmail you into silence an outrage against the fundamental principles of democracy and an insult to Africans and people of African descent throughout the world." Padmore praised Du Bois as "the finest representative of our people's hopes, dreams and aspirations. You have done more than any other man during the first half of the twentieth century to blaze the way and chart the course for Negro rights in America and African and Colonial freedom."[40] Frederic Joliot-Curie, France's high commissioner for atomic energy and president of the World Peace Council, praised Du Bois's "perseverance and courage in the struggle for a just cause."[41] The International Union of Students, an organization numbering five million youths in seventy-one nations, declared that Du Bois's "work for peace is in the best traditions of the American people. Prosecution is an attack upon peace supporters, upon Negro people and upon [the] right of professors and students to act for peace."[42] An International Defense Committee was created, composed of representatives from Brazil, Switzerland, Italy, Belgium, Romania, the Netherlands, France, and other nations.

Even within the United States, many courageous voices rallied to Du Bois's defense. The senior bishop of the African Methodist Episcopal Church, Reverdy C. Ransom, denounced the indictment as a "strike against the intelligentsia of Negro Americans and the millions who trust and follow their leadership." A conviction would be "the most powerful blow against Negro Freedom and Equality that has happened since Abraham Lincoln issued his proclamation emancipating the slaves. We are not turning back a single inch."[43] Albert Einstein contacted Du Bois asking to do whatever possible to help his case. And a prominent black judge, Hubert T. Delany, who was subpoenaed to testify in the trial, informed Du Bois that while he was not called, "I would have considered it an honor to have given testimony to [your] excellent reputation. . . . I know of no single individual in this country who has fought longer, harder, more consistently and more militantly for the rights of Negroes than you."[44]

For the rest of his life, however, Du Bois would be treated as a convicted felon in his native land. Black newspapers that had proudly carried his columns and occasional essays for decades now refused even to mention his name. FBI and local police agents quizzed residents in Du Bois's Brooklyn neighborhood about his visitors and habits. Large commercial publishers who once competed for his manuscripts now rejected his works out of hand. "From being a person whom every Negro in the nation knew by name at least and hastened always to entertain or praise, churches and Negroes' conferences refused to mention my past or present existence," Du Bois notes in his *Autobiography*. "The central office of the NAACP refused to let local branches invite me or sponsor any lectures. I was refused the right to speak on the University of California campus, because of NAACP protest."[45]

On February 12, 1952, Du Bois was informed by the State Department that he would not be permitted a passport, because "your proposed travel would be contrary to the best interests of the United States."[46] Until 1958, when the Supreme Court overruled the State Department's actions, he was strictly confined to the United States. In May 1952 Du Bois and his second wife, Shirley Graham Du Bois, were even refused entry into Canada, despite the fact that no passport was necessary to visit that country. Now a political pariah, even to many of his own people, Du Bois had private moments of doubt and despair. "The white world which had never liked me but was forced in the past to respect me, now ignored me or deliberately distorted my work," he noted. "It was a bitter experience and I bowed before the storm. But I did not break."[47]

Nearly ninety years of age, Du Bois fearlessly continued the battle for peace and racial justice as before. In journals at home and abroad, he continued to criticize the foreign policy of the Truman and Eisenhower administrations. In a *Monthly Review* essay, he observed that the crisis of world capitalism would bring about a united front of colored people across the globe into a program for socialism.[48] In a speech in Los Angeles on June 3, 1954, he argued that Vice President Richard M. Nixon was trying to send U.S. "troops into Indo-China." The threat to world peace largely "lies in the continued insistence" of the United States "that the existence of Socialist and Communist states are in themselves reasons for fear of aggression."[49] In *Jewish Life*, he cautioned readers that America was attempting to manipulate war with Communist China over the Formosa issue.[50] By 1956, if not well before, Du Bois had concluded that the gains achieved by the Bolshevik Revolution outweighed its flaws, and more specifically, that the Soviet state's continued existence had a progressive and positive role in the collapse of European colonial regimes and in the struggle against white supremacy.[51]

Perhaps most decisively, Du Bois continued to have a significant impact upon developments in the African Diaspora, and in his writings he repeatedly linked the question of world peace with the politics of African liberation. He advised Padmore and Nkrumah to be wary of British and American corporate investment in the period of postindependence. In 1957, he assisted Dr. Carlton B. Goodlett, publisher of the *Sun-Reporter* newspaper in San Francisco, in establishing a medical team for service in West Africa. To a West Indian correspondent, he urged the creation of a West Indian Federation. Clearly and in detail, he provided an analysis that placed black liberation and self-determination within a geopolitical framework of detente between the USSR and the United States. Peace, in short, was vital to the winning of black freedom.[52]

IV

Du Bois's final years were spent largely outside the United States. First, in 1958–1959, he went on a world tour that included the Soviet Union and China. Then he left the United States on October 5, 1961, for Nkrumah's Ghana, where he died at the age of ninety-five on August 27, 1963. Du Bois's departure was prompted in part by the U.S. Supreme Court's decision to uphold the infamous "McCarran Act," which again jeopardized his right to a passport. On October 1, 1961, he applied for admission to the Communist Party of the United States. Characteristically, in a letter to General Secretary Gus Hall, Du Bois wrote, "I have been long and slow in coming to this conclusion, but at last my mind is settled."[53]

His decision to join the Communist Party and, even earlier, his work for peace brought ridicule from historians and other academic detractors. In 1959 historian Francis Broderick wrote:

> No single work [of Du Bois] except *The Philadelphia Negro*, is first-class. *Black Reconstruction* will be remembered, but more because of its eccentric racist-Marxist interpretations than because of its assemblage of new material. . . . It seems unlikely that Du Bois will be remembered as a literary artist. . . . If there was a sharp break in Du Bois's ideas, it came not in 1934, when he separated from the NAACP, but in 1952, when he abandoned the struggle for Negro rights to concentrate on world movements for peace and socialism.[54]

The intellectual dishonesty and racism within these lines are evident. To this day, Du Bois suffers from a host of detractors and "defenders," both those who vigorously dissent from certain aspects of his later life and work and those who applaud only his earlier contributions. But the full measure of the man is to be found not merely in his voluminous and formidable academic studies, nor in his work for the NAACP, and not even in his central role as the Father of Pan-Africanism. It is found in his dialectical method of analysis, his constant care for the fine details and practical experience of human societies and cultures, and their relationship to the broader processes of economic and material life.

His method of research, which carefully linked the integral themes of peace, African liberation, and socialism, had its impact upon scores of social theorists and political leaders who came later. One example is provided by Martin Luther King Jr. Six weeks before his assassination, King spoke at a Carnegie Hall tribute on the centennial of the birth of Du Bois. Like Du Bois, King had now taken a public stand against another Democratic administration, in opposition to U.S.-provoked foreign wars. Du Bois "defied" his powerful opponents, King declared, "and though they heaped venom and scorn upon him, his powerful voice was never still." King did not skirt Du Bois's long-standing identification with Marxism. "So many would like to ignore the fact that Du Bois was a Communist in his last years." In a deliberate reference to Vietnam, King said, "Our irrational, obsessive anti-Communism has led us into too many quagmires."[55] King's principled commitment to nonviolent direct action did not dictate that he remain silent on national liberation struggles abroad or on the necessity for economic justice at home.

Most of the people of color across the world, consciously or not, define "peace" in Du Boisian terms—the absence of imperialist aggression, the achievement of national self-determination, the end of apartheid and racial segregation, the realization of what is needed for a decent and humane material and social life for themselves and for their children. Throughout his entire career as a public figure, W. E. B. Du Bois spoke eloquently for these social goals. If, after the end of World War II, he emphasized with greater sharpness the necessity for world peace, it was no sudden departure from his fundamental principles or method of analysis.

The change occurred within American society itself, and within the direction of the government and corporations of the United States, toward a clear and very real prospect of war. Such a war would have obliterated the prospects of African liberation, for a decent life for American working people, black and white, and for the realization of a socialist future for humanity. This new reality motivated Du Bois to dedicate his life to what he termed the "battle for peace." In the end, his legacy can—and will—motivate others to end war and racism in our time. It can succeed, however, only if white American peace activists finally come to terms with their own unconscious or explicit racism, if they understand in theory and in fact the direct relationship of U.S. aggression in Central America, Africa, and Asia to the larger process of exploitation that spawns racism and human suffering. The specter of nuclear madness, for Du Bois's time and for our own, will not be lifted unless the battle for peace is directly joined to the struggle for economic justice, national liberation, and racial equality. Without real justice, there can be no peace.

9

Harold Washington's Chicago:
Race, Class Conflict, and Political Change

In 1983 Chicago elected its first black mayor, Congressman Harold Washington, in a political contest highly charged with racism and social-class conflict. Breaking out of a two-generations-long pattern of electoral apathy and political repression, nearly three-fourths of all black voters turned out on April 12 of that year to give Washington more than 514,000 votes. The black Democrat combined that total with votes from other key constituencies—79 percent of the Puerto Rican vote, 68 percent of the Mexican American vote, and 38 percent of the Jewish vote—to defeat Bernard Epton, his previously obscure Republican opponent.[1] During the next four years Washington tried to reform the city's byzantine government while addressing the basic grievances and problems of blacks and other constituents in the areas of housing, health care, employment, police brutality, and social services.

The central political dilemma confronting Washington was the need to create a broad-based, progressive, radical-reformist, multiethnic, multiclass coalition that would, in theory, embrace African Americans, Hispanics, Asian Americans, low-income working people, and the unemployed. Evidence provided by the mayoral campaign of 1987, when Mayor Washington sought and won reelection, suggests that the difficulties inherent in such a strategy—a "Rainbow Coalition"—may be underestimated by its proponents. Moreover, the coalition's more progressive elements failed to develop independent structures outside of government to influence the mayor's agenda, and that failure directly contributed to the difficulty of consolidating a Rainbow Coalition in Chicago.

I

Washington's inability to dominate the city council for the first three years of his tenure undermined his efforts to transform Chicago's political system. The boss of the Cook County Democratic Party machine, Alderman E. R. "Fast Eddie" Vrdolyak, deprived the mayor of any real authority by controlling twenty-nine of the fifty aldermen. Vrdolyak's majority bloc changed the city council's rules to require a two-thirds vote to take bills away from committees that refused to act on them. "Regular" Democrats dominated by the machine held the powerful committee chairmanships, and independents aligned with Washington held nothing. Normal governmental processes were totally disrupted by these "council wars."

Superficially, the conflicts between the Vrdolyak and Washington blocs seemed to be motivated solely by race. During the 1983 Democratic mayoral primary, Vrdolyak had mobilized white supporters by resorting to crude race-baiting: "It's a racial thing. Don't kid yourself. . . . We're fighting to keep the city the way it is."[2] The fundamental factors motivating these political skirmishes, however, were patronage and power, not race. Vrdolyak and his allies were "concerned about loss of power and patronage and opportunities," observed Edwin C. Berry, former director of the Chicago Urban League. "If Harold Washington were as white as the driven snow and he took away those privileges, they would be equally against him."[3]

Despite the disruption caused by the council wars, Washington's administration successfully addressed many social problems. In the area of public housing, the city built 9,596 new residential units in 1983–1985. Washington's housing staff was reduced by one-fourth, but it was able to rehabilitate more than twice the number of homes restored under the previous administration. The Housing Department gave emergency grants to nonprofit groups to save low-income hotels and apartment buildings. The administration also cooperated with housing experts to initiate the Chicago Equity Fund and the Chicago Housing Partnership, which provided funds to nonprofit organizations renovating low-income houses.

In the field of health care, the record was mixed. Under Washington, the city's infant mortality rate dropped from 18.6 per thousand live births to 16.4, but this rate was still 55 percent higher than the national average. And in several black communities in Chicago, the infant mortality rate remained much higher—between 24 and 30 deaths per thousand live births. Inflation had severely shrunk the Health Department's budget, and the number of staff and professional workers was cut from 2,234 to 1,962. But this fiscally strapped department continued to manage six large health care centers and numerous small clinics and to serve as "the basic health care provider for 230,000 Chicagoans a year."[4] Despite their financial difficulties, these public agencies and others continued to improve methods of service.

With some difficulty, the new administration attempted to revise the city's budgetary priorities. Its task was complicated by reductions in the amount of community development funds granted to the city by the federal government, which declined from $140 million in 1983 to $85 million in 1985. But Washington believed that most Chicagoans would support additional user fees and taxes if the budgetary process was honest and if financial alternatives were clearly outlined.

By late 1983 Washington had begun a process of collective bargaining with all employees, introducing "new cost controls, efficient management, and personnel cuts" in city departments swollen by patronage. Approximately $13.5 million of the remaining federal community development funds was "shifted from administrative salaries and into a variety of neighborhood and service improvements."[5] Washington also initiated a series of tax hikes amounting to $312 million over a three-year period. Consequently, the mayor was able to reduce the city's long-term debt by $27.5 million. But the city council blocked many efforts to locate additional sources of revenue. Proposals to tax health clubs and boat moorings were tabled by the council's finance committee, and a plan for a $79 million commercial lease tax on corporations was halted in court.

Washington faced two major difficulties in addressing the city's economic problems. First, his prime constituency suffered disproportionately from employment discrimination and high rates of joblessness, and it expected the administration to act in a "social-democratic" manner by creating jobs. Hispanic and black entrepreneurs who had endorsed Washington urged the administration to expand "minority business enterprise" and affirmative-action plans. Sensitive to these demands, Washington signed an executive order in April 1985 setting aside at least 30 percent of city contracts for minority-owned and women-owned firms.[6] The next year, the city's Department of Economic Development issued a report advocating expanded business growth in the Hispanic community. All city departments were urged to set specific targets for purchases from Latino-owned companies, and $280,000 was set aside to fund ten Hispanic business organizations.[7]

Washington's 1983 appointment of Robert Mier as commissioner of economic development was also a partial signal in favor of a moderately left economic strategy. Mier advocated public support for cooperative and worker-owned enterprises, as well as financing for joint ventures with large corporations. Throughout his first term, Washington repeatedly insisted that his long-term goal was "full employment" and a "booming general economy." But this social-democratic desire was tempered by the political constraints of his own office, and the mayor cautiously cooled the economic expectations of his own supporters: "Fiscal prudence in municipal government leads to a better economic climate for business. . . . The employer of last resort must be the Federal Government, if government at all."[8]

Washington's second difficulty in addressing Chicago's economic problems was the cold disdain with which he was regarded by corporate leaders. It had begun with his mobilization in 1982 for the 1983 mayoral race and never really abated, despite repeated overtures by his administration. Business leaders originally perceived Mier as "too pro-neighborhood and left-wing," and they "particularly disliked Mier's and Washington's ideas that economic development must not be left in the hands of business executives with little accountability to the mayor's office and that economic development and manpower training should be closely linked."[9] By the middle of Washington's first term, corporate "paranoia" toward the administration persisted. Business leaders recognized that the struggle between Washington and Vrdolyak's majority bloc in the city council was about "power, not race," in the words of one corporate attorney. "But by that standard, they don't see [Washington] winning. . . . They want to see him making compromises with his opponents." Large developers complained that conducting business with new city officials was "slower" than before, but they admitted that procedures were also "fairer and more professional."[10]

By August 1986 the Department of Economic Development had created approximately sixteen thousand new jobs through ninety different types of loans and financial-assistance packages to aid businesses. Washington initiated the general obligation bond, designed to fund capital improvements in the city's infrastructure and in neighborhoods. Overall employment citywide under Washington increased by 2.2 percent in 1983–1984, including a 5.1 percent increase in jobs on the South Side.[11] Most bankers and corporate executives, however, remained pessimistic about the city's economic climate under a black mayor.

It was not until early 1986 that the administration won a decisive victory against Vrdolyak's bloc, after a federal court ordered special elections in seven gerrymandered wards. On March 18, 1986, candidates aligned with the machine won three seats, Washington supporters gained two, and runoff elections were scheduled for two races in which no candidate had won a clear

majority. The races in these two wards would largely prefigure the 1987 mayoral election, and both sides mobilized their forces. The Democratic
machine basically conceded its hold on the Fifteenth Ward, which was 75
percent black. With active campaign support from Washington and the
Reverend Jesse Jackson, Marlene Carter, a progressive neighborhood activist
and clerical worker, trounced her machine-backed black opponent by a two-
to-one margin. But the aldermanic contest in the Hispanic Twenty-sixth
Ward was perceived as highly marginal by both factions. Hispanic incumbent Manuel Torres had voted faithfully behind the Vrdolyak faction in the
city council, and he was the recipient of ample financial and political support
from former mayor Jane Byrne, state's attorney Richard M. Daley, and other
white Democrats. Challenger Luis V. Gutierrez, an advocate of Puerto Rican independence, was viciously smeared as a communist, a supporter of ter-
rorists, and even an atheist—despite his prominent membership in the
United Church of Christ and his campaign slogan, "Church, Family, Community." Gutierrez's superior grassroots organizing effort, which helped to
increase voter turnout from 47 percent in the March 1986 election to 62 percent six weeks later, defeated Torres and the machine.

The victories of Gutierrez and Carter ended the Democratic machine's
council mandate of twenty-nine to twenty-one and created a balance of
twenty-five aldermen on each side—which permitted the mayor to cast
tie-breaking votes and thus control the city government. Several white and
Hispanic aldermen who had previously supported Vrdolyak immediately
announced their "independence" and cast votes with the mayor on several
occasions. Washington was finally able to win approval of major proposals
and to place his nominees on various boards, some of whose appointments
had been stalled by the council's majority since late 1983.[12]

On September 24, 1986, the "reformed" city council narrowly passed
the mayor's budget, which included an $80 million property tax increase.
Machine leader Edward Burke was removed as chairman of the council's
finance committee and replaced by Washington lieutenant Timothy Evans.
Democratic Party committee member Edmund Kelly was replaced as superintendent of Chicago's Park District by independent black leader Jesse
Madison.[13]

II

Increasingly, the Regular Democrats found themselves on the defensive.
Their only solution was the removal of Washington from office. To accomplish this, they had to re-create the chaotic conditions of the general election
of April 1983, when a little-known Republican challenger had nearly upset

Washington in a racially charged political environment. The white Democrats also recognized that they had to avoid at all costs an election that pitted Washington against two or more well-known white candidates. What was required, in short, was a "white united front"—or in Vrdolyak's words, "anyone but Harold." Setting the theme for the machine was powerful U.S. Congressman Dan Rostenkowski: "I'd love to see a united front."[14]

The initial strategy to guarantee a two-way mayoral race was advanced by the supporters of state's attorney Richard M. Daley, son of Chicago's former political boss and an unsuccessful candidate for mayor in 1983. Daley proposed to replace the traditional two-party primary system with a nonpartisan election. The two candidates receiving the highest number of votes would subsequently face each other in a runoff if neither had received at least 50 percent of the vote. Daley explained his proposal as an attempt to promote racial harmony within the electoral process: "The current system encourages the politics of factions which have no incentive to reach beyond themselves to the entire Chicago community. It encourages an attitude of 'us against them.'"[15] Black leaders immediately denounced the proposed referendum on the issue as a transparently racist maneuver.

Sixty volunteers from the Chicago Urban League, the NAACP, and other civic associations found thousands of irregularities in the petitions for the referendum. Many signatures were forgeries or were those of nonresidents; about five thousand signatures were actually photocopies from other names on the petition sheets. Although the city's Board of Elections initially approved the referendum, circuit court judge Joseph Schneider blocked it from the February 24, 1987, ballot. In early November 1986, the Illinois Supreme Court ruled that Daley's referendum was "too ambiguous" to be "constitutionally valid."[16]

The next machine scenario was to pressure white prospective candidates to fall behind a single challenger against Washington in either the Democratic primary or the general election. The chief difficulty here was that the personal and political ambitions of the individual white candidates transcended party loyalties and racial solidarity. The Republicans had opposed the nonpartisan scheme because it would have voided any practical opportunity to elect a Republican mayor. Several candidates soon volunteered for the GOP mayoral primary, including Northwestern University professor Donald Haider, who had been a Democratic aide to Mayor Byrne; Chicago police officer Chester Hornowski; and local entertainer Ray Wardingley, professionally known as Spanky the Clown. All were "political unknowns," but any of them might siphon off several thousand votes from a major white independent challenger in the general election, thus throwing the race to

Washington.[17] For this reason, such prominent Illinois Republicans as former governor Richard Ogilvie and former U.S. attorney Dan K. Webb declined to run.

Jane Byrne complicated matters in July 1985 by announcing her candidacy for mayor in the Democratic primary. She gradually won the endorsements of several influential machine leaders, including Alderman Roman Pucinski and former Park District head Edmund Kelly, and collected a campaign treasury exceeding one million dollars. But Byrne had too many liabilities as a potential "white united front candidate." Throughout 1986 Byrne consistently scored from six to sixteen points behind Washington in public opinion polls. The former mayor's highly controversial record in office had created the widespread perception that she could never be reelected.[18] The Daley wing of the Regular Democrats, based on Chicago's Southwest Side, decided to support Cook County assessor Thomas C. Hynes, though he was little known to most Chicago voters. Hynes's chief asset was the political support of Daley and U.S. representatives Dan Rostenkowski and William Lipinski. He filed to enter the Democratic primary but simultaneously prepared to run on a third-party ticket in the general election.[19]

These intricate machinations failed to take into account the ambitions of Vrdolyak, Washington's most prominent white critic. The machine boss's controversial image as a vulgar racist demagogue was not popular with a majority of Chicago's electorate, whether white, Hispanic, or black. White voters polled in late 1986 gave the Democratic Party leader a 53 percent "unfavorable" rating and a "favorable" rating of 37 percent, while blacks gave him an unfavorable score of 82 percent. In a hypothetical head-to-head race against Washington, polls indicated that the mayor would win, 62 percent to 29 percent. Many white leaders immediately dismissed Vrdolyak's candidacy as "political suicide" or, at best, a duplicitous effort to "lure the Mayor into the Democratic primary" against himself and Byrne and then drop out, leaving Washington and Byrne in a two-way race.[20]

This critique underestimated Vrdolyak's subterranean talents and assets. In mid-1986, he had established his own political action committee, Save Chicago, and opened six political offices in all-white neighborhoods. Vrdolyak led the city council fight against Washington's property tax hike, and the millionaire lawyer rhetorically cast himself as an "anti-establishment populist."[21] Moreover, Vrdolyak had served on the city council since 1971, and over the years he had acquired detailed, damaging information on his friends and opponents, which he used astutely at critical junctures. Newly elected alderman Luis Gutierrez described

Vrdolyak's normal blackmail-type pressure on Washington's city council supporters:

> There [are] only about six or seven of us of the twenty-five [pro-Washington aldermen] that say anything. You could say there's only six or seven that have big mouths and want to talk all the time. But I figured it out—there's only six or seven of us that Eddie Vrdolyak doesn't have anything on, that Eddie Vrdolyak hasn't done a favor for, that Eddie Vrdolyak hasn't taken care of some problem, that Eddie Vrdolyak doesn't have some dirt on. So when you want to get up and take Eddie on, you got to be clean.[22]

Vrdolyak intuitively sensed that racism had to be a central component of any successful strategy to defeat Washington. Large numbers of white voters would not turn out on election day unless they were motivated by hatred and fear. Vrdolyak's means were vulgar—one leading member of his city council bloc "always referred to the mayor as 'that f--king nigger.'" Vrdolyak himself told white community groups that "Washington wanted to drive whites out of the city and 'blacken' it."[23]

The racist polemics of the Vrdolyak bloc created a social environment in which vigilante violence against people of color could occur unchecked. In the March 1986 special ward elections, members of the Ku Klux Klan openly campaigned for at least one Regular Democratic candidate. On June 28, 1986, the Klan held a "White Pride Rally" at Marquette Park that initially attracted between three hundred and five hundred white residents. When a small interracial group tried to rally against the Klan's demonstration, several hundred local whites physically attacked them. Throughout the summer of 1986 other similar incidents occurred. In Dolton, Illinois, a white mob verbally assaulted and stoned a black marching corps during a Fourth of July parade; in the white suburb of Lynwood, a black family found racist graffiti defacing their home; and at least one local black home was firebombed.[24] These random acts of terror were not planned, committed, or openly endorsed by Vrdolyak and his Democratic machine supporters, but they served that group's general political objectives. The most effective way to coordinate an anti-Washington organization and agenda among white working people was the manipulation of racism.

Washington's troubles were compounded by the disarray in his own electoral coalition. His seizure of control within the city council was a mixed blessing in that it created the dangerous perception that the incumbent would easily be reelected. It also fueled unrealistic patronage demands by various ethnic and political constituencies within his own bloc, who were impatient with the pace of reform. To address the former, a voter registration drive was launched in August 1986 to sign up most of the 177,000 voters who had been purged from electoral rolls since the previous election. Partly because of political apathy, only 60,000 people were registered in about six weeks, but they lived mostly in black and Latino neighborhoods.

Contributing to the problem for progressives were the discriminatory policies of the Chicago Board of Elections, which regularly deprived thousands of poor and minority voters of their voting rights. The Chicago Coalition for Voter Registration estimated that "20 percent of voters termed ineligible by election judges are illegally disfranchised."[25] The difficulties in registering low-income voters meant that the size of Washington's core constituency would be considerably smaller than it had been in 1983.

Washington also had to decide whether to contest the mayoral election as a Democrat—within the Democratic Party primary, in other words—or as an independent in the general election. Numerous factors pointed toward an independent campaign. Washington had broken with the Regular Democratic organization in 1977, during his unsuccessful mayoral race against Michael Bilandic. As an Illinois state senator, he had helped to block Hynes's election as Senate president for five weeks; he had also sponsored a bill to permit Chicago voters to recall Mayor Byrne. In 1977 Washington had told a group of black journalists: "I'm going to do that which maybe I should have done ten or twelve years ago. I'm going to stay outside that damned Democratic Party and give it hell."[26]

Throughout his first term, close advisers reiterated that the mayor had no ideological or partisan commitment to the Democratic Party's national leadership. In the spring of 1984 more than a hundred community activists and leftists, including Robert Starks, Luis Gutierrez, and Marlene Carter, formed the Cook County Coalition for New Politics. Although the coalition was short-lived, it advanced the notion of a progressive, multiracial third party within the city. In Gutierrez's district, 250 voters had joined his Westtown Twenty-sixth Ward Independent Political Organization by 1986. His prime supporters, like most Chicago-area progressives, "could give a damn about the Democratic Party," Gutierrez insisted. "They're ready to work on whatever it is that moves socioeconomic justice ahead."[27] Moreover, the Democratic Party's national leaders refused to condemn public efforts by Washington's opponents to splinter the local party on narrow racial lines. "We keep the [Democratic] party in power," reflected Washington deputy campaign manager Jacky Grimshaw, "and the party allows racists like Vrdolyak to remain in power."[28]

The question of a third-party mayoral candidacy was not merely tacti-
cal but fundamental to the entire scope of black and progressive politics for
the post-Reagan era. Richard Saks, a leader of Common Ground Network,
a Chicago-based community group, astutely outlined the issues in 1986:

> [There are] two parties, and they both call themselves Democratic.
> One is the Vrdolyakers, who base themselves on a straight-up racial
> appeal; and the second is the Mayor's coalition, which includes virtu-
> ally the entire black community, a majority of the Latino community,
> and a section of poor whites and progressive-minded whites. . . .
> [Either] one or the other is going to be forced out of the Democratic
> party. Either the Vrdolyakers will sell themselves to the Republican
> party officially; or the Washington forces will be forced to form some
> type of third party.[29]

The local outcome would have a profound impact on national politics,
because Washington's defeat might prompt the conservative wing of the
Democratic Party to accelerate its offensive against "special interests" such
as national minorities, feminists, organized labor, and the peace movement.

After some hesitation, Washington finally decided to run in the Democratic primary, even if Byrne challenged him as the sole white opponent.
One factor was the need to support progressive Democratic allies running
in aldermanic races. Another was the finding of opinion polls indicating
that he would lose some electoral support if he ran as an independent.
There was also the public perception of weakness, which might be fostered
if the incumbent mayor abandoned his own party's line to his opponents.[30]

III

The racial, ethnic, political, and social-class elements supporting Washington's candidacy in 1983 had been highly divergent, and the mayor's chief
challenge now was to create viable linkages among them. Each constituency seemed to view the administration's reform agenda narrowly, through
the prism of its own specific interests.

One representative example is provided by the black-Latino controversy over the city clerk's race. Black attorney William Walls announced his
candidacy for the post, and support for him began to coalesce among
Washington allies. A citywide coalition of Latino leaders, however, decided to field its own candidate for the post—Gloria Chevere, the deputy
commissioner for planning and former director of the city's largest Puerto
Rican credit union. Washington, Jesse Jackson, and other black leaders endorsed Chevere, and Walls was pressured to leave the race. Black colum-

nist Vernon Jarrett charged that Walls had become an "unwitting ally of Jane Byrne," because his campaign would only assist incumbent Walter Kozubowski, a Regular Democrat. But many black nationalists and several black politicians saw Washington's support for Chevere as a betrayal of blacks' interests. Chicago Metro News editor Nathaniel Clay deplored the mayor's endorsement of Chevere as an act of "political expediency." If Hispanics were seriously committed to a coalition, Clay insisted, they should have "deferred to Walls. . . . They didn't do this because their real goal is to maximize Hispanic political clout . . . this can only be done at the expense of blacks; coalition politics in this instance is simply a convenient cloak for ethnic ambitions."[31]

The Chevere-Walls conflict highlighted the underlying divisions and conflicts that have long characterized relations between African Americans and Latinos. For decades, black and brown reformers and progressives have advocated a political alliance, based on common experiences of discrimination, economic exploitation, and political domination. Yet American social history provides few models of "natural alliances" being formed among oppressed sectors of society via joint recognition of suffering and common self-interest.

Sociologically, Chicago's Latino population, unlike black America, is neither a racially oppressed group nor a social group defined by a unified historical, political, and cultural background. The first substantial number of Spanish-speaking immigrants to the city were Mexican laborers who found work in local steel mills and railroad yards shortly after World War I. The initial influx of Puerto Ricans occurred two decades later. The local populations of both national minorities expanded dramatically only during the past quarter century. In 1960 Chicago's Puerto Rican population numbered only 32,371. Ten years later, Cook County's Latin America–born population had grown to 81,811, and 47,397 of these were Mexicans. By 1980 the Census Bureau reported 499,322 Hispanics in Cook County; included among this growing population were 310,428 Mexicans (about 62 percent of all Hispanics); 116,597 Puerto Ricans (23 percent); 15,961 Cubans (3 percent); and 56,336 Spanish-speaking residents from Central and South America and the Caribbean.

There are significant socioeconomic and racial distinctions within this community. Puerto Ricans are nearly two times more likely than Mexicans to live below the poverty level (31.6 percent versus 17.5 percent in 1980). Cubans have a significantly higher median income than other Hispanics (in 1980, for example, $20,168 versus $11,959 for Puerto Ricans and $16,566 for Mexican Americans). Nearly 40 percent of all Puerto Ricans have an eighth-grade education or less, and two-thirds have not finished high school, statistics well below those for other Hispanics, blacks, and whites. Most Cubans and many Mexicans have been culturally and socially assimilated by the local white mainstream, while Puerto Ricans and perhaps a majority of Chicanos share with blacks a profound alienation from prevailing sociopolitical conditions.[32]

Both black and Hispanic communities harbor other barriers to the joint development of a progressive political bloc. Before 1980, only one Latino had been elected to public office in Chicago. Hispanic churches were seldom involved in electoral political activities or radical social welfare work until Washington's first mayoral race. With relatively low voter-turnout rates, and under the omnipresent influence of the Democratic Party's machine, Latino neighborhoods frequently produced politicians aligned behind Vrdolyak, such as state representative Joseph Verrios and Thirty-first Ward alderman Miguel Santiago, both from Puerto Rican constituencies. Washington appointed three Puerto Ricans to high-level positions after his election in April 1983: Miguel del Valle, chairperson of the Mayor's Advisory Commission on Latino Affairs (MACLA); Benjamin Reyes, a mayoral assistant; and Maria Cerda, director of the Department of Employment and Training.

But moderate Hispanic leaders such as Twenty-fifth Ward alderman Juan Soliz, who also generally voted with Vrdolyak's bloc, repeatedly charged that Washington's administration had not given Latinos their "fair share." In 1987 MACLA released a statement defending the Washington administration's affirmative-action hiring policies for blacks, but it also asserted that "for Latinos the results have lagged far behind what was expected and what is considered equitable." Ramiro Borja, a leader of Chicago's Mexican American community, was far more critical and expressed a widely held belief that "it's almost impossible to build a strong coalition between Hispanics and Blacks." Borja asserted that blacks cooperate only with "those Hispanics who can agree with them" and that, in any case, "usually they treat us pretty much as tokens." Conversely, many African American leaders perceived Latino political demands as selfish and excessive. Prominent journalist Lu Palmer, head of the Black Independent Political Organization, suggested that "tradition and history have shown us that Hispanics lean toward whites. . . . It's inevitable that there will be significant conflict between Blacks and Hispanics."[33]

Similar tensions existed between African Americans and Chicago's other ethnic groups. The Asian community in recent years has grown even faster than the Hispanic group has. In 1970 the total Asian-born population in metropolitan Chicago was 35,341; ten years later, 128,293 Asian-born immigrants lived in the area. There was tremendous linguistic, social, cultural, and economic diversity within this population, which was 27 percent Filipino, 21 percent Indian, 14 percent Korean, 3 percent Vietnamese, and 35 percent "other Asians," including Japanese and Chinese. In several respects, part of the Asian community shares political and economic characteristics with Cuban Americans. Many fled their homelands to escape Marxism-Leninism and then adopted conservative Republican politics as residents of the United States. Other Asians, particularly the Indians, Pakistanis, and Filipinos, generally entered the Chicago area with fluency in English and advanced academic or technical backgrounds that permitted quick assimilation into a petit bourgeois environment. Koreans draw historical parallels between their own entrepreneurial efforts to promote capital accumulation and the earlier strategies of Jewish immigrants who took "the small-business route to success."[34]

Washington partially responded to Asian political concerns in 1984 by creating the Advisory Committee on Asian American Affairs and by appointing Japanese American lawyer Paul Igasaki as permanent liaison to the Asian American community. Nevertheless, Washington remained highly unpopular among Koreans, Chinese, and many other Asians, despite his appointment of Asians to Chicago's library and public health boards. No Asian Americans were members of the mayor's cabinet or held seats on the board of education. In June 1987 the Advisory Committee called for a "stronger commitment to finding and hiring qualified Asian-Americans at all levels of city government."[35]

Nearly as large as the Asian American community is the Arab American community, which numbered more than 120,000 in the Chicago metropolitan area in 1980. Socioeconomic divisions split the Arab American community, much as they did other ethnic groups. The Lebanese (26 percent of all Chicago Arabs), the Iraqis (12 percent), and the Egyptians (4 percent) represent a relatively affluent, well-educated, middle-income stratum. Conversely, the 41,850 Palestinians (35 percent) in the area exhibit several socioeconomic traits paralleling those of African Americans—high rates of unemployment, low household income (56 percent of all families earn less than $15,000 annually), subjection to random racist violence and police surveillance.

Since many Arab Americans own small businesses in interracial markets, some conflicts with black patrons and entrepreneurs were perhaps inevitable. Black community leaders increasingly charged that Arab Americans exploited their black clientele: that their grocery and liquor stores refused to buy wholesale goods from black vendors, charged exorbitant prices for dated items, and employed clerks who harassed black customers. Black-Arab tensions polarized sharply in mid-1985, when a Jordanian grocer shot and killed a young black man on Chicago's South Side. The National Black United Front's local chapter, led by Northeastern Illinois University professor Conrad Worrill, protested the killing and denounced the Arab grocer's actions. Subsequently, Worrill began receiving telephone death threats. Although black-Arab meetings were held to reconcile differences, conflicts between the two communities persisted, undermining joint political activities.[36]

Tensions between Washington and many elements of the liberal white community also flared up occasionally. For example, most white gay and lesbian organizations had opposed Washington during his 1983 primary campaign. After the campaign, the mayor spoke frequently on behalf of gay and lesbian rights; in June 1986 he prominently attended a Gay Pride parade that drew thirty thousand participants. But Washington's political overtures to white gays were frequently viewed as inadequate. The administration failed to hire a full-time, paid liaison to the gay community until mid-1987. Washington personally endorsed a gay-rights ordinance before the city council in 1986 but did not press his allies to support it, and the measure died. Ten of the nineteen black aldermen and two of the four Hispanic aldermen voted against the proposed ordinance. Some gay activists perceived Washington's shortcomings as symbolic of the general homophobia of nearly all black leaders, which made long-term coalitions highly problematic. Al Wardell, co-chairperson of the Illinois Gay and Lesbian Task Force, insisted: "We have never been successful in getting strong black support. . . . We haven't even been able to get Operation PUSH to do much of anything."[37]

The Washington administration's efforts to create political linkages among various racial and ethnic constituencies even extended to white, blue-collar neighborhoods. In 1984 white ethnic groups organized a Save Our Neighborhoods, Save Our City convention, which promoted a self-defined "white ethnic agenda." One of their specific demands was the creation of a "home equity insurance plan" to establish an insurance fund that would "guarantee that people would not lose money when selling their homes in racially changing neighborhoods." Washington not only endorsed their proposal but also boldly agreed to speak before the hostile white ethnic convention.[38]

Such political overtures seemed foolish to many black critics, since low-to-moderate-income white ethnics formed Vrdolyak's reactionary political base. Moreover, they contributed to a sense of frustration and cynicism among many black activists. Efforts to expand the administration's political base among Hispanics, Asians, and others didn't address festering problems within the African American community. By 1985 Lu Palmer was stating publicly that thousands of black Chicagoans were "disillusioned" with Washington and had "turned off from politics."[39] Even black progressives who generally sympathized with the mayor's ambitious multiracial focus questioned the immediate viability of his strategy. "The mayor has reached out to those communities and yet there has been little reciprocity," observed Robert Starks. "How much longer can the public expect Black people to reach out and make efforts to coalesce when they are continually rejected?"[40]

IV

Had Jane Byrne seized upon these discontented elements within Washington's bloc and developed a coherent, programmatic alternative to the incumbent's agenda, results of the February 24, 1987, Democratic primary might have been different. But Byrne's campaign never developed popular enthusiasm or mass support, for several reasons. She repeatedly attacked the incumbent's administration for bureaucratic scandals, tax increases, and rising crime figures, but she was unable to justify or explain away the chaos and disorder of her own administration. Byrne had been responsible for a $94 million deficit, which Washington had eliminated. During her tenure, the total number of jobs in the city declined 6.1 percent. Her own public record, in short, was a major liability.

Byrne also attempted to distance herself from her former political ally, Vrdolyak, and the continuing charges that her conduct of the 1983 campaign had been overtly racist. Rhetorically subdued, she appealed to racial and ethnic unity and condemned what she termed Washington's racially "divisive tactics." Although the media applauded this strategy, it failed to provoke the active support of the hard-core Vrdolyak-oriented ethnics, who generally perceived the election in crude racial terms. Finally, Byrne made special efforts to take the decisive Hispanic vote away from Washington. But, in the words of Illinois commerce commissioner Ricardo Tostado, Byrne frequently appeared "silly" by "doing political spots in broken Spanish and making commercials for Mexican restaurants."[41]

What was remarkable was not that Byrne lost but that she very nearly won. Washington received 575,020 votes, representing 53.1 percent of the electorate, while his two opponents received 505,919, 46.7 percent.[42] In the city's ten wards where blacks total 95 percent or more of the electorate,

Washington earned 239,836 votes, or 98.8 percent of all ballots. But in the six white ethnic wards with 95 percent or more white voters, Washington obtained 1,245 fewer votes than he had in the 1983 general election. In the six liberal North Lakefront wards, Byrne defeated Washington by a 54-to-46 popular-vote margin, and the incumbent received 9,599 fewer votes than in the 1983 general election.

The limitations of Washington's multiethnic strategy were most painfully evident in the city's 129 predominantly Hispanic precincts. Despite the incumbent's many Latino appointments and special programs for Hispanic constituents, the overall Hispanic vote went to Byrne by a 48-to-45 margin. Washington won the Puerto Rican precincts with 62.2 percent, but Byrne carried the fifty-eight heavily Mexican American precincts by a 57-to-37 margin. Some Chicanos voted for Byrne because of their political ties to the Democratic machine; for others, racism was a prime factor, and they cast their votes against the mayor solely because he was black. Washington's failure to win the Hispanic vote probably contributed to the defeat of city clerk candidate Gloria Chevere. The Puerto Rican candidate easily won in black wards, garnering 77 percent of the vote. Her margin over Kozubowski was smaller in Puerto Rican precincts, where she received 62.2 percent. But in Mexican precincts, Chevere split evenly with her pro-Byrne opponent, 41.8 to 41.4 percent. The Washington campaign was able to claim a "victory" in the Hispanic community only because his 1987 totals there were dramatically higher than in the 1983 Democratic primary. Nevertheless, a strong Hispanic-black electoral alliance did not materialize, and Washington won the Democratic nomination largely because of Byrne's ineptitude.[43]

Other ethnic minorities courted by the Washington administration failed to provide majorities. In the Thirty-ninth Ward, the six largely Korean precincts gave Washington only 22.5 percent of the vote. Chinese precincts voted overwhelmingly for Byrne, giving the incumbent 11.3 percent. Jewish voters, traditionally strong supporters of liberal Democrats, endorsed Byrne by a 60-to-40 margin.[44]

Washington's three white opponents in the general election—Republican nominee Donald Haider, Vrdolyak as the candidate of the Solidarity Party, and Hynes as head of the Chicago First Party—recognized the mayor's vulnerabilities. But none of them was prepared to initiate a common strategy to produce a single white challenger for the April 7, 1987, general election. Haider's campaign was underfinanced and all but ignored by Illinois Republican leaders, and the former Democrat had difficulty attracting media attention. Hynes and Vrdolyak virtually ignored the mayor and hurled accusations at each other, in an effort to consolidate the white vote. Hynes levied the charge that Vrdolyak had met with and received support from Chicago's organized crime leader. These polemics only partially obscured the fact that both major white candidates were in substantial agreement on virtually all policy issues. Both opposed affirmative action, gay and lesbian rights, and economic and social welfare reforms, and both favored property-tax reduction and hiring increases in the police department. The struggle was essentially over which faction, the Daley bloc or Vrdolyak's organization, would control the broken remnants of the old Regular Democratic machine.[45]

This dissension among Washington's opponents worked to the mayor's advantage. Both downtown newspapers endorsed him, and the Chicago Federation of Labor threw him its support. Byrne endorsed Washington and urged her supporters to vote for the incumbent in the general election. Several aldermen who belonged to the Vrdolyak bloc and represented all-white wards pledged neutrality or made private overtures to the Washington campaign. By late March, Washington held a commanding 51 percent in opinion polls, with Hynes at 17 percent, Vrdolyak at 13 percent, and Haider at 4 percent.

Political pressure from Rostenkowski, Lipinski, and other influential white leaders for a single white challenger finally forced Hynes to quit the mayoral race only two days before the election. Hynes admitted that his decision was designed solely to block Washington's reelection: "Harold Washington will win if they both remain in the race." Although polls had indicated that only 40 percent of Hynes's supporters would vote for Vrdolyak, Hynes's last-minute departure gave Vrdolyak's struggling campaign a tremendous boost. Nearly all of the white officials who had encouraged Hynes to run immediately shifted their allegiance to Vrdolyak. Washington's allies curiously underestimated the racist motives behind Hynes's action and erroneously assumed that the black incumbent would pick up a major share of Hynes's votes. Deputy campaign manager Jacky Grimshaw confidently predicted that Washington would "pick up Lakefront voter support" and even some voters on the all-white Northwest and Southwest Sides, elevating the mayor's total "to nearly 60 percent of the vote."[46]

As forecast, Washington easily carried the general election, winning 600,290 votes (53.4 percent) to his opponents' combined 524,622 votes (46.6 percent). The incumbent's share of support in the black wards was still impressive at 99 percent. But in other electoral sectors, there were some signs of erosion. Washington's overall 1987 vote was actually 19,636 votes below Republican Bernard Epton's 1983 mayoral vote. In less than one week, Vrdolyak more than doubled his electoral base, winning 42 percent of the vote; Haider received a minuscule 4 percent. Liberal and moderate white Democrats who had long opposed Vrdolyak's vulgar race-baiting tactics could not summon the courage of their ideological convictions to cast a vote for a black progressive candidate. By the tens of thousands, at the last possible moment, they embraced the local advocate of white supremacy. Despite Byrne's endorsement, only 6 percent of the former mayor's primary voters went to Washington in the general election; Vrdolyak received 85 percent. Vrdolyak scored heavily in wards previously committed to Hynes; in Lipinski's Twenty-third Ward on the Southwest Side, for example, Vrdolyak held a 35-to-1 margin over the mayor. Overall, Washington won about 15 percent of the white vote citywide, compared to 74 percent for Vrdolyak. In the six wards where 95 percent or more of the voters were white, Washington's share dropped to 4.6 percent. A majority of Jewish voters also endorsed Vrdolyak by 51 percent, compared to 36 percent for Washington. The mayor's own public estimate that he would receive approximately 24 percent of the white vote not only was unrealistic but also seriously underestimated the power of racism as a motivating factor in white American electoral behavior.[47]

More sobering were the electoral returns from minority precincts. The small Indochinese community went for Washington by 58.5 percent. But most Asians voted like whites of all ideological persuasions. The city's two predominantly Chinese precincts voted heavily for Vrdolyak, giving the incumbent 16.7 percent. Korean precincts were only somewhat better, voting 24.4 percent for Washington. The Hispanic wards were sharply divided. Chevere had worked vigorously as one of Washington's deputy campaign managers, and tremendous mobilization efforts had targeted Latino neighborhoods. Puerto Rican voters responded positively, giving Washington 74 percent to Vrdolyak's 17.8 percent and Haider's 2.4 percent, according to precinct analyses conducted by the *Chicago Reporter*. Some election observers claimed that a majority of Mexican Americans had actually voted for Washington.[48] But the interpretation of many political analysts was that the Hispanic community had been deeply divided over the Washington reelection campaign and that thousands of Latinos strongly opposed any strategic alliance with the African American community.

The meaning of Vrdolyak's defeat was understood by every Democrat, reformer, and Regular in the city. White Northwest Side state representative Alfred Ronan delivered the political consensus: "Mayor Washington is the boss of the city of Chicago." The mayor expanded his majority bloc on the city council with the addition of several progressives and liberals.[49]

Vrdolyak was forced to resign as chairman of the Cook County Democratic Party, to be replaced by white moderate George Dunne, who had been one of the few leading Democrats to endorse Washington in the 1983 general election.

What was much less certain were the implications of Washington's re-election for the city's diverse ethnic and racial constituencies. Washington had promised the initiation of the "Action Agenda" to promote improvements in public housing, education, health, and employment.[50] But the persistence of fiscal problems and an uncertain tax base threatened to turn such promised reforms into a bitter illusion. Within weeks of the election, conflicts began to erupt inside city hall between administrators of a fiscally conservative bent and those who favored more radical social change.

Some leftist elements within the Washington coalition strongly suggested that Chicago's black middle class was incapable of transcending its programmatic and ideological positions to move toward a more radical transformation of the political economy of race, ethnicity, and class. Abdul Alkalimat of Chicago's People's College argued that while Washington was a "progressive Democrat he [was] not a revolutionary." The mayor had given "a great nod to a partnership with business. This partnership helps to push a conservative model in solving Chicago's problems." In contrast, Alkalimat observed, the progressive elements that supported Washington should have done so critically and with reservations, by consolidating their "power on the basis of broad-based democratic people's organizations" and by clarifying "the class content of Black power."[51] In this regard, leftists in Chicago critically failed to develop structures outside of governmental agencies that could simultaneously support and critique the Washington administration's policies from the Left. The failure to do so has meant that the contradictions that separated blacks, Hispanics, and various ethnic minorities remain partially unaddressed; the structural economic and social problems that plagued Chicago's working class were discussed in a limited and truncated fashion.

V

This essay was originally written only days before Harold Washington's unexpected death in late 1987. Washington had failed to identify a logical successor who would support and defend the progressive accomplishments of his administration.

When Washington died no one in his coalition was prepared to continue his struggle against the Cook County Democratic organization. African Americans soon became divided ideologically, between progressive alderman Timothy Evans and conservative deputy mayor Eugene Sawyer. Latinos who had been a central force within the Washington coalition began to defect to the Democratic machine. In 1989 state's attorney Richard Daley completed the machine's return to power, trouncing Sawyer by a massive margin of 100,000 votes. Daley consolidated his political position immediately after becoming mayor. By the mid-1990s Daley appeared to be just as secure a mayor as his father was at the peak of his political influence.

The lesson of Harold Washington is that black leadership in the civil rights and Black Power periods depended too heavily upon personalities. The charisma of a Harold Washington was no substitute for an effective political organization, which could have kept together the various class and ethnic forces that had challenged the Democratic machine during the 1980s. Black leadership must go beyond the model of personal political activism symbolized by the life and legacy of Harold Washington.

PART FOUR

Beyond Boundaries:
The Future of Black History in the Present

10

The Rhetoric of Racial Harmony

I

In terms of race relations, America's society is more thoroughly integrated today than at any point in its history. The number of black elected officials increased from barely 100 in 1964 to about 7,000 when I wrote this essay in 1990. The figure just a few years later is more than 11,000. The number of African Americans enrolled in colleges and universities has quadrupled; the number of black-owned banks and financial institutions has increased tenfold; the percentage of African Americans in the middle class and professions has significantly expanded.

Perhaps the most striking changes in public perceptions of race have occurred in popular culture, social institutions, and the media. American music, theater, public education, sports, and the arts are now heavily influenced by the rhythms and patterns of African American life. Black images in commercial advertisements are commonplace. Blacks remain underrepresented in the ownership and management of cultural and social institutions, but as employees and prominent public representatives, they are nearly everywhere.

Despite these symbols of racial advancement, however, incidents of racist harassment, vigilante violence, and social disruption have escalated in recent years. In the late 1980s, a pattern emerged—and continues: hundreds of African American students have been victimized by intimidation or outright threats on university campuses across the country. White youth have formed "white student unions" at several institutions to push back affirmative action and the preferential recruitment of minorities as faculty and students.

Civil rights organizations point to a disturbing pattern of legal indictments and political harassment of black elected officials and to the growth of violence against black-owned property and individuals in urban areas. Racial tensions in cities such as New York have culminated in a series of massive public demonstrations by both blacks and whites, with each side accusing the other of "racism." A generation removed from the Civil Rights Act of 1964, which abolished legal racial discrimination in public accommodations, and the Voting Rights Act of 1965, which extended the electoral franchise to all Americans regardless of race, the goal of racial harmony and integration seems more distant than ever before.

What explains this racial paradox—this emergence of a black middle class and this acceptance of black cultural achievements within a society experiencing such a deepening crisis of race relations? Any analysis of the contemporary status of African Americans in the United States must begin with analysis of the accomplishments and the contradictions of the Civil Rights Movement of the 1950s and 1960s.

A generation ago, the leaders of the social protest movement for desegregation mobilized millions with one simple demand—"freedom." In the context of the Jim Crow South after World War II, freedom meant the elimination of all social, political, legal, and economic barriers that forced black Americans into a subordinate status.

Implicit in the demand for desegregation were several assumptions. Desegregation would increase opportunities for blacks in business, government, and society overall. Desegregated educational institutions would promote greater racial harmony and understanding among young people from different ethnic communities, which in turn would promote residential integration. Affirmative-action policies, the strategy of compensating for past discrimination against minorities, would gradually increase the numbers of African Americans, Hispanics, and other people of color in administrative and managerial positions.

It seemed evident that as African Americans escaped the ghetto and were more broadly distributed across the social-class structure and institutions of society, racial tensions and bigotry would decline in significance. As blacks were more thoroughly integrated into the economic system, it was thought, the basis for racial confrontation would diminish.

This thesis was fundamentally flawed. In the first place, desegregation did not benefit the entire black community uniformly. Black professionals and managers, those who had attended colleges and technical schools, were the principal beneficiaries. Working-class African Americans also benefited: incomes increased as new opportunities were created in the upper-income levels of the labor force, and their children for the first time had access to higher education.

But opportunity in a capitalist society is always a function of social-class position, which means ownership of capital, material resources, education, and access to power. For the unemployed, the poor, and those without marketable skills or resources; for those whose lives were circumscribed by illiteracy, disease, and desperation, "race" continued to occupy a central place as a factor in their marginal existence.

Legal desegregation contributed to the popular illusion that the basis for racial discrimination and conflict no longer existed. The abolition of racially separate residential districts, hotels, schools, and other public institutions convinced many white Americans that the "Negro question" had finally been firmly resolved. Black American leaders such as Martin Luther King Jr. had always insisted upon the achievement of a "color-blind society." The passage of antidiscriminatory legislation had eliminated all basic impediments to the socioeconomic and cultural advancement of African Americans, according to this view.

Thus, as many black leaders continued to speak out against current social injustices or pointed to the growing economic disparities between blacks and the majority of middle-class whites, their complaints were easily dismissed as anachronistic, self-serving rhetoric. By raising the issue of racism, many whites now believed, blacks themselves must be "racist."

The American civil rights leadership and the black political establishment now find themselves in a quandary largely of their own making. Their failure to develop a body of politics that takes a qualitative step beyond the discourse and strategies of the Civil Rights Movement of a generation ago is directly linked to the poverty of their theoretical outlook.

II

The central weakness of this African American leadership—largely middle-class—is its inability to distinguish between *ethnicity* and *race* and to apply both terms to the realities of American capital, power, and the state. African American people are both an ethnic group (or more precisely, a national minority) and a racial group. Our ethnicity derives from the cultural synthesis of our African heritage and our experiences in American society, first as slaves and then as sharecroppers, industrial laborers, the unemployed, and now as the core of the postindustrial urban underclass in the semi-destroyed central cities of North America.

As W. E. B. Du Bois observed nearly a century ago, black Americans are both African and American, "two souls, two thoughts, two unreconciled strivings; two warring ideals in one dark body, whose dogged strength alone keeps it from being torn asunder." This central duality is at the core of our ethnic consciousness, forming the fundamental matrix for all expressions of African American music, art, language patterns, folklore, religious rituals, belief systems, the structure of our families, and other manifestations of our culture and society. Blackness in the cultural context is the expression and affirmation of a set of traditional values, beliefs, rituals, and social patterns, rather than physical appearance or social-class position.

Race is a totally different dynamic, rooted in the structures of exploitation, power, and privilege. "Race" is an artificial social construction that was deliberately imposed on various subordinated groups of people at the outset of the expansion of European capitalism into the Western Hemisphere five centuries ago. The "racial" consciousness and discourse of the West was forged above the bowels of slave ships, as they carted their human cargoes into the slave depots of the Caribbean and the Americas. The search for agricultural commodities and profits from the extreme exploitation of involuntary workers deemed less than human gave birth to the notion of racial inequality.

In the United States, a race is frequently defined as a group of individuals who share certain physical or biological traits, particularly phenotype (skin color), body structure, and facial features. But race has no scientific validity as a meaningful biological or genetic concept. Beyond this, the meaning of race shifts according to the power relations among the racial groups.

For instance, in apartheid South Africa, Japanese people were considered "white" by the regime, whereas Chinese were classified as "colored." In Brazil, a person of color could be "white," "mulatto," or "black," depending upon the individual's vocation, income, family connections, and level of education.

Even in rigidly segregated societies such as the American South before the modern Civil Rights Movement, race was frequently situational—a function not just of physical appearance but also of the explicit or implied power relations that connect the individual of color to local or external constituencies. In many segregated cities such as Washington, D.C., Arab and African diplomats and foreign representatives were permitted to stay in "whites only" hotels, which were strictly off-limits to local blacks. African Americans who owned property or who were well-respected professionals, university professors, or ministers were occasionally granted social privileges usually extended solely to whites.

Race, therefore, is not an abstract thing but an unequal relationship between social aggregates, which is also historically specific. The subordinated racial group finds itself divorced from the levers of power and authority within the socioeconomic order. The oppressed racial group's labor power, its ability to produce commodities, is systematically exploited, chiefly through abnormally low wage rates. It is denied ownership of the major means of production. It lacks full access to sources of capital and credit. The racial group's political status is marginal or peripheral, as full participation and legislative representation are blocked.

Finally, dominant and subordinate racial categories are constantly reinforced in the behaviors and social expectations of all groups by the manipulation of social stereotypes and by using the legal system to coerce. The popular American myth of the Negro's sexual promiscuity, prowess, and great physical attributes, for example, was designed to denigrate the intellectual abilities and the scientific and cultural accomplishments of blacks.

The racist stereotype of the black race's inclination toward antisocial behavior, criminality, and violence reinforces the series of discriminatory codes, employment patterns, and legal harassment aimed at nonwhites. Institutional and vigilante violence, including lynching, the death penalty, and the disproportionately large number of African Americans arrested for crimes that whites commit with impunity, help to justify and reinforce the stereotypes.

To be white in the United States says nothing directly about an individual's culture, ethnic heritage, or biological background. A society created to preserve "white culture" would be either very confused or tremendously disappointed. White culture does not exist. White power, privileges, and prerogatives within capitalist society do exist.

Whiteness is fundamentally a statement of the continued patterns of exploitation of subordinated racial groups, which create economic surpluses for privileged groups. To be white means that one's "life chances," in the lexicon of American sociologists, improve dramatically. Any white person, regardless of personal appearance, income, or education, usually finds it much easier to establish credit, purchase a good home, or start a business than the average nonwhite person does.

To be white in the United States statistically means that police officers rarely harass you, that your life expectancy is significantly longer than that of others, and that your children will probably inherit property and social position. Blackness in American racial terms has meant enduring a hundred different insults, harassments, and liabilities experienced daily; living with the reality that a black university graduate will make less money in his or her lifetime than the average white graduate of secondary school; experiencing higher death rates due to the absence of adequate health care facilities in one's neighborhood; accepting the grim fact that, in 1990, a young white American male's statistical likelihood of becoming a victim of homicide was roughly one chance in 186, while a young black male's statistical chance was one in 20.

III

The ambiguity and confusion concerning the crucial differences between race and ethnicity in the United States are directly attributable to the uneven merger of the two concepts as they relate to black Americans. People of African American nationality, whose cultural patterns and social traditions are derived in part from Africa, have been made to be the subordinate "race." Physical appearance and phenotype were convenient, if not always predictable, measures for isolating the members of the oppressed racial group, "the blacks."

For white Americans this racial-ethnic overdetermination did not occur, for several reasons. White Americans originated from many different countries and cultures, ethnic intermarriage was frequent, and the rigid economic and legal barriers that confined blacks behind ghetto walls usually did not exist. By the middle of the twentieth century, millions of white Americans had no clear ethnic or cultural identity beyond vague generalizations. Their sense of aesthetics derived largely from the lowest cultural common denominator—the mass media and the entertainment industry.

Whites' racial identity was ruptured from ethnicity and was politically or socially relevant only insofar as it affected issues of direct personal interest—such as whether a Hispanic or African American family intended to purchase a home in their neighborhood, or whether their employer planned an affirmative-action hiring program for minorities. Whiteness was fundamentally a measure of personal privilege and power, not a cultural statement.

White capitalist America's cultural vacuity, its historical inability to nurture or sustain a vibrant "national culture" drawing upon the most creative elements of its various ethnicities, helps to explain the present paradox of desegregation. Millions of white Americans, devoid of their own cultural compass, have absorbed critical elements of African American music, dance, literature, and language. They now accept black participation in professional athletics and extend acclaim to African American film stars and entertainers. In a desperate search for collective identity, whites have mimicked blacks in countless ways, from the black-faced minstrels of the nineteenth century to the contemporary white musical groups who sing reggae and rap.

But whites' affinity and tolerance for blackness are largely cultural, not racial. Many whites have learned to appreciate African-derived elements of music, dance, and religious rituals but would not endorse the sharing of power or material privileges—because that would undermine the stratification of race.

For example, the late Lee Atwater, who ran the Republican National Committee during President George Bush's administration, was the architect of a viciously racist media campaign that was largely responsible for electing Bush. Atwater's infamous television advertisement of convicted felon Willie Horton linked the specter of the black rapist to the Democrats' supposed weakness on law-and-order issues. Yet Atwater's much beloved personal hobby was playing the blues on his guitar, weakly imitating African American blues artist B. B. King.

The central characteristic of race relations in the 1990s is "interaction without understanding." White students purchase the latest recordings of black singers and cheer the latest exploits of black athletes while at the same time bitterly protesting the imposition of course requirements that mandate classes in African American politics, history, or literature. White employers encourage the recruitment of black junior executives to their firms but shudder at the prospect of minorities' moving into their exclusive neighborhoods or joining their elite private clubs. White religious leaders espouse pious platitudes about ethnic understanding and racial reconciliation while doing relatively little to bring their white, upper-class congregations into close contact with the gritty problems of the ghetto. Racial integration, within the framework of capitalism, has produced the symbols of progress and the rhetoric of racial harmony without empowering the oppressed.

IV

Perhaps the greatest irony in this post–civil rights situation is that African Americans born after 1960 often have great difficulty identifying the realities of the oppressive race and class structures they encounter today. And that's because of the transformation of white racial etiquette.

No white politician, corporate executive, or religious leader now uses the term *nigger* in public. African Americans coming to maturity in the 1980s and 1990s have never personally experienced Jim Crow segregation.

They cannot say how they feel about being denied the right to vote, because their electoral rights are guaranteed by law. They have never personally participated in street demonstrations, boycotts, picket lines, and seizures of government and academic buildings. Few have tasted the pungent fumes of tear gas or felt the fiery hatred of racist mobs. The absence of a personal background of struggle casts a troubled shadow over the current generation of black Americans, who are poorly equipped to grapple with the complexities of the racial and class domination that they face.

Integration has also crippled African Americans in terms of their "cultural literacy." Under traditional racial segregation, the strict barriers that were established forced a wide variety of professions and social classes into intimate interaction. Black physicians had to look for patients in the black community. African American attorneys depended upon black clients. Black storekeepers looked to blacks for patronage.

Black social organizations, civic associations, and religious institutions reflected the broad spectrum of social class, from custodians to schoolteachers and civil servants. The sense of shared suffering and collective cooperation was the basis for an appreciation of the community's racial identity and heritage. African American history was taught in segregated schools and churches, and pictures of prominent black leaders were frequently displayed.

Denied access to the white media, blacks established their own network of race-oriented publications. A separate cultural and artistic underground developed in the cities, creative enclaves that produced the classical legacy of modern jazz and the urban blues.

But as the racial boundaries were lowered and as white public discourse became largely race-neutral, the terrain for black cultural awareness diminished. Young African Americans no longer were forced to confront their ethnicity or cultural history. In effect, we are witnessing the development of a substantial segment of our black population that is *post-black*—without any cultural awareness, historical appreciation, or political commitment to the traditions, customs, values, and networks that have been the basis for black identity in America.

In all racially bifurcated societies, the government, legal system, major political parties, and other institutions of state power are designed—explicitly or implicitly—to preserve white power and perpetuate the domination of nonwhites. In the United States, racial superiority and racial prerogatives retain tremendous influence within the actual power relations and public policies of governmental structures and political parties.

By the decade of the 1980s, racial polarization in America had crystallized into an apartheid-type, two-tiered political system. Blacks, as a racial group, will often vote for a white liberal candidate over a black one, if in their judgment the former's agenda is more progressive. But most whites, taken as a racial group, find it difficult if not impossible to vote for any African American candidate, regardless of his or her qualifications, experience, or education. When white Democrats are confronted at the polling booth with a choice between a black Democrat who clearly articulates their class and political interests versus a white Republican, the vast majority consistently defect to the white candidate.

Under the leadership of former president Ronald Reagan, who vigorously opposed civil rights legislation, affirmative action, and other racial reforms achieved in the 1960s, the Republican Party transformed itself into a multiclass, white united front, dedicated largely to the ideology of conservatism, anticommunism abroad, and preservation of the hegemony of corporate capital over labor.

This ideological drift to the right has influenced the behavior of a growing number of black politicians, who seek to further their own careers outside the boundaries of traditional civil rights politics. Positioning themselves further to the right to capture the support of upper-class white voters, they increasingly advance positions that are alien to the black freedom struggle. A recent example of this nascent trend is Douglas Wilder, elected governor of Virginia in 1989, in the Southern state that was the home of the Confederacy during the Civil War.

Wilder's campaign largely ignored the state's black electorate and concentrated exclusively on winning one-third of the state's white vote. This percentage, combined with a strong black turnout, would guarantee victory over his Republican opponent. To achieve this goal, Wilder reversed himself on many liberal policy positions that he had taken before. During the campaign, he embraced the death penalty, opposed statehood for the District of Columbia, and supported anti-union right-to-work laws.

Wilder's case illustrates two political realities of the post–civil rights period. First, with the end of racial segregation, the black community, ironically, lacks structures of accountability that would modify or effectively check the public or political behavior of its own elected officials. Second, growing numbers of African Americans in government, in the legal system, and in political parties are trying to transcend their own racial designation of *black* in order to further their own careers.

This creates an ever-growing sense of alienation and frustration for the millions of African American poor, working-class, and unemployed, who are still trapped in the ghetto and who see little real significance in the elevation of a Wilder to high office. Black representation in government rarely improves the quality of their lives, and their actual material conditions have become worse overall since 1980. The "post-black politicians" are irrelevant to the problems of the oppressed.

The challenges of race, class, and power confronting black Americans are far more complicated than Martin Luther King Jr. ever anticipated when he stood on the steps of the Lincoln Memorial at the 1963 March on Washington, delivering his "I Have a Dream" speech. The objective should not be the realization of a utopian, color-blind society. The objective should be a democratic social order that seeks to achieve certain goals: First, democratic principles must be extended from the electoral system into the structures of the economy and the social order, making a job or guaranteed income a human right. Also, public health-care facilities, housing, and access to transportation must be available to all. Finally, ethnicity must be clearly separated from race, a distinction that would preserve America's diverse cultural and ethnic heritages while abolishing all the forms of institutional discrimination that are justified by the perpetuation of racial categories. We must destroy *race* without uprooting culture and ethnicity.

V

Will whites be willing to give up their centuries of power and privilege over oppressed African Americans, Hispanics, and other people defined by racial categories of subordination? Will the white elites who control the banks and financial institutions, the factories and corporations, the exclusive real estate and country clubs, recognize that a truly multicultural democracy will exist only when the power within the economic system and the government is redistributed—*fundamentally* redistributed?

This could require a radical restructuring of capitalism itself, as those who are most disadvantaged generate new social protest movements demanding a more equitable division of resources. It is also possible that white American politicians, corporate leaders, educators, and intellectuals will try to follow the model for race relations developed in post-apartheid South Africa: nonwhite domination of the government and public institutions and the concomitant expansion of the black middle class, all the while preserving white domination of the legal system, private property, and the economy.

What is the role of the religious community in addressing America's crisis of race and class inequality? It is relatively easy to stand before one's congregation and solicit funds for a Hispanic or African American vocational training center or request canned goods and secondhand clothing for minority women on welfare. It is a very different thing to ask one's peers and associates to question the preferential status and material benefits they possess simply by the fact of being white.

There will be no racial peace in America until millions of whites come to terms with the uncomfortable truth that black oppression, poverty, and high unemployment rates are hardly accidental, are hardly the symptoms of an absence of the work ethic among blacks. Institutional racism and class domination are structural and elaborate, benefiting certain privileged classes at the cost of common misery for others.

The major contribution that religious institutions can make to human relations is a commitment to achieve the deconstruction of white racial privilege within society as a whole. More succinctly, this would mean a commitment to "racial suicide" for the social category "white."

So long as millions of white Americans confuse race with ethnicity and perceive their world in immutably racial terms tied to an eclectic mixture of biological myths, racist stereotypes, and IQ tests, they will be unable to fully overcome their own crippled consciousness. And without a cultural metamorphosis among middle-class whites, one that would force them to confront the terrible social and economic consequences of institutional racism, no racial dialogue or peace with the ghetto will be possible. Without social justice, there will be no peace.

11

Black Fundamentalism: Louis Farrakhan and the Politics of Conservative Black Nationalism

I

On October 16, 1995, the largest public gathering of African Americans in history occurred in Washington, D.C., in the shadow of the nation's Capitol. They had come together under the slogan the Million Man March, with an agenda emphasizing racial pride, personal responsibility, and patriarchal family relations. Estimates of the crowd's size ranged from a low of five hundred thousand to well over one million.[1] Black men made the pilgrimage from thousands of cities, towns, and communities throughout the country and represented many different social classes, religious faiths, and political orientations. The African American who initiated this demonstration had been vilified in the national media for more than a decade as racist and anti-Semitic. Yet this leader had the political insight to recognize and respond to the deep sense of social crisis within this community, the levels of rage, social alienation, and violence that were destroying an entire population of young African American males. In a language both spiritual and visionary, he exhorted black men to transform their lives, to protect their families, to give their time and financial support to black institutions. Participants often felt emotionally overwhelmed, surrounded by a virtual sea of black humanity, responding to a historic moment.

Louis Farrakhan had brought off an event of a type achieved by no previous African American leader—not even Martin Luther King Jr. King had been the main orator, originator, and chief political architect of the historic March on Washington, D.C., of August 28, 1963, which represented the height of the Second Reconstruction. But the 1963 protest march had been approved in advance by the Kennedy administration, and its goal had been pressure on the U.S. Congress to pass the legislation that would outlaw racial segregation in public accommodations. The larger audience that day was the American public, and the overall theme was interracial harmony and cooperation.

The Million Man March, in contrast, did not focus primarily on issues of public policy or the passage of new legislation aimed at African Americans. The social philosophy behind its agenda was deeply conservative and pessimistic about the likelihood that whites would ever recognize or respond to blacks' grievances. With the exception of several prominent speakers such as Jesse Jackson, few addresses at the march called extensively for militant actions against the Republican-controlled Congress or the most conservative Democratic president since Woodrow Wilson. The political logic behind this was relatively clear. Reaganism, the "Contract with America," and the growing ideological conservatism of both major parties constituted a retreat from the programs and policies of the Civil Rights Movement. White liberals and liberalism had virtually ceased to exist, and affirmative-action policies were widely denounced as "reverse discrimination." To most of the African American men who responded to Farrakhan's call to Washington, it seemed that black people had little alternative but to turn inward. If white institutions, politics, and society could not be transformed democratically to include racialized minorities, African Americans on their own had to employ their resources and skills for the survival and uplift of their race. In the language of an earlier racial conservative, Booker T. Washington, black folk had to "cast down their buckets where they are."

In the immediate aftermath of the Million Man March, many black organizations reported significant increases in membership. Even groups that had not endorsed the march or that had long histories of hostility toward Farrakhan personally, such as the National Urban League and the National Association for the Advancement of Colored People, gained fresh recruits and renewed commitment. One measure of the long-term impact of the Million Man March was seen a year later, on election day in November 1996. The total number of American voters declined from 104.4 million in 1992 to 95.8 million in 1996, despite the addition of 5 million more registered voters during this four-year period. Turnout declined from 55.2 percent in 1992 to only 48.8 percent in 1996, the lowest rate since 1924. Nearly 500,000 fewer African American women voted in 1996 than in

1992. Against this downward trend were African American male voters. Exit polls estimated that approximately 1.5 million *more* African American men participated in the 1996 presidential election than in the election of four years earlier.

Ideologically, this black male electorate was clearly more conservative than its black female counterpart. David Bositis, an analyst at the Joint Center for Political and Economic Studies, observed that "black women were 11 percentage points more Democratic in their presidential vote than black men, 89 to 78 percent. The comparatively large black Republican congressional vote—18 percent—is likewise undoubtedly attributable to the increased number of black male voters." In 1996 labor unions, civil rights organizations, and the Democratic Party had all initiated many efforts to increase the size and turnout percentage of the African American electorate. What, then, explains the decline in the number of black women voters and the dramatic increase in involvement by African American males in the political process? Weighing the evidence, Bositis observed:

> There was only one major relevant event of note in the past year or so that focused primarily on black men, and that was the Million Man March . . . at which Farrakhan exhorted black American men to take more responsibility for their lives by registering to vote and by voting. In reviewing a variety of possible alternative hypotheses to account for the sharp increase in the black male vote, I find it highly implausible that there was another factor that rivaled the Million Man March in bringing about this change.[1]

While the great majority of African Americans had endorsed, with varying degrees of enthusiasm, the Million Man March, by no means was that support universal. Prominent African American feminists such as Angela Davis and Julianne Malveaux denounced the deliberate exclusion of women from the mobilization, arguing that Farrakhan's reactionary concepts of women were patriarchal and misogynist. Lesbian and gay rights activists pointed to the many blatantly homophobic statements made by Farrakhan and the Nation of Islam (NOI) about black homosexuality. Many liberal elected officials, trade unionists, and civil rights leaders who feared being identified with Farrakhan's long history of vicious anti-Semitism, including his characterization of Judaism as a "gutter religion," refused to support the march. The response of black progressives and radicals to the mobilization often seemed contradictory. The entire black Left understood the factors that underlay the widespread popular response to Farrakhan's call for the march: high levels of unemployment, the deterioration of central cities, cutbacks in social services, the rapid expansion of the criminal justice system and the mass incarceration and institutionalization of several million African American young men, the abandonment of affirmative action, the general disarray of moderate black leaders and civil rights organizations in addressing the contemporary social crisis. It was indeed true that Farrakhan was an anti-Semite, but this was not central to his overall program and was not a significant factor in his growing appeal to a young generation of African Americans.

The aspects of the social phenomenon surrounding Farrakhan that were most disturbing were its dynamic yet deeply reactionary character, its clever manipulation of racial slogans and symbols evoking black pride and militancy, and an economic analysis taken almost verbatim from Booker T. Washington's program of black petty entrepreneurship and political cooperation with white conservatives. The march had contributed to some extent to a revitalization of black male activism and civic engagement. Yet it had also provoked bitter divisions over such issues as patriarchy, reproductive rights, homophobia, and the meaning and social construction of gender within the black community. The deeper fear was that Farrakhan would consolidate the enormous political capital generated by the march's success toward utterly reactionary purposes. Despite the militancy of his rhetoric, Farrakhan would inevitably find common cause with the most reactionary and even racist elements in white political life.

Within less than a year, many of the worst fears about where Farrakhan intended to take the black movement became apparent. In June 1994, the Reverend Benjamin Chavis, then executive secretary of the NAACP, had initiated the National African American Leadership Summit, an effort to forge a united front across ideological and political perspectives within the black community. After Chavis was fired from his NAACP position, he became essentially a client of Farrakhan, financially and politically dependent. In 1995 and 1996, the National African American Leadership Summit's constituency became increasingly smaller and ideologically narrower. Organized labor, civil rights organizations, and elected officials largely kept their distance, because it was soon clear that the summit had degenerated into a front organization controlled by Farrakhan. Many prominent cultural nationalists such as Maulana Karenga and Haki Madhubuti backed away from the summit, partially because its leadership failed to hold a comprehensive evaluation of the strengths and weaknesses of the march. The summit failed to maintain contact with thousands of volunteers and was plagued by organizational problems.

Nevertheless, when the National African American Leadership Summit called for a national political convention at St. Louis in September 1996, at least three thousand representatives gathered to participate. On the convention's final day, the Reverend James Bevel, one of Martin Luther King Jr.'s former lieutenants and a recent ideological convert to political conservatism, was given the podium. Bevel proudly introduced as a major speaker to the convention delegates "the man of the hour," Lyndon La Rouche. Many African Americans in the audience were stunned: they immediately recognized La Rouche as a leader of fascist extremism in the United States and a racist defender of the former apartheid regime of South Africa. To others, who were unfamiliar with La Rouche's public record, it remained inexplicable why this white man was invited to speak from the central podium to an audience of black nationalists and activists. What did this all mean? Instantly the crowd turned against Bevel and La Rouche, booing them off the stage and intimidating them into silence. A fistfight erupted between several black nationalists and some supporters of La Rouche, which was broken up by Farrakhan's security force, members of the Fruit of Islam. Throughout the country, perplexed African American activists asked themselves why a notorious white supremacist and fascist would be permitted to address a black political convention. Only Farrakhan could have given permission for La Rouche to speak.

What seems at first to be a curious paradox was no puzzle at all. There were significant elements in their respective ideologies that brought Farrakhan and La Rouche into agreement. Months earlier, in a similar vein, Republican vice presidential candidate Jack Kemp had publicly praised Farrakhan's emphasis on "personal responsibility," black self-sufficiency, and morality. There was a logical convergence between the black Right and the white Right, which embraced capitalist economics, morality, and patriarchy.

The reason that Farrakhan's message of personal responsibility, patriarchy, and racial self-help resonated so profoundly among millions of black people was that it was not new. The political consciousness of African Americans harbored distinct memories of earlier formations and movements with strikingly similar goals and objectives. The contemporary influence of Farrakhan can be understood only against a background of the inner history of black folk, who through their own experiences and in their own language constructed an approach toward social development that would ensure their collective survival in a hostile world. It is partially in this sense that Farrakhan can be understood only as a conservative: his entire program presumes the permanent boundaries of race and racial antagonisms and the need to construct racial institutions that promote order, social stability, and patriarchal households within the black community. To explain the widespread popularity and appeal of Farrakhan today, at least within a significant segment of black America, we must examine the historical roots of his conservative ideology.

II

Historians of the African American experience have tended to emphasize the long struggle by black people for equal treatment and civil rights. Although the quest for equality has always been the central feature of black activism, it was by no means universal as a response to white domination. Just as influential as inclusion or integration has been the idea of black nationalism. Over the past 150 years, many divergent organizations identified with black nationalism have emerged, reflecting a wide spectrum of ideologies, but several core elements have been characteristic of this tradition. First and foremost was the belief that African Americans were an oppressed nation or national minority trapped inside a predominantly white society, a nation that had developed its own culture, social institutions, and collective interests. Instead of perceiving themselves as Americans who "happened to be black," black nationalists often viewed themselves as either people of African descent or Africans who happened to reside in the United States. Ontologically, the realization of critical self-awareness could be achieved only by grounding oneself in the rituals, culture, and traditions generated by and among black people. Also central to black nationalism was the logical insight that an oppressed people could survive in a hostile environment only if they constructed institutions and enterprises to provide goods, services, and resources to their own group. Black nationalists were therefore skeptical about the long-term viability of relationships or alliances with Euro-Americans and tended to link their own struggles domestically to larger efforts to achieve black empowerment and self-determination globally.

With some variations, these tenets have been the foundation of black nationalist politics from the militant emigrationism of Martin Delany in the 1850s to Marcus Garvey's Universal Negro Improvement Association (UNIA) in the 1920s. For decades, many black nationalists have advocated some type of territorial separation between the races inside the United States, since they see interracial harmony as impossible. As early as 1916, writer Arthur Anderson suggested that one Southern state should be occupied solely by blacks, who would be permitted to secede and create their own government. By the late 1920s, the Communist International partially recognized the political claims of the Garveyites by defining the thousand-mile crescent of millions of African Americans across the Deep South as a "black belt nation." Even W. E. B. Du Bois, often a hostile critic of black nationalism, described black America during the nadir of the Great Depression as "a nation in a nation."[2]

The Garvey movement was largely responsible for transforming the ideology of black nationalism into a mass protest movement with large numbers of working-class, poor, and rural supporters. The historical context for this transformation was World War I and its immediate aftermath, as national independence and "home rule" movements erupted in Asia, the Caribbean, and Europe. In the United States, the Red Summer of 1919 culminated in widespread lynchings and racist violence against blacks. Among white Americans, a nativist movement developed with the rebirth of the Ku Klux Klan, which claimed three million members by the early 1920s. Garvey was an astute student of these nationalist movements and incorporated many of their techniques and strategies into his own program.

First, Garvey inspired the development of a political organization that often seemed decentralized and chaotic, yet was based on himself as the central, dominant personality of the movement. To become a "Garveyite" was not merely to acquire a distinct political outlook or to become a member of a UNIA local branch. Political loyalty within the organization rested on a deep personal attachment to Garvey himself. Garvey's understanding of Caribbean and African American rural cultures, traditions, and histories of resistance during slavery and colonialism was extremely complex. By holding great public demonstrations and rituals, the UNIA incorporated many of these cultural themes. The UNIA's African Legion nurtured the image of a black paramilitary force that would someday overturn the system of white power. Garvey's Negro Factories Corporation and Black Star Steamship Line symbolized the desire of poor and working-class blacks to provide for their own economic welfare. Sociologist E. Franklin Frazier described Garvey's brand of black nationalism as a deep spiritual and otherworldly movement, which merged black religiosity with the pageantry of grand rituals:

> [Garvey] not only promised the despised Negro a paradise on earth, but he made the Negro an important person in his immediate environment. He invented honors and social distinctions and converted every social invention to his use in his effort to make his followers feel important. While everyone was not a "knight or sir," all his followers were fellow-men of the Negro race. . . . The women were organized into Black Cross Nurses and the men became uniformed members of the vanguard of the great African army.[3]

But Garveyism was, at the same time, deeply conservative. Although there were "left-wing Garveyites" who incorporated a socialist analysis into their black nationalist politics, Garveyism was a social philosophy most clearly expressed by the slogan Race First. Garvey himself appreciated revolutionary movements throughout the world, and even to some extent patterned UNIA programs after those developed by insurgents in the Irish revolution of 1916–1921 against Great Britain. Yet Garvey's challenge, as he saw it, was basically the construction of a distinctly racial political culture of solidarity and resistance, giving self-confidence and hope to the most oppressed sectors of his people. As sociologist Doug Gutknecht observed: "Garvey rather than trying to create a movement based on traditional class politics, believed cultural and racial questions were primary: the struggle for mobility and opportunity to compete rested on a viable set of cultural institutions and race self-pride. Garvey's symbolic style of politics often alienated him from those possessing resources, political contacts, formal means of disseminating information, etc."[4]

In practical terms, Garvey's version of racial solidarity required an explicit rejection of liberal black intellectuals such as W. E. B. Du Bois and reformist organizations like the NAACP. Black elites who favored racial integration, from this perspective, were clearly working against the best interests of Negroes. Blacks should not "beg" whites for social equality and acceptance but should establish their own racial standards and values for group development. It was only a short step from this Race First dogma to the argument that the only whites who were capable of honest and sincere dialogue with black people were overt racists and white supremacists. In the early 1920s, Garvey made contacts with representatives of the Anglo-Saxon Club and the White American Society, which were part of a growing Ku Klux Klan–oriented movement in the post–World War I period. A decade later, Garvey even identified his political accomplishments with those of European fascism, proclaiming that UNIA activists were "the first fascists."[5]

Another essential element of Garveyism was the charismatic personality of the leader. Max Weber originally defined *charisma* as a type of leadership generated by great moments of social instability and unrest. The charismatic leader challenges the status quo by evoking the deepest emotions and energies of his audience, revealing the power "to revolutionize men from within."[6] Such powerful personalities articulate an alternative vision of the world as it should be, and motivate their followers to construct that world. Garvey's entire career as a black leader closely follows Weber's classic model: he was simultaneously prophetic, personally courageous, intensely emotional, ambitious, and deeply aware of his mission in history.

A critical reciprocity intimately bound together the leader and his follow-ers. In most charismatic relationships, according to Thomas Spence Smith, "the leader is a vehicle for the idealizing transferences of his audience, the audience for the leader's mirroring transferences." The charismatic leader "needs his idealizing disciples or followers. He is nothing without a follow-er: with one, he is a prophet or a lord."[7] It was difficult for such leadership to acknowledge mistakes or accept criticism from subordinates. Either one embraces every element of the leader's agenda and his personal authority or one is judged disloyal and potentially a traitor to the cause.

When these distinct elements were combined—charismatic leader-ship, autocratic hierarchies, social conservatism, a reductionist definition of racial categories, extreme hostility toward external critics—a new ten-dency emerged in the black nationalist tradition that could be termed *black fundamentalism*. Unlike the black nationalist formations of the nine-teenth century, this conservative tendency manifested itself in strict disci-plinary terms, and members of the UNIA were routinely silenced, expelled, or harassed if they challenged or criticized Garvey's authority. This was particularly the case for those who had risen high in the organization's hierarchy and those who had close personal relations with the leader. The best illustration of this is provided by Garvey's first wife, Amy Ashwood Garvey. Ashwood had been the "lady secretary" of the UNIA, traveling in Garvey's behalf as a noted public lecturer and political organizer. She con-tributed to the UNIA's newspaper, *Negro World*, and served as an officer of the Black Star Steamship Line. In late December 1919, Ashwood and Garvey were married before thousands of UNIA members and supporters. Within several months, the marriage fell apart. Garvey accused his wife of infidelity and drunkenness, while Ashwood responded with charges of infidelity against him. For the next six years, the pair was constantly in court, charging each other with a series of offenses, including bigamy. In 1922 Garvey married Ashwood's former roommate, Amy Jacques, who had been the maid of honor at their 1919 wedding.

Both the U.S. and British governments were largely responsible for the destruction of the Garvey movement. Despite Garvey's advocacy of racial separatism, the UNIA challenged white authorities by its emphasis on colo-nial independence and militant protests. When Garvey named himself the "provisional president of Africa," Du Bois and other middle-class Negro leaders thought him ridiculous. Those in power did not share their opin-ion. *Negro World* was banned in several countries and territories in Africa and the Caribbean. UNIA leaders and organizers were subjected to harass-ment, arrest, and in some cases death. The U.S. government launched an effort to destroy the UNIA from within and charged Garvey himself with mail fraud. The UNIA leader was convicted and imprisoned; in 1927 he was expelled from the United States, never to return. Although the UNIA had virtually disappeared as an organization, Garvey had forever transformed the ideology of black nationalism as a mass movement. The charismatic legacy of Garveyism brought together a series of contradictory ideas and themes: racial awareness and cultural pride, social conservatism, black capitalism, anticolonial protest, political militancy.[8]

III

From its founding by Fard Muhammad in Detroit during the late 1920s and early 1930s, the Nation of Islam reflected most of the core themes of traditional black nationalism. This small religious sect mixed an unorthodox Islam with a patriarchal, conservative outlook on black issues and interests. Under the patriarchal guidance of Elijah Muhammad, the organization grew from its marginal existence in the ghettos of Chicago and the Midwest to its development as a significant voice within black America during the period of the Second Reconstruction. The genius of Elijah Muhammad lay in his construction of a religious community that resonated with the familiar values of conservative black nationalism, such as racial pride and self-sufficiency, combined with a number of innovations that permitted an autocratic and highly centralized formation. These innovations would expand the tendency toward racial fundamentalism established by Garvey into a truly autocratic, hierarchical movement.

Theologically, the Nation of Islam taught its members that Euro-Americans were literally "devils," incapable of overcoming their racial hatred. Since no spiritual dialogue or reconciliation with white America was possible, African Americans had to separate themselves from its evil influences. Divine intervention would one day eliminate the sickness of white domination. Meanwhile, from the standpoint of racial survival, Elijah Muhammad taught that blacks should seek their own separate territory. An all-black state could be administered and controlled by African Americans as a protective shield; behind it they could develop economic enterprises, schools, social institutions, and families. Consequently, the Nation of Islam did not seek to challenge white authorities in government or throughout American society. They minimized their involvement in politics and elections and opposed any overt protest for desegregation and civil rights. Muhammad defined miscegenation as a type of "mongolization" that would culminate in the genetic and social destruction of the black race. African American leaders who favored integration, such as Martin Luther King Jr., were clearly disloyal to their own people's best interests. Muhammad met with King on one occasion, but he frequently denounced the civil rights leader for encouraging African Americans "to submit to the white man and to become one of them."[9]

Like other conservative black nationalists before him, Elijah Muhammad advocated the creation of black-owned businesses and thought them central to the collective advancement of the race. By the 1960s and early 1970s, for example, the Nation of Islam had established a series of successful commercial enterprises, including restaurants, supermarkets, and farms. It had purchased thousands of acres of land to produce grain, beef, and dairy products for urban black markets. According to Claude Andrew Clegg III, Muhammad's biographer, by 1971 the Nation of Islam's farm in Michigan had "roughly one hundred cows [which] were being milked every day, and twenty thousand chickens were producing enough eggs to keep Chicago retail operations well supplied." The Temple Farms holding in Georgia "consisted of a large dairy, a cannery, seven hundred head of cattle, and almost a thousand acres of corn, soybeans, and peanuts."[10] Although most of the agricultural enterprises were unsuccessful, the attempt to gain a measure of black economic sufficiency won the support of many of the Nation of Islam's critics.

In effect, the Nation of Islam preached an economic strategy of "black capitalism" strikingly similar to that championed more than a century ago by Booker T. Washington. Like the founder of Tuskegee Institute, Muhammad believed that capitalism had no color line. Anyone with the will and energy to build an enterprise providing goods and services to his people should be rewarded. This faith in black entrepreneurship explained Washington's hostility to labor unions, socialism, and racial politics. Similarly, Muhammad was deeply opposed to communism, partly on the grounds that it was atheistic. The Nation as a whole was apathetic toward black militancy and activism inside organized labor and maintained its distance from Marxist politics of any kind. When Malcolm X caucused with Fidel Castro during the Cuban leader's visit to the United Nations in 1960, for instance, Muhammad was furious.[11]

It is in these contexts—strict racial separatism, autocratic leadership, defense of capitalism, and opposition to communism—that the Nation of Islam must be interpreted as a deeply conservative and fundamentalist movement among black people. Militancy is, after all, a "style" rather than a coherent philosophy of politics. The members of the Nation were militant believers in a creed that projected an alternative racial universe, a way of viewing the world through an inverted prism of race. Ideologically, the orientation of this sect was inherently antidemocratic, patriarchal, and intolerant.

Given its fundamentalist orientation, it is not at all surprising that the Nation of Islam inevitably sought to establish relationships with white conservatives. In Chicago, the national headquarters of the Nation, Muhammad cultivated a cordial understanding with that city's powerful political boss, Richard J. Daley. The Cook County Democratic machine's vast resources ruthlessly dominated the politics of the black community, silencing critics and preserving the most rigid system of residential segregation in the country. The Chicago police department routinely harassed and victimized black residents, with Daley's consent. Yet the Nation of Islam in Chicago rarely experienced the sort of police raids and harassment that occurred frequently in other cities. Both the Daley machine and the Nation feared the rise of a black radical movement that might challenge the political status quo. Clegg speculates that "Muhammad and Daley apparently shared common ground that minimized the chances of confrontation between them. Perhaps the Muslims greased the machine with money from time to time. Possibly the mayor feared offending the black electorate by openly persecuting Muhammad, who was definitely one of the more influential and affluent African-Americans in the city. Whatever the case, the result was a political symbiosis that lasted until Muhammad's death in 1975."[12]

Muhammad developed even more cordial relationships with white supremacists. John X. Ali, who was appointed national secretary of the Nation of Islam in 1958, served as the primary contact with the far Right. Authors Louis Lomax and Karl Evanzz have suggested that Ali was also working covertly as the top informant for the Federal Bureau of Investigation inside the Nation. It was through Ali that eccentric Texas millionaire H. L. Hunt made a substantial donation to the Nation of Islam. Hunt apparently endorsed the racial separatism and political conservatism of the group as an alternative to the Civil Rights Movement.

As mosques were organized in Atlanta, Richmond, Miami, and other Southern cities, the Nation of Islam more aggressively pushed its call for a separate black territory or "homeland." The first practical step toward this objective was to establish a land base somewhere in the Deep South. This may have been the motivation for the Nation of Islam's secret dialogue with the Ku Klux Klan. On January 28, 1961, Malcolm X and Jeremiah X, the minister of the Atlanta mosque, met with leaders of the KKK. Unknown to both parties, however, the FBI was present, and the agency secretly recorded the discussion. The Nation's representatives and the Klansmen first shared their views on race and quickly found common ground. Malcolm X reportedly attributed "the whole struggle to a Jewish conspiracy carried out by unsuspecting blacks." The two parties agreed to establish a truce between their respective organizations, as long as the Nation continued its opposition to the movement for desegregation. To establish good faith, the Klan offered to help the Nation of Islam obtain as much as twenty thousand acres of land in either Georgia or South Carolina. Only days before his assassination four years later, Malcolm X publicly revealed his detailed negotiations with the Ku Klux Klan:

> They wanted to make this land available to him so that his program of separation would sound more feasible to Negroes and therefore lessen the pressure that the separationists were putting upon the white man. I sat there. I negotiated it. I listened to their offer. And I was the one who went back to Chicago and told Elijah Muhammad what they had offered. . . . From that day onward the Klan never interfered with the Black Muslim movement in the South. Jeremiah attended Klan rallies . . . they never bothered him, never touched him. . . . When the brothers in Monroe, Louisiana, were involved in trouble with the police . . . Elijah Muhammad got old [James] Venable. Venable is the Ku Klux Klan lawyer. He's a Ku Klux Klan chieftain, according to the *Saturday Evening Post*, that was up on the witness stand. Go back and read the paper and you'll see that Venable was the one who represented the Black Muslim movement in Louisiana.[13]

An even more bizarre relationship subsequently developed between the Nation of Islam and the American Nazi Party, led by George Lincoln Rockwell. The Nazis, like the KKK, bitterly opposed civil rights and social equality for black people and espoused a program of race hatred and anti-Semitism. But Rockwell viewed the racial policies of the Nation of Islam as worthy of his support. Muhammad biographer Clegg observed that Rockwell and Elijah Muhammad "exchanged correspondence and apparently worked out an agreement of mutual assistance." Both Malcolm X and Raymond Sharrieff, the supreme captain of the Fruit of Islam (the Nation's security force), privately questioned the public relationship with Rockwell and the Nazis. But Muhammad insisted that Rockwell be permitted to appear at Muslim meetings. On June 25, 1961, Rockwell and twenty others wearing Nazi uniforms attended a speech by Malcolm X in Washington, D.C. On February 25, 1962, Elijah Muhammad himself spoke publicly on "Savior's Day" at the Chicago International Amphitheatre, before an audience that included Rockwell and other Nazi Party members. Malcolm X would later charge that there was a "conspiracy" among the Nation of Islam, the Ku Klux Klan, and the Nazis. Clegg also observed, "When black separatists seek accommodation and rapprochement with racists and reactionary elements of a society, they compromise the moral force behind their struggle for liberation regardless of how noble their intentions may be. To a certain extent, Muhammad had done exactly that by entertaining the Georgia Klan and countenancing Rockwell. Even worse, he had allowed the Nation to stray dangerously close to the ideological pathway of white supremacy."[14]

The larger political question to be answered here is why Elijah Muhammad sought an informal alliance with fascists and racists. In one of his last speeches, Malcolm X provides part of the answer. Through the beginning of the 1960s, he declared, "there was not a better organization among black people in this country than the Muslim movement. It was militant. It made the whole struggle of the black man in this country pick up momentum because of the unity, the militancy, the tendency to be uncompromising. All of these images created by the Muslim movement lent weight to the struggle of the black man in this country against oppression." But beginning in 1960, Elijah Muhammad began to move the organization in a new, more conservative direction. Malcolm focused his attention primarily on Muhammad's corrupt personal behavior, which he described as "more mercenary . . . more interested in wealth . . . and, yes, more interested in girls." Muhammad had fathered several children by his private secretaries, acts of adultery for which any other Muslim would have been summarily punished or expelled. But a more probable cause was the rapid acceleration of the black freedom movement during these years. Beginning in January 1960, the sit-in desegregation protests erupted across the South. In 1961 the Congress of Racial Equality was leading "freedom rides" throughout Georgia and Alabama. Medgar Evers was at the forefront of the fight for desegregation as state leader of the NAACP in Mississippi. Hundreds of idealistic, militant young people established the Student Nonviolent Coordinating Committee in late 1960, to campaign for civil rights and to register African American voters. It was precisely at this historical moment that the Nation of Islam deemphasized politics, became overtly antagonistic to the Civil Rights Movement, and grew ever more autocratic and conservative ideologically. Malcolm suggested that the Nation would never attack the Klan or the Nazis: "I defy them to do so. They can't do it. Because they both have the same paymaster."[15]

IV

Louis Farrakhan emerged as a prominent spokesperson for conservative black nationalism directly as a result of Malcolm X's assassination. He was born Louis Eugene Walcott in Boston; his West Indian mother had been a Garveyite, and she supported his involvement in the Nation of Islam, beginning in 1955. Given the name Louis X, the young man moved quickly up the organizational hierarchy. At Harlem's Temple No. 7, he was a lieutenant in the Fruit of Islam and Malcolm X's protégé. In 1957 Louis X became the leader of the Boston mosque. When Malcolm X broke from the Nation in 1964, his most bitter critic was Louis X. Defending the black patriarch of the Nation, Louis X denounced Malcolm X as a "hypocrite" and a traitor "worthy of death." Following Malcolm's assassination, Louis X later was named to lead Harlem's Temple No. 7 mosque. Renamed Louis Farrakhan, the charismatic minister had, by the late 1960s, been appointed "national representative" of the Nation of Islam.

With the death of Elijah Muhammad in 1975, the Nation of Islam was thrown into organizational chaos. One of Muhammad's sons had sided with Malcolm X during the schism with his father. This was Wallace Muhammad, who, surprisingly, emerged as the new leader. He rapidly transformed the Nation; renouncing the group's separatist ideology, he brought it into compliance with the formal tenets and practices of orthodox Islam. During these years Farrakhan withdrew from the reformed Islamic organization and "reestablished" the old Nation of Islam—going back to the fundamentalist precepts and practices of its former patriarch. Although the majority of former Nation members remained loyal to Wallace Muhammad and adapted themselves to the new rituals of mainstream Islam, Farrakhan carved out his own public image as a militant spokesperson for contemporary black nationalism. In the 1984 presidential campaign of Jesse Jackson, Farrakhan's Nation of Islam provided security for the black candidate for a time. Farrakhan's articulate, charismatic style won over a new generation of black activists in the 1980s and 1990s—an ironic situation for many of them, who had been inspired by the powerful personality of the late Malcolm X.

Over the next several years, Farrakhan tried to "repackage" himself as a mainstream leader of the African American community. Although Jackson disavowed Farrakhan's support during his 1988 presidential campaign, the Nation of Islam won praise as it involved itself in voter-registration campaigns and electoral activity. Farrakhan crusaded against the illegal drug market within black communities, which destroyed the lives of thousands of blacks. He encouraged a dialogue among prominent gangs in the ghettos of major cities, to reduce the level of social violence. Under Farrakhan's leadership, the Nation of Islam dramatically increased its international visibility in many different ways. Libya offered an estimated $1 billion to finance the Nation of Islam's various programs within the United States. In early 1996 Farrakhan traveled across the globe on a well-publicized nineteen-nation tour, highlighted by personal audiences with the leaders of Iraq, Nigeria, Sudan, and South Africa. Later that year he challenged the U.S. embargo of Cuba by visiting that island nation and engaging in a lengthy political dialogue with Fidel Castro. Despite all of these external changes, the central ideology of the Nation of Islam remained as fundamentalist and conservative as ever. Farrakhan astutely employed the radical style he had learned from Malcolm X in his personal and political overtures to Castro, Nelson Mandela, and other Third World revolutionaries. But the actual content of the Nation's program was strict racial separatism, patriarchy, and extreme intolerance of any critics of the movement.

On issue after issue, Farrakhan's positions on major public policies are as reactionary as those of Newt Gingrich and his "Contract with America" Republican Congress. To this day, Farrakhan retains his belief in "racial purity" and opposes integration as a strategy for black advancement. He still supports in principle a separate state for all African Americans and a territorial division of the country along racial lines. On several occasions, he has expressed support for the death penalty as a punishment for many different "crimes," such as interracial sex. He has described homosexuality as "unnatural and sick."[15] His economic philosophy, like that of Elijah Muhammad, is a version of black entrepreneurial capitalism, the political economy of Booker T. Washington.

From the vantage point of white extreme conservatism, Farrakhan's racial fundamentalism has unmistakable parallels with fascist and white racist ideologies and organizations. By the early 1980s, Farrakhan's activities and speeches had come to the attention of British fascists, who quickly embraced the black Muslim's program of racial separatism. The publication of the National Front, a paramilitary organization with a record of racist assaults and attacks against black people in Great Britain, praised Farrakhan as "God-sent." The National Front subsequently distributed leaflets defending the Nation of Islam's positions. Back in the United States, in the wake of the controversies surrounding Farrakhan's statements about Jews and Zionism, white American racists developed an appreciation for him as well. At the 1985 Savior's Day conference, one guest speaker was Arthur Butz, a so-called revisionist critic of the Holocaust and author of *The Hoax of the*

Twentieth Century. Farrakhan was publicly praised by Ku Klux Klan leader Tom Metzger for his recognition that the American system was a "rotting carcass" and that the Jews were "parasites." The Nation of Islam occasionally initiated the dialogue with the white Right. For example the July 1990 issue of *The Spotlight*, the publication of the fascist, racist Liberty Lobby, featured an interview with Farrakhan. The Muslim leader is quoted as observing that "America was founded by white people for white people."[16]

An evaluation of Farrakhan's current relationship with racist extremist Lyndon La Rouche requires some background information on the latter's political history. From 1949 until his expulsion in 1966, La Rouche was an activist in the Socialist Workers Party, a Trotskyist organization. At the height of the mobilization against the Vietnam War, La Rouche established his own radical sect, the National Caucus of Labor Committees. Within a few short years, the La Rouche group mutated from the Left to the ultra-Right, embracing a fascist agenda of extreme anticommunism, racism, and anti-Semitism. In 1973 the La Rouchites initiated "Operation Mop Up," a series of violent assaults against members of the U.S. Communist Party. Armed with clubs, pipes, and other weapons, La Rouche's cult tried to disrupt public meetings and physically intimidate radical activists. Much of La Rouche's violence and hatred focused on the black movement. In 1977 La Rouche declared that African Americans who fight for equal rights are obsessed with "zoological specifications of microconstituencies' self interests" and "distinctions which would be proper to the classification of varieties of monkeys and baboons." La Rouche's publications and organization aggressively attacked black leaders who represented a variety of political perspectives, including Congressman Parren Mitchell, then head of the Congressional Black Caucus, Atlanta mayor Andrew Young, and Jesse Jackson. La Rouche's followers also carried out a racist assault against prominent activist/artist Amiri Baraka.[17]

In these same years, La Rouche actively courted leaders of the Ku Klux Klan and white fascism. In 1974 his front organization, the National Democratic Policy Committee, collaborated with racist groups in Boston to support an anti-busing candidate for Congress. The following year, the NDPC initiated a legal defense campaign on behalf of Roy Frankhouser, Grand Dragon of the Pennsylvania chapter of the Ku Klux Klan. La Rouche later provided intelligence information on the U.S. anti-apartheid movement to the Bureau of State Security (BOSS) of the apartheid regime in South Africa.

As La Rouche's cult grew to perhaps one thousand dedicated members and supporters, it began an extensive involvement in electoral politics. As the NDPC's presidential candidate in the 1980 Democratic primaries, La Rouche won 185,000 votes in fifteen states and received $526,000 in public funds from the Federal Election Commission. La Rouche's public addresses revealed a bizarre philosophy—a mixture of paranoia, racism, and right-wing ideology. For example, La Rouche insisted that Queen Elizabeth II of England was "a kingpin of the global drug traffic"; that former secretary of state Henry Kissinger and Vice President Walter Mondale were "Soviet agents"; and that David Rockefeller's "program for world reorganization is modeled after the conceptions of Hitler's finance minister." At the same time, La Rouche as a presidential candidate strongly defended the expansion of nuclear power and praised the call for the Star Wars nuclear weapons system aimed at the Soviet Union.[18]

According to the *Village Voice* of May 17, 1988, "By early 1981 La Rouche was well received within the upper reaches of the Reagan administration. His advocacy of fusion won him support in the Department of Energy, and the Pentagon was receptive because of Star Wars, which La Rouche claims to have invented. He became an ally in Reagan's war on drugs. La Rouche and his wife Helga met with top CIA officials to brief them on political and military matters in West Germany, where La Rouche is also well known. More importantly, La Rouche had access to the National Security Council adviser Judge William Clark."[19] Through the early years of the Reagan administration, La Rouche's political influence grew dramatically. His front organizations, which generated millions of dollars in contributions each year, included the Schiller Institute, the National Anti-Drug Coalition, and the pro-nuclear Fusion Energy Foundation, which, according to researcher Eugene H. Methvin, "rakes in tax-exempt dollars without disclosing to donors its bizarre political links." An expensive weekly newsmagazine, the *Executive Intelligence Review*, and a national newspaper, *New Solidarity*, promoted La Rouche's political analysis to hundreds of thousands of readers. La Rouche became recognized as a major political force. He was granted private audiences with Indian prime minister Indira Gandhi, Mexican president José López Portillo, Argentinian president Raul Alfonsin, and CIA deputy director Bobby Ray Inman. La Rouche's fundraising efforts generated $30 million in 1984 alone, to finance his unsuccessful campaign in that year's Democratic presidential primaries. Dennis King, author of *Lyndon La Rouche and the New American Fascism*, estimated that La Rouche's organization generated more than $200 million between 1980 and 1988.[20]

La Rouche's successes in electoral politics led him to reevaluate his racist positions on civil rights and black politics in general. Perhaps he took careful notes from Reagan's cultivation of a coterie of black apologists for his reactionary policies, such as economists Thomas Sowell and Walter Williams, television journalist Tony Brown, U.S. Civil Rights Commission chairman Clarence Pendleton, and the director of the Equal Employment Opportunity Commission, Clarence Thomas.

In any case, by the mid-1980s La Rouche had concluded that his organization had to develop allies within the African American community. The first significant step toward this goal was the organization of a rally at Washington, D.C.'s Lincoln Memorial in January 1985. La Rouche front organizations sponsored the event, which was theoretically held in honor of Dr. Martin Luther King Jr.'s birthday. At least five thousand African Americans attended the rally, which also featured banners in support of President Reagan's Star Wars nuclear weapons scheme: "I Have a Dream, and Build the Beam." Quietly La Rouche began to recruit dozens of African Americans into his organization and to develop close relationships with others who might benefit from his financial contributions. In the latter category was Congress of Racial Equality leader Roy Innis, who first met La Rouche in the early 1980s. In October 1984 Innis testified as a "character witness" for La Rouche in a slander suit against NBC. Innis claimed in the trial that La Rouche was neither a racist nor an anti-Semite and that "the composition of his organization indicates to me that he's not a racist."[21] La Rouche's prize recruit, however, was the Reverend James Bevel, who had been a top aide to King.

The mainstream leadership of the black community was not fooled by La Rouche's new tactics. The NDPC was without question a dangerous, anti-black, anti-Semitic cult. In the *Atlanta Voice* of April 12–18, 1986, the A. Philip Randolph Institute declared: "La Rouche appeals to fear, hatred and ignorance. He seeks to exploit and exacerbate the anxieties and frustrations of Americans by offering an array of scapegoats and enemies—Jews, Zionists, international bankers, blacks, labor unions—much the way Hitler did in Germany." In 1985 African American leader Julian Bond accused La Rouche of "using the elderly and the politically unsophisticated to promote his brand of right-wing totalitarianism, his alliance with Nazis and the Klan, his support for the white supremacists in South Africa, and for President Reagan's 'Star Wars' Program."[22]

One of La Rouche's sharpest and most perceptive black critics was the Reverend Benjamin Chavis, a former political prisoner and at that time executive director of the United Church of Christ's Commission on Racial Justice. In his nationally syndicated column, in August 1986, Chavis sharply denounced "La Rouche and his band of fanatics" for attempting "to win black recruits." La Rouche's front organizations have played upon "the black community's fear of the growing drug problem and the AIDS epidemic. They have gotten black recruits with their strong anti-drug line and their suggestion that all AIDS victims be quarantined." Through his NDPC, La Rouche "dupe[d] some black and Hispanic candidates into running on his ticket and to vote for his candidates." Chavis warned African Americans that the "La Rouche organization is clearly racist, works closely with the Klan, and is a supporter of the South African government as well. . . . It is trying, through its many tentacles, to infiltrate the black community." La Rouche's supporters responded to these and other African Americans' criticisms with racist and inflammatory rhetoric. One of La Rouche's white candidates in Baltimore, Debra Freeman, smeared Congressman Parren Mitchell as "a house nigger for the Zionists."[23] In March 1985, the La Rouchite newspaper *New Solidarity* bitterly denounced Farrakhan for "building a Nazi-communist terrorist movement closely linked to the Greens and their backers in the United States."[24]

La Rouche's empire was seriously threatened when in 1989 the cult leader and six of his top aides were convicted of federal fraud and tax evasion charges, receiving prison sentences of up to fifteen years. From his cell, La Rouche vowed, "They can't crush the organization. . . . It has a tough leadership and no matter how many people get bumped off, it will survive for generations to come." It was during the federal government's successful prosecution of La Rouche that the organization accelerated its efforts to cultivate friends and allies among black Americans. In 1992 La Rouche launched his presidential campaign by selecting the Reverend James Bevel as his vice presidential running mate. A surprising number of African American leaders were recruited to endorse the campaign; among the most prominent were the Reverend Hosea Williams, field director of the Southern Christian Leadership Conference and county commissioner of De Kalb County, Georgia, and Amelia Boynton Robinson, a Civil Rights Movement veteran and a 1990 recipient of the Martin Luther King Jr. Freedom Medal. In a press statement published in the La Rouche newspaper *New Federalist* on October 26, 1992, African American supporters of La Rouche stated: "It is time to secure the victories of the civil rights movement that was led by Dr. Martin Luther King, and guarantee the economic and moral future of our posterity. For these reasons we hereby endorse the La Rouche–Bevel candidacy, and encourage all citizens to join our new movement and vote La Rouche–Bevel on Nov. 3." The endorsers of this statement included (besides Williams and Robinson) Joseph Dickson, publisher of the *Birmingham World* newspaper; the Reverend Floyd

Rose, former editor of the *Macon Reporter*, and Mattie Harkness, former president of the Pickens County, Alabama, chapter of the NAACP.[25]

La Rouche's publications began to make favorable references to Farrakhan and the activities of the Nation of Islam. The Nation gradually reciprocated, citing data generated by La Rouche's research for its own publications. According to the *New Federalist* of September 28, 1990, Dr. Abdul Alim Muhammad, an NOI spokesman, told a meeting of La Rouchites: "To Mr Lyndon La Rouche and his wife, and to those members of his organization, especially those of his organization . . . who put out the *New Federalist* newspaper and the *Executive Intelligence Review*, I want to say on behalf of Minister Louis Farrakhan and the entire Nation of Islam, how much we admire you and respect you for the great work that you are doing." The NOI publication *The Final Call* of December 24, 1990, reported that Dr. Muhammad spoke in Paris at an international conference sponsored by the Schiller Institute. In the next few years, the Nation of Islam and the Schiller Institute collaborated in public forums at Howard University and the University of the District of Columbia. In 1994, following Chavis's ouster as head of the NAACP, representatives of the Nation of Islam once again joined forces with the La Rouchites. On September 1, 1994, the Schiller Institute organized and paid for a public forum in Washington. It featured Dr. Muhammad, who in turn accused the Anti-Defamation League of B'nai B'rith of "engineering" Chavis's removal. Dr. Muhammad also used the occasion to attack Imam W. Deen Mohammed, Elijah Muhammad's son, as "this functionary of the ADL network."[26]

When La Rouche was paroled from federal prison in 1994, Farrakhan's political influence had never been greater. The La Rouche organization then moved aggressively to deepen its extensive relationship with the Nation. After the Million Man March, Bevel began working closely with Farrakhan's representatives and with Chavis, as head of the National African American Leadership Summit. At the first anniversary of the march, some 50,000 to 100,000 people gathered before the United Nations to mark the "World Day of Atonement." According to the La Rouche publication *New Federalist*, the demonstration's major themes were "Atonement, Reconciliation, and Responsibility" and were "jointly agreed upon by the rally leaders," Farrakhan, Chavis, and Bevel. The rally's keynote address was delivered by Farrakhan, who spoke for nearly three hours.

But Bevel, in a rambling, virtually incoherent statement, characterized the 1995 Million Man March and the 1996 World Day of Atonement as "God breaking in, and people breaking out, to join forces to create a new nation." Bevel declared: "So, the new people, like a new baby, must not follow the old beaten path of the errant elders who are lost and have gone astray. The new people must listen to the voice of God, atone for the sin and crime of violence, murder, and war, and create a new world devoid of this old pagan, heathen, barbaric, human-sacrificing ritual. . . . And those who argue that there is a greater priority than addressing this human and social disease are likened unto the shoeshine boys who were fighting over which one was going to have the number-one shoeshine stand as the Titanic was making its descent." Despite Bevel's bizarre statements and his role as a La Rouche lieutenant, many prominent African Americans joined him on the platform at the Day of Atonement demonstration, including Harvard University professor Cornel West, the Reverend Al Sharpton, comedian and social critic Dick Gregory, and Pan-Africanist activist Kwame Toure.[27]

It was supremely ironic that Chavis, who had so clearly comprehended the dangers of La Rouche's fascist and racist politics a decade earlier, became politically and even financially dependent upon the La Rouche–Farrakhan liaison. Chavis's personal tragedy symbolizes the political contradictions of black fundamentalist nationalism: its autocratic character, its conservative economic ideology, and its active collaboration with white supremacy and fascism. The dangerous connections between Farrakhan and La Rouche only repeat the historical pattern of Garvey's associations with white racists in the 1920s, and Elijah Muhammad's relationship with the Nazis and the Ku Klux Klan a generation later. Perhaps the greatest tragedy of all is that the vast majority of African Americans are still unaware that some of their most prominent and charismatic leaders have fundamentally compromised and betrayed their interests by consorting with those who oppose their very existence as a people. In 1985, Julian Bond suggested that if La Rouche became successful, "a section of black America will have become allied with its own worst enemy." Unfortunately, Bond's prediction proved to be all too true.

12

Black Leadership and Organized Labor:
From Workplace to Community

For well over a century, there has been an ongoing debate within the African American community regarding different strategies that could be employed to promote group economic advancement and greater income equality with white Americans. The personalities advocating specific programs and organizational affiliations have shifted dramatically over the decades, but the general ideological conflict over what strategic vision is appropriate for black economic development has remained remarkably consistent. In its most basic terms, the debate concerns the complex relationships among race, class, and economic power. How does a minority group, with limited resources of capital and credit, devise a strategy to lift incomes and to promote group economic development?

One approach to this challenge of black economics has started with *race.* The argument here is simple: race is the most important factor in determining the availability of jobs, career advancement, access to credit and capital. Race must therefore be used as a framework for coordinating black producers and consumers to achieve empowerment within the capitalist system. The opposite approach begins from the point of view of *class.* Black Americans overwhelmingly are working people, who share common class interests with workers of different racial and ethnic backgrounds. By building solidarity between African American leadership and the labor union movement, and by increasing black union membership and participation, the black community will increase its political and economic clout. The enhanced power of the African American and labor movements will place greater pressure on government to support more-progressive social policies like affirmative action and vocational training programs, which disproportionately aid racialized minorities. An increase in the incomes and standard of living for the entire working population, combined with liberal government policies aimed at reducing poverty and joblessness, will dramatically improve the economic condition of the black community.

While it is certainly true that these two arguments are not mutually exclusive—labor unions and capitalism have coexisted for many years—nevertheless, the division between these two poles has fostered very different perspectives among African American leaders. The first architect of the blueprint for black capitalist development was Booker T. Washington, founder of Tuskegee Institute in 1881 and the National Negro Business League in 1900. Washington aggressively opposed labor unions and urged African Americans to seek employment as scabs to undercut racist white workers. By building black-owned businesses that provided goods and services to a mostly segregated market, African Americans would create jobs for themselves. This strategy of economic self-reliance was later accompanied by an explicit rejection of government as a tool for addressing income inequality. In the generations of black leadership since Washington, the strategy of capitalist development has been embraced by advocates of both racial integration and black nationalism. Marcus Garvey, the Jamaican black nationalist and leader of the Universal Negro Improvement Association in the 1920s, was a staunch proponent of Washington's economic strategy. In the 1980s black conservatives who were aligned with the Reagan administration, including economists Thomas Sowell, Glen Loury, and Walter Williams, preached racial self-help, black private entrepreneurship, and a reduction of government regulations and restrictions on the market. Today many of the same economic ideas are being championed by two seemingly very different black leaders: Colin Powell and Louis Farrakhan. Both men would favor blacks becoming "less reliant" on government programs; both support efforts at black entrepreneurship; both probably believe that the black middle class has the unique responsibility to uplift the rest of the black community. Although one leader is the darling of moderate Republicanism and white suburbia and the other has his core constituency in the black inner cities, that does not alter the similarities of their economic argument. As Peter Drier has noted: "According to Farrakhan, the road to black success is through entrepreneurship: by blacks owning businesses and keeping economic resources in the African American community. This goal resonates with the American Dream, but it is a far cry from economic reality." What was "tragically absent" from Farrakhan's address at the 1995 Million Man March, notes Drier, was any mention of "the institution that has played perhaps the largest role in improving the economic condition of black Americans: unions."[1]

The case against the economic strategy of black-labor solidarity rests partially on the long history of racial discrimination within the white working class. Historian William H. Harris has eloquently characterized racial exclusion as a central theme for the entire history of American labor:

> The importance and centrality of race in America comes forth in so much that has been part of the American labor movement, and raises without question the most important issue with which organized labor must contend if labor will continue to have a major place in American society. History is replete with examples of why this is so. For instance, railway engineers were not solely responsible for the failure of Eugene V. Debs' Pullman strike. The decision of numerous black workers to refuse to join the American Railway Union, and thus, in effect, become strikebreakers, contributed to Debs' failure as well. Yet, the very reason that black workers did not make common cause with the American Railway Union, namely because white railway unionists would not permit blacks to join the unions or to take certain railroad jobs such as engineers, brakemen, and conductors, requires historians to question whether the term scab really fits their actions. Is one a scab or strikebreaker when one takes a job during a strike that the striking workers, all of whom are white, have themselves gone on strike to keep black workers out? During the late 19th and 20th centuries, white workers initiated more than 100 strikes in order to keep black workers from gaining access to certain jobs.[2]

The pattern of racial exclusion was deeply entrenched in the American Federation of Labor (AFL) and was only partially broken when the Congress of Industrial Organizations (CIO) organized workers of both races. Racial progress was particularly slow in many craft trades. In 1960, for example, only 1.5 percent of all employed electricians were nonwhite. It was only when the Department of Labor under President Lyndon Johnson decided to pressure the skilled trade unions to desegregate that this rigid pattern of exclusion began to soften. In 1969 the Nixon administration began to implement what was termed the Philadelphia Plan, which was specifically designed to increase the number of African Americans and other racial minorities in the skilled trades. The Department of Labor directly funded several minority apprenticeship programs, such as the National Urban League's Labor Education and Advancement Program, which trained African Americans for skilled jobs as carpenters, ironworkers, heavy-equipment operators, and electricians. By 1980 nearly 5 percent of all employed electricians were African Americans. By 1995 approximately 15 percent of the one million jobs in the skilled trade unions belonged to black workers.

But black workers have learned that access to apprenticeship programs does not necessarily mean regular full-time employment. Under the Philadelphia Plan, contractors who bid for government-financed construction projects were required to meet goals for minority employment established by affirmative-action guidelines. The contractors shifted the burden of achieving these goals to the union locals that supplied the workers. And it is at the local level that racial bias is still perpetuated. In Philadelphia, Local 542, for example, once maintained mandatory hiring halls, where all job assignments were placed. But as competition for jobs increased, the white-dominated locals allowed contractors to hire union members without going through the hiring halls. In effect, this permitted white foremen to select their relatives and friends for positions and to discriminate against minorities. One report of Local 542 indicated that while 30 percent of all workers sent out for jobs were minorities, they worked only 16 percent of all hours worked by local members.

The retreat from equality represented by the Philadephia Plan is also symbolic of the distinctly different experiences that African Americans and whites have in the workplace, regardless of whether they are members of unions. The critics of African American–labor solidarity would make the argument that race is a more profound factor in determining what happens on the job, or in the availability of employment, than class is. There is considerable evidence to support this thesis.

First, social scientists for decades have observed a wage gap between whites and African Americans that is profoundly structural—regardless of education, vocational training, or other factors, nearly all blacks at all levels still earn less than whites. During the Civil Rights and Black Power Movements, and especially with the implementation of affirmative-action and equal employment opportunity measures, the income gap between blacks and whites narrowed dramatically. In 1967 black men earned 45 percent less than white men. By 1977 the wage gap had diminished to 29 percent. After that, the racial wage gap stagnated and to some extent was eroded.[3] Economist James P. Smith illustrates the racial stratification of wages by isolating the work experiences of college-educated African American men since the 1960s. Smith observes: "Among new college graduates, black men earned 83 percent as much as comparable white men in 1967–1968; by 1971–1972 there was complete wage parity. After 1971–1972, wage gains of young black workers steadily eroded. For college graduates, this erosion marked both decades until we had come roughly full circle with a wage differential in 1990 little different than that with which we started." What was even more striking was the decline of wages between races within the same cohorts. Smith notes that "among college graduates who entered the job market in 1971, wages of blacks exceeded those of comparable whites by 2 percent. Within this cohort, black males' wages were only 75 percent as much as those of their white counterparts 18 years into their careers in 1989."[4]

The racial wage gap also persists among union members. In 1987 African American union workers earned an average of $387 per week, compared with $458 per week for white union members. By 1994 white unionists received $514 a week on average, compared with $405 for black union members. The African American unionists' wage was only a small amount above the average weekly wage of $385 for all unionized and non-unionized, non-supervisory workers.[5]

The racial stratification of the work experience even extends to the rates of joblessness and reemployment. In periods of economic hardship, whites are far more likely than blacks to gain reemployment. For example, in the period 1979–1983, 77.9 percent of white men were reemployed, compared with only 63.1 percent of black men. For women workers, the figures were 62.9 percent for whites, 53.8 percent for blacks. The racial division of displaced workers who found reemployment was particularly sharp for workers who had less than three years' tenure on their last job. In 1984–1986, a period of relative economic growth, for displaced workers who had been employed on their previous job for less than one year, 81.7 percent of all white men were reemployed, compared with only 66.6 percent of the African American men. For displaced women workers in this category, white women again had higher rates of reemployment over black women, 61.2 percent versus 52.4 percent. In the managerial, administrative, and professional occupations, sectors where there are still relatively small numbers of minorities, African American displaced workers are at least as competitive as their white peers in obtaining new jobs. This is also the case when blacks had been employed at their previous jobs for eleven or more years.[6]

Once African Americans are out of work, it takes most of them a much longer time to be reemployed in the same occupation or industry than it does whites. Citing data from a 1988 Department of Labor survey, economist Lori G. Kletzer observes: "In the 1984–86 period, 15.5 percent of white men and 11.4 percent of white women reported experiencing no joblessness following displacement; among blacks, the percentages were much smaller, 5.4 percent of men and 6.6 percent of women. At the other end of the joblessness distribution, long-term joblessness—that exceeding 26 weeks—was more prevalent for sampled blacks than for sampled whites. For the 1984–86 period, 37.8 percent of black men and 29.5 percent of black women reported at least 26 weeks without work, compared with 18.8 percent of white men and 22.4 percent of white women." For displaced workers who had been unemployed for more than one full year, the racial stratification of experience remained: for men, the jobless rates were 5.0 percent for whites, 9.5 percent for blacks; for women, 6.6 percent for whites and 14.8 percent for African Americans.[7]

As a consequence of the racialized patterns of discrimination in career advancement, unequal wages, job displacement, and reemployment, most black American workers have been losing ground economically over the past two decades. Only a minority of African American workers who have high levels of skills and education, and those located in professional, technical, and administrative positions, have done comparatively well. Lou Ferleger and Jay R. Mandle note that "while the proportion of black families with incomes of more than $50,000 (adjusted for inflation) increased from 4.7 percent in 1970 to 8.8 percent in 1986, the percentage of poor black families—those with incomes of less than $10,000—also increased, from 26.8 percent to 30.2 percent."[8] About one-fourth of all black adults are no longer in the formal labor force, and in some urban communities like Harlem, that measurement exceeds 40 percent. The informal economy, both legal and illegal enterprises and markets, increasingly supports growing numbers of black working people. This development has had a devastating impact, particularly among young African Americans, many of whom have no experience or expectation of obtaining a real job in their lifetimes.

There is no question that race remains a critically important factor in determining the life chances—employment, income mobility, housing, health care, education—of all African Americans, even a generation after the Civil Rights Movement. But African Americans as a group have always understood that race does not and cannot explain everything. Much more than white American voters, the black electorate usually makes its political choices based on ideology, rather than the race of individual candidates. Similarly, from their practical experiences in the workplace, most blacks and other minorities have concluded that a strategy of class solidarity and unions, with all of their problems and contradictions, still represents the best approach for increasing income and improving the economic life of their communities. The best evidence of this is provided by public opinion polls. In one 1989 Associated Press/Media General national survey, more than 1,100 adults were asked about their attitudes toward organized labor. When non-union workers were asked, "Would you join a union at your place of work?" those responding "yes" included 56 percent of all African Americans, 46 percent of all Hispanics, and only 35 percent of non-Hispanic whites. When asked whether they had a generally "favorable" opinion of unions, 62 percent of both blacks and Hispanics responded positively, compared with only 43 percent of whites.[9]

This pro-union perspective is deeply rooted in the social consciousness and the political terrain of black history. Particularly, this intimate connection to the labor movement is based on the activist leadership of black trade unionists like A. Philip Randolph, who founded the Brotherhood of Sleeping Car Porters in 1925. Randolph directly linked the struggles of the black working class for higher wages and better working conditions with the cause for desegregation and civil rights. In the 1950s and 1960s, despite all of its many contradictions, organized labor provided critical support for the mass desegregation campaigns across the South. It was labor, not the mainstream of the Democratic Party, that endorsed the 1963 March on Washington, calling for the adoption of the Civil Rights Act. During the Black Power movement in the late sixties, the most significant radical tendency of African American activism was arguably not the highly publicized Black Panther Party but the League of Revolutionary Black Workers. From Montgomery to Memphis, black trade unionists and working-class people generally were central to the African American struggle.

There is a common recognition among black workers that their earnings, fringe benefits, and general working conditions improve with unionization, relative to black non-union labor. In 1987, for example, black union members earned an average of $387 per week, 51.8 percent more than black non-union workers, who averaged $255 per week.[10] It is for these reasons that African Americans are assuming an increasingly important role within the labor movement. While white male membership in unions has declined from 55.8 percent of all white male workers in 1986 to 49.7 percent in 1994, African American representation has increased in these same years from 14 percent to 15.5 percent. Even more important is the race and gender profile of organized labor today. As of 1995, only 14.8 percent of all white workers age sixteen and above were union members. Black men now have the highest union membership rate, 23.3 percent, followed by black women workers, at 18.1 percent.[11]

With their growing numbers, African Americans in recent years have become more directly involved in politics. As late as 1984, African Americans were leaders of only two of the AFL-CIO's ninety-five affiliates: Henry Nicholas headed the predominantly black National Union of Hospital and Health Care Employees, and Frederick O'Neal was president of the Associated Actors and Artists of America. By the end of the 1980s, a group of powerful black leaders had emerged: William Lucy, secretary-treasurer of the American Federation of State, County, and Municipal Employees (1 million members); Mary H. Futrell, president of the National Education Association (1.6 million members); John N. Sturdivant, president of the American Federation of Government Employees (at 700,000 members, the largest union of federal workers); Marc Stepp, vice president of the United Automobile Aerospace and Agricultural Implement Workers of America; Leon Lynch, vice president of the United Steelworkers of America; Henry Nicholas, still president of the National Union of Hospital and Health Care Employees; and Robert L. White, president of the National Alliance of Postal and Federal Employees.[12] With this new concentration of black leadership, the Coalition of Black Trade Unionists (CBTU), founded in 1972 as a pressure group for African Americans within the labor movement, exerted greater political influence.

This new power became apparent during the 1995 contest between John J. Sweeney, president of the Service Employees International Union, and AFL-CIO secretary-treasurer Thomas R. Donahue, for the AFL-CIO presidency. Black union leaders were not consulted in the selection of the candidates, and the CBTU decided to pressure both to accept fundamental changes in the federation. Among the CBTU's list of demands were that more minorities and women be included in the delegations sent to AFL-CIO conventions; that more African Americans be hired for federation staff positions; and that black labor leaders be consulted in the future "in drafting of strategies for organizing industries and plants that employ a higher percentage of minorities." Sweeney's October 1995 election as president pointed the federation toward a more progressive position on issues of race and gender. The AFL-CIO 1995 convention voted to increase the number of racial minorities and women on its executive council. With these changes, the number of minorities on the executive council increased from four out of thirty-five (11 percent) to eleven out of fifty-four (20 percent).[13]

What are the prospects for African American and other minority workers as they enter a new century? The globalization of capital and the information revolution have greatly transformed the system of production and even the character of work in the United States. Demographically the racial, ethnic, and gender composition of the American working class is changing rapidly. For the period 1990–2005, the Bureau of Labor Statistics projects an increase in the percentage of white males sixteen years and over in the civilian labor force of 17.4 percent. For women and minorities, the projected percentages are significantly higher: women workers, 26.2 percent; African Americans, 31.7 percent; Asian/Pacific Island Americans, 74.4 percent; and Hispanic Americans, 75.3 percent from their 1990 numbers.[14]

The current national debate about competitiveness in the global economy, for example, must take into account the demographic transformation of the U.S. labor force. For many years, both organized labor and capital largely ignored the black worker. They can no longer afford to do so. As Lou Ferleger and Jay R. Mandle observe:

> More than at any time in the past, the interests of the black labor force coincide with those of the nation as a whole. . . . If the United States is to compete effectively in the future, it will require a renewed attention to the productive competence of its labor force—including its sizable African-American component. If this is not done, not only will African-Americans suffer economically, but the country's businesses will continue to decline in world marketplaces.[15]

In the growing trend toward multiculturalism, at least at the present time, the corporations are in some respects ahead of both organized labor and public and private institutions such as universities. Globalization has forced multinational corporations to approach markets in entirely new ways. Both employees and consumers are increasingly multiethnic and transnational. Managers recognize that cross-cultural awareness and fluency enhance efforts to enter and exploit new markets. Global corporations that traditionally were run exclusively by Europeans and white North Americans now frequently recruit managers from non-western societies or from black, Asian, and Latino populations inside the United States. Large firms have initiated "cultural audits" or diversity workshops for their managers and sales personnel. In the United States, corporations now often fund multicultural events for employees during African American History Month or on Cinco de Mayo. "Corporate multiculturalism" is the coordinated attempt to manipulate diversity to maximize profits. Labor must surely be as "multicultural" as capital as it considers the demographic trends and social composition of the U.S. and global workforce.

The long-term question confronting organized labor, however, is whether it will merge the interests of the black freedom movement with its own agenda for social reform. "Race-based" politics cannot address the basic economic interests and problems within the African American communities, and the majority of black workers implicitly understand this. But organized labor will not make its case for solidarity to minority workers unless it develops the capacity to address class and racial issues simultaneously. An example is provided by Randolph's Negro March on Washington Movement of 1941, which pressured the Roosevelt administration to sign an executive order outlawing segregation in defense industries. To Randolph, racial equality as a goal was always tied to economic parity, but the issue of race could not be simplistically reduced or subordinated to the category of class. Historian William H. Harris reminds us that "Randolph saw the Brotherhood of Sleeping Car Porters as an agency to be involved in fomenting social change across the fabric of America and, if he had his way, across the fabric of the world."[16] The twelve-year struggle to achieve a contract for the members of the Brotherhood with the Pullman Company was important but not enough. Labor had the moral and political obligation to fight for social justice and the dismantling of institutional racism.

The basic challenge ahead of black labor is the construction of an alternative political culture, which can transcend the ideological boundaries and the political limitations of black liberal leadership in the Democratic Party and the civil rights community. "Organizing" is not just a means to articulate grievances or to demand higher wages. Its power lies in the transformation of its subjects. Ordinary people begin to see themselves in a different way. Workers acquire a new sense of power and possibility—that they can change the way things are, both at the workplace and at home. The rhetoric of divisiveness and racial exclusivity offers no hope for black working people to challenge corporate capital or to reverse the conservative trends in public policy on issues of race. Most black people really understand this. The act of organizing requires people to make effective connections with others who speak different languages or who represent different cultural traditions, nationalities, ethnicities, and religions. There is no monochromatic model for democratic social change in a pluralistic society.

To restate the political query raised by Martin Luther King Jr. in the aftermath of the triumph over legal segregation: "Where do we go from here?"—black labor will be able to lead only when it is able to incorporate critical elements of African American popular culture into its approach to organizing and into its normal political discourse. The model I have in mind here is the Civil Rights Movement. Oppressed people throughout the world for centuries engaged in civil disobedience, the disruption of the normal activities of the state and civil society. But in the context of the desegregation struggles across the South, civil disobedience was articulated as the "sit-in movement." The creative site of popular protest moved from the courtroom to the street, to the segregated lunch counters and department stores. Black workers saw themselves as actors in their own history. The new protest terminologies, such as "sit-ins" and "freedom rides," established a way of talking about empowerment and resistance. That new language must come from the expressions of daily life and the reflections of struggle that black workers themselves feel and know as their reality.

1. The Racial Contours of the Constitution

Originally published in *Howard Law Journal* 30, no. 4 (1987): 661–73.

1. For example, the Virginia slave code of 1694 stipulated that no slave was permitted to leave any plantation without written permission of the master. Slaves accused and convicted of robbing a store or residence were usually given sixty lashes and were then secured to a public pillory with their ears nailed to the posts. After a period of time, their ears were lashed from their heads. In South Carolina, the legislature was somewhat less tolerant of black misconduct. In 1686 South Carolina blacks were barred from engaging in certain types of trade. In 1722 sheriffs were permitted to search blacks for weapons and to whip them on the spot. For serious offenses, such as running away, slaves could be killed; for petty crimes, blacks were branded on their faces. Northern colonies were equally repressive. In 1703 Massachusetts passed a statewide curfew, requiring blacks to be off the streets by nine o'clock in the evening. Two years later interracial marriages were outlawed. Before 1700 Pennsylvania had no separate laws for free Negroes or slaves, but in the early eighteenth century blacks were barred from white courts. Interracial marriages were declared illegal; blacks accused of rape were castrated; no slave was permitted to travel more than ten miles from the master's residence without a written pass. See Paul C. Palmer, "Servant Into Slave: The Evolution of the Legal Status of the Negro Laborer in Colonial Virginia," *South Atlantic Quarterly* 65 (Summer 1966): 355–70; Adele Hast, "The Legal Status of the Negro in Virginia, 1705–1765," *Journal of Negro History* 54 (July 1969): 217–39; and Robert C. Twombly

and Robert H. Moore, "Black Puritan: The Negro in Seventeenth-Century Massachusetts," *William and Mary Quarterly* 24 (April 1967): 224–42.

2. Vincent Harding observes: "The threat of Black struggle was used as a means to solidify white people, to array lower-class whites into a colony-wide police force against the Black quest for freedom" (Harding, *There Is a River: The Black Struggle for Freedom in America* [New York: Harcourt Brace Jovanovich, 1981], p. 33).

3. About 40 percent of the population was essentially a landless proletariat, and at least 80 percent of all white indentured servants "died, became landless workers, or returned to England."

4. John Adams admitted candidly, "The state of Connecticut has always been governed by an aristocracy, more decisively than the empire of Great Britain is. Half a dozen, or at most a dozen families have controlled that country when [it was] a colony, as well as since it has been a state" (Staughton Lynd, "Beyond Beard," in Barton J. Bernstein, ed., *Towards a New Past: Dissenting Essays in American History*, p. 48 [New York: Pantheon, 1968]).

5. Poor whites often harbored and assisted black runaway slaves. Colonial historian Gerald W. Mullin notes: "Some whites openly aided fugitive slaves. . . . Many slaves evidently knew which White men, especially among watermen and officials, were lenient enough or sufficiently gullible enough to let them pass as free. . . . The insurrectionist, Gabriel Prosser, and his lieutenants made extensive use of rivers and watermen, bogus passes, whites who sold them supplies, and religious revivals in order to plan the wholesale destruction of the new capital city." See Mullin, *Flight and Rebellion: Slave Resistance in Eighteenth Century Virginia* (New York: Oxford University Press, 1972), pp. 113, 117, 128.

6. See Julian D. Mason, ed., *The Poems of Phillis Wheatley* (Chapel Hill: University of North Carolina Press, 1966), pp. 33–35.

7. Herbert Aptheker, *A Documentary History of the Negro People in the United States, from Colonial Times Through the Civil War* (New York: Citadel, 1951), pp. 7–8.

8. Harding, *There Is a River*, p. 43.

9. David Brion Davis, *The Problem of Slavery in the Age of Revolution, 1770–1823* (Ithaca, N.Y.: Cornell University Press, 1975), pp. 279–80.

10. Donald L. Robinson, *Slavery in the Structure of American Politics, 1765–1820* (New York: Harcourt, 1971), pp. 81–83, as quoted in Harding, *There Is a River*, p. 45.

11. Davis, *The Problem of Slavery*, p. 282.

12. Winthrop D. Jordan, *White Over Black: American Attitudes Toward the Negro, 1550–1812* (Chapel Hill: University of North Carolina Press, 1968), p. 342.

13. Davis, *The Problem of Slavery*, pp. 24, 173–74.

14. Herbert Aptheker, *American Negro Slave Revolts* (New York: International Publishers, 1963), pp. 207–8.

15. Benjamin Franklin led antislavery forces in Philadelphia and subsequently

became chairman of the Pennsylvania Abolition Society. Virginia governor James Wood later became president of the Virginia Abolition Society.

16. In 1780 Pennsylvania adopted provisions for emancipating all blacks when they achieved the age of twenty-eight. Two years later Virginia passed a bill allowing individual slaveholders to free their own chattel.

17. Davis, *The Problem of Slavery*, p. 87.

18. Ibid.

19. Ibid., p. 170; Mullin, *Flight and Rebellion*, pp. 11, 29, 60–61. See also Robert McColley, *Slavery and Jeffersonian Virginia* (Urbana: University of Illinois Press, 1964). Mullin notes that Washington used "less substantial, pre-fab"–type shacks for his slaves, which were "small, temporary, and were moved from quarter to quarter following the seasonal crop" (p. 51). Washington also believed that his slaves stole "everything they could lay their hands on." He kept his meat and corn houses always locked and closely watched his hogs and sheep. Washington even ordered the killing of all slaves' dogs, because the animals "aid[ed] them in their night robberies" (pp. 60–61).

20. Thomas Jefferson, *Notes on Virginia, 1784–1785*, as quoted in Jordan, *White Over Black*, pp. 374 and 436.

21. Jordan, *White Over Black*, p. 436; William Cohen, "Thomas Jefferson and the Problem of Slavery," *Journal of American History* 36 (December 1969): 503–26; William W. Freehling, "The Founding Fathers and Slavery," *American Historical Review* 77 (February 1972): 81–93.

22. During the war, he had proposed that young free blacks "be colonized to such place as the circumstances of the time should render most proper, sending out with arms, implements of household and of the handicraft arts . . . to declare them a free and independent people, and extend to them our alliance and protection" (Jordan, *White Over Black*, pp. 546, 552). Madison's definition of political democracy explicitly excluded Negroes. In 1820 the former president insisted that the removal of all Negroes from the United States was imperative: "The repugnance of the Whites to their continuance among them is founded on prejudices themselves founded on physical distinctions, which are not likely soon if ever to be eradicated" (ibid., p. 533).

23. Theoretically, a democratic society required the "complete incorporation" of freed blacks, Madison wrote in 1788. But racial integration was "rendered impossible by the prejudice of whites, prejudices which proceeding principally from the difference in colour must be considered as permanent and insuperable"(ibid., pp. 533–34).

24. Lynd, "Beyond Beard," p. 50.

25. Davis, *The Problem of Slavery*, pp. 323–25.

26. Ibid., pp. 100, 123–24.

27. US Const, Art I, 9, Clause 1.

28. Davis, *The Problem of Slavery*, pp. 127–28.

29. US Const, Art I, 2, Clause 3.

30. US Const, Art IV, 2, Clause 3.

31. *Somerset v. Steward*, Lofft 1, Eng. Rep. 98, pp. 499, 510 (K.B., 1772) (per Lord Mansfield, Chief Justice of the King's Bench).

32. US Const, Art IV, 2, Clause 3.

33. John Hope Franklin, *From Slavery to Freedom*, 3d ed. (New York: Knopf, 1967), pp. 151–52.

34. Davis, *The Problem of Slavery*, pp. 130, 323–25.

35. Ibid.

36. Ibid., p. 323; see also Jordan, *White Over Black*, p. 324.

37. Ibid.

38. Aptheker, *A Documentary History of the Negro People*, pp. 209–10.

39. Ibid.

40. Ibid.

41. Ibid., pp. 27, 102.

42. Jordan, *White Over Black*, p. 374.

43. US Const, Amend XIV, 1.

44. Jordan, *White Over Black*, p. 374.

2. Black History and the Vision of Democracy

Originally published in Harry C. Boyte and Frank Riessman, eds., *The New Populism: The Politics of Empowerment*, pp. 198–206 (Philadelphia: Temple University Press, 1986).

Aptheker, Herbert. *American Negro Slave Revolts*. New York: International Publishers, 1963.

Douglass, Frederick. "What to the Slave Is the Fourth of July?" *Black Scholar* 7 (July–August 1976): 33–37.

Edet, Edna M. "One Hundred Years of Black Protest Music." *Black Scholar* 7 (July–August 1976): 38–48.

Fite, Gilbert C. *Cotton Fields No More: Southern Agriculture, 1865–1980*. Lexington: University of Kentucky Press, 1984.

Focus 13 (March 1985): 4–5.

Levine, Lawrence W. *Black Culture and Black Consciousness: Afro-American Folk Thought from Slavery to Freedom*. Oxford: Oxford University Press, 1977.

Litwack, Leon F. *Been in the Storm So Long: The Aftermath of Slavery*. New York: Knopf, 1979.

Marable, Manning. *How Capitalism Underdeveloped Black America*. Boston: South End Press, 1983.

Ransom, Roger L., and Richard Sutch. *One Kind of Freedom: The Economic Consequences of Emancipation*. Cambridge: Cambridge University Press, 1977.

U.S. Bureau of the Census. *1977 Survey of Minority-Owned Business Enterprises*. Washington, D.C.: Government Printing Office, 1979.

White, Walter. *Rope and Faggot*. New York: Arno, 1969.

Woodward, C. Vann. *Origins of the New South, 1877–1913*. Baton Rouge: Louisiana State University Press, 1951.

3. Booker T. Washington and the Political Economy of Black Accommodation

Originally published in Thomas D. Boston, ed., *African American Economic Thought*, Vol. 2, *Methodology and Policy*, pp. 157–73 (New York and London: Routledge, 1996); and in Charles W. Eagles, ed., *Is There a Southern Political Tradition?* pp. 51–71 (Jackson: University Press of Mississippi, 1996).

1. Thomas Holt, *Black Over White: Negro Political Leadership in South Carolina During Reconstruction* (Urbana: University of Illinois Press, 1977), p. 68.

2. Benjamin E. Mays, "Black Colleges: Past, Present, and Future," *Black Scholar* 6 (September 1974): 32.

3. J. John Harris, Cleopatra Figgures, and David G. Carter, "A Historical Perspective of the Emergence of Higher Education in Black Colleges," *Journal of Black Studies* 6 (September 1975): 56.

4. Mays, "Black Colleges," p. 32.

5. Daniel C. Thompson, "Black Colleges: Continuing Challenges," *Phylon* 40 (June 1979): 185.

6. U.S. Bureau of the Census, *The Social and Economic Status of the Black Population in the United States: An Historical View, 1790–1978 (Washington, D.C.: Government Printing Office, 1979), pp. 13, 92, 96, 120, 138; Robert William Fogel and Stanley L. Engerman, Time on the Cross: The Economics of American Negro Slavery* (Boston: Little, Brown, 1974), p. 125; and Roger Ransom and Richard Sutch, *One Kind of Freedom: The Economic Consequences of Emancipation* (New York: Cambridge University Press, 1977), pp. 150–54, 182–85.

7. Gilbert C. Fite, *Cotton Fields No More: Southern Agriculture, 1865–1980* (Lexington: University of Kentucky Press, 1984), p. 32.

8. Florette Henri, *Black Migration: Movement North 1900–1920* (Garden City, N.Y.: Anchor Books, 1976), pp. 39–40; and C. Vann Woodward, *Origins of the New South, 1877–1913* (Baton Rouge: Louisiana State University Press, 1951), p. 213. The average annual death rate of black prisoners leased to private contractors was 11 percent in Mississippi in 1880–1885. In Arkansas, the death rate was 25 percent in 1881.

9. Sterling D. Spero and Abram L. Harris, *The Black Worker: The Negro and the Labor Movement* (New York: Atheneum, 1968), pp. 49–50.

10. Monroe Work, *Negro Year Book and Annual Encyclopedia of the Negro* (Tuskegee, Ala.: Tuskegee Institute Press, 1912), pp. 22, 168, 176–78.

11. Louis R. Harlan, *Booker T. Washington: The Making of a Black Leader, 1856–1901* (New York: Oxford University Press, 1972), pp. 144–46, 255, 272–73, 278–80.

12. Bureau of the Census, *Social and Economic Status of the Black Population*, pp. 14, 72, 73, 76, 78; and August Meier, *Negro Thought in America, 1880–1915* (Ann Arbor: University of Michigan Press, 1963), p. 127.

13. Harlan, *Washington: Black Leader*, p. 141; and Louis R. Harlan, *Booker T. Washington: The Wizard of Tuskegee, 1901–1915* (New York: Oxford University Press, 1983), pp. 130–31, 135.

14. Jack T. Kirby, *Darkness at the Dawning: Race and Reform in the Progressive South* (Philadelphia: Lippincott, 1972), p. 171.

15. Meier, *Negro Thought*, pp. 123–24, 253.

16. Manning Marable, "Booker T. Washington and African Nationalism," *Phylon* 35 (December 1974): 398.

17. P. Olisanwuche Esedebe, *Pan-Africanism: The Idea and Movement, 1776–1963* (Washington, D.C.: Howard University Press, 1982), p. 48.

18. Harlan, *Washington: Wizard of Tuskegee*, pp. 267–69; and Manning Marable, "A Black School in South Africa," *Negro History Bulletin* 37 (June–July 1974): 258–61.

19. Harlan, *Washington: Black Leader*, p. 227.

20. Booker T. Washington, *Up from Slavery* (1901), in *Three Negro Classics* (New York: Avon, 1965), pp. 146–50.

21. Harlan, *Washington: Black Leader*, pp. 222, 224.

22. Meier, *Negro Thought*, p. 111.

23. Harlan, *Washington: Black Leader*, pp. 90–91.

24. Spero and Harris, *The Black Worker*, pp. 129, 131; and Philip S. Foner, *Organized Labor and the Black Worker, 1619–1973* (New York: International Publishers, 1974), p. 79.

25. Foner, *Organized Labor and the Black Worker*, p. 99; Woodward, *Origins of the New South*, pp. 363–64; and Spero and Harris, *The Black Worker*, pp. 359, 363–66.

26. Meier, *Negro Thought*, p. 101.

27. Henri, *Black Migration*, p. 33.

28. Woodward, *Origins of the New South*, p. 368; and Fite, *Cotton Fields No More*, p. 21.

29. W. E. B. Du Bois, "The Talented Tenth," in Booker T. Washington et al., eds., *The Negro Problem*, pp. 31–75 (New York: Arno, 1969).

30. W. E. B. Du Bois, "Lecture in Baltimore," December 1903, in Herbert Aptheker, ed., *Against Racism: Unpublished Essays, Papers, Addresses, 1887–1961, 1887–1961, by W. E. B. Du Bois* (Amherst: University of Massachusetts Press, 1985), pp. 75–77.

31. Harlan, *Washington: Wizard of Tuskegee*, pp. 153–55.

32. Oliver Cromwell Cox, "The Leadership of Booker T. Washington," *Social Forces* 30 (1951): 91–97.

33. Louis R. Harlan, *Separate and Unequal: Public School Campaigns and Racism in the Southern Seaboard States, 1901–1915* (New York: Atheneum, 1969), pp. 12,

13, 250, 255–58; and Bureau of the Census, *Social and Economic Status of the Black Population*, p. 17.

34. Woodward, *Origins of the New South*, pp. 437–39.

35. Henri, *Black Migration*, p. 37.

36. Harlan, *Separate and Unequal*, pp. 134, 256.

37. Woodward, *Origins of the New South*, pp. 351–55; C. Vann Woodward, *The Strange Career of Jim Crow* (New York: Oxford University Press, 1974), pp. 99, 116–18; and Monroe N. Work, *Negro Year Book, 1918–1919* (Tuskegee, Ala.: Tuskegee Institute Press, 1919), p. 374.

38. See Michael Reich, *Racial Inequality: A Political-Economic Analysis* (Princeton, N.J.: Princeton University Press, 1981), p. 269.

39. Foner, *Organized Labor and the Black Worker*, pp. 74, 102.

40. Woodward, *Origins of the New South*, p. 361.

41. Manning Marable, "The Land Question in Historical Perspective: The Economics of Poverty in the Blackbelt South, 1865–1920," in Leo McGee and Robert Boone, eds., *The Black Rural Landowner—Endangered Species: Social, Political and Economic Implications*, pp. 15–19 (Westport, Conn.: Greenwood, 1979); and Bureau of the Census, *Social and Economic Status of the Black Population*, p. 15.

42. W. E. B. Du Bois, "The Negro and Social Reconstruction," in Aptheker, *Against Racism*, p. 114.

4. W. E. B. Du Bois and the Politics of Culture

Originally published in Hartmut Heuermann, ed., *Classics in Cultural Criticism*, Vol. 2, pp. 173–94 (Frankfurt: Peter Lang, 1990).

1. W. E. B. Du Bois, *The Suppression of the African Slave Trade to the United States of America, 1638–1870* (New York: Longman, Green, 1896; reissued, New York: Social Science Press, 1954).

2. W. E. B. Du Bois, *The Philadelphia Negro: A Social Study* (Philadelphia: Ginn, 1899).

3. W. E. B. Du Bois, *The Negro* (New York: Henry Holt, 1915); and W. E. B. Du Bois, *Black Folk Then and Now: An Essay in the History and Sociology of the Negro Race* (New York: Henry Holt, 1939).

4. W. E. B. Du Bois, *Black Reconstruction in America: An Essay Toward a History of the Part Which Black Folk Played in the Attempt to Reconstruct Democracy in America* (New York: Harcourt, Brace, 1935).

5. W. E. B. Du Bois, *The Souls of Black Folk: Essays and Sketches* (Chicago: McClurg, 1903).

6. Ibid., pp. 3–4.

7. W. E. B. Du Bois, "Scientific Reasons Against Race Antagonism," *Boston Globe*, July 19, 1914.

8. W. E. B. Du Bois, *Darkwater: Voices from Within the Veil* (New York: Harcourt, Brace, 1921; reprint, New York: Schocken, 1969), pp. 30, 42.

9. W. E. B. Du Bois, "Freedom of Speech," *Crisis* 37 (August 1930): 280.

10. W. E. B. Du Bois, "In Black," *Crisis* 20 (October 1920): 263, 266.

11. W. E. B. Du Bois, "Criteria of Negro Art," *Crisis* 36 (October 1926): 290, 292, 294, 295–97.

12. W. E. B. Du Bois, *A Bibliography of Negro Folk Songs* (Atlanta: Atlanta University Press, 1903).

13. Du Bois, *The Souls of Black Folk*, p. 251.

14. W. E. B. Du Bois, "John Work: Martyr and Singer," *Crisis* 32 (May 1926): 32–34.

15. W. E. B. Du Bois, review of *Congaree Sketches*, by Edward Clarkson Leverett Adams, *Amsterdam News*, August 27, 1927.

16. W. E. B. Du Bois, "Our Music," *Crisis* 40 (July 1933): 165.

17. Gerald Horne, *Black and Red: W. E. B. Du Bois and the Afro-American Response to the Cold War, 1944–1963* (Albany: State University of New York Press, 1986), p. 15.

18. W. E. B. Du Bois, "Elizabeth Prophet, Sculptor," *Crisis* 36 (December 1929): 407, 427–29. Also see Du Bois, "Can I Become a Sculptor? The Story of Elizabeth Prophet," *Crisis* 39 (October 1932): 315.

19. W. E. B. Du Bois, "Possibilities of the Negro: The Advance Guard of the Race," *Booklover's Magazine* 2 (July 1903): 3–15.

20. W. E. B. Du Bois, "Tanner," *Crisis* 28 (May 1924): 12.

21. W. E. B. Du Bois, "A Chronicle of Race Relations," *Phylon* 1 (1940): 175–92.

22. W. E. B. Du Bois, "The Drama Among Black Folk," *Crisis* 12 (August 1916): 169, 171–72.

23. W. E. B. Du Bois, "The Negro and the American Stage," *Crisis* 28 (June 1924): 56–57.

24. W. E. B. Du Bois, *The Autobiography of W. E. B. Du Bois: A Soliloquy on Viewing My Life from the Last Decade of Its First Century* (New York: International Publishers, 1968), pp. 85, 137.

25. Ibid., p. 270; and Paul Buhle, *Marxism in the USA: From 1870 to the Present Day* (London: Verso, 1987), p. 107.

26. Du Bois, "The Drama Among Black Folk."

27. W. E. B. Du Bois, "Can the Negro Serve the Drama," *Theatre Magazine* 38 (July 1923): 12, 68.

28. W. E. B. Du Bois, "The Ethiopian Art Theatre," *Crisis* 26 (July 1923): 103–4.

29. W. E. B. Du Bois, "The Krigwa Players' Little Negro Theatre," *Amsterdam News*, October 5, 1927; and Du Bois, "Krigwa," *Crisis* 30 (June 1925): 59.

30. W. E. B. Du Bois, "Beside the Still Water," *Crisis* 38 (May 1931): 168–69.

31. W. E. B. Du Bois, "The Humor of Negroes," *Mark Twain Quarterly* 5 (Fall–Winter 1942–1943): 12.

32. W. E. B. Du Bois, "The Prize Fighter," *Crisis* 8 (August 1914): 181; and Du Bois, "As to Pugilism," *Crisis* 25 (April 1923): 247.

33. W. E. B. Du Bois, "A Chronicle of Race Relations," *Phylon* 1 (1940): 90–97; 2 (1941): 388–406.

34. Horne, *Black and Red*, p. 15; and W. E. B. Du Bois, "The Winds of Time," *Chicago Defender*, May 10, 1947.

35. W. E. B. Du Bois, "The Problem of Amusement," *Southern Workman* 26 (September 1897): 181–84.

36. W. E. B. Du Bois, "Christmas," *Crisis* 3 (December 1911): 65, 68.

37. W. E. B. Du Bois, "Of the Giving of Life," "Of the Shielding Arm," "Of the Grim Thrust," and "The Frank Truth," *Crisis* 4 (October 1912): 287–89.

38. W. E. B. Du Bois, *Brownies' Book* 1 (January 1920): 23–25; Du Bois, *Brownies' Book* 1 (August 1920): 234; and Du Bois, *Brownies' Book* 2 (February 1921): 52–53.

39. W. E. B. Du Bois, *Dusk of Dawn: An Essay Toward an Autobiography of a Race Concept* (New York: Schocken, 1968), pp. 271–72.

40. Elinor Desverney Sinnette " 'The Brownies' Book': A Pioneer Publication for Children," in John Henrik Clarke, Esther Jackson, Ernest Kaiser, and J. H. O'Dell, eds., *Black Titan: W. E. B. Du Bois*, pp. 164–75 (Boston: Beacon Press, 1970).

41. W. E. B. Du Bois, letter published in the *New York Globe*, September 8, 1883.

42. W. E. B. Du Bois, letters published in the *New York Globe*, December 6, 1884, and December 27, 1884.

43. W. E. B. Du Bois, *Moon* (March 1906). The only copy in existence is available at the Moreland Room of the library at Howard University, Washington, D.C.

44. W. E. B. Du Bois, "Negro Writers," *Crisis* 19 (April 1920): 298–99.

45. W. E. B. Du Bois, "An Institute of Negro Art," *Crisis* 24 (June 1922): 58–59.

46. W. E. B. Du Bois, "The Du Bois Literary Prize," *Crisis* 38 (April 1931): 137.

47. See W. E. B. Du Bois, *The Quest of the Silver Fleece: A Novel* (Chicago: A. C. McClurg, 1911).

48. See W. E. B. Du Bois, *Dark Princess: A Romance* (New York: Harcourt, Brace, 1928); and Manning Marable, *W. E. B. Du Bois: Black Radical Democrat* (Boston: Twayne, 1986), p. 133.

49. See W. E. B. Du Bois, *The Black Flame: A Trilogy* (New York: Mainstream Publishers): Book 1, *The Ordeal of Mansart* (1957); Book 2, *Mansart Builds a School* (1959); Book 3, *Worlds of Color* (1961).

50. W. E. B. Du Bois, "The Song of the Smoke," *Horizon* 1 (February 1907): 4–6.

51. W. E. B. Du Bois, "The Tragedy of Atlanta, From the Point of View of the Negroes," *World Today* 11 (November 1906): 1173–75.

52. W. E. B. Du Bois, "A Litany of Atlanta," *The Independent* 61 (October 11, 1906): 856–58.

53. Horne, *Black and Red*, pp. 256–59, 266.

54. "Says Dr. DuBois Would Have Faced Charges," *Afro-American*, May 20,

1944, quoted in W. E. B. Du Bois, *The Correspondence of W. E. B. Du Bois*, Vol. 2, *Selections, 1934–1944*, ed. Herbert Aptheker (Amherst: University of Massachusetts Press, 1976), pp. 401–2.

55. Du Bois, *Dusk of Dawn*, p. 94.

56. Du Bois, *Black Reconstruction in America*, p. 703.

5. The Black Faith of W. E. B. Du Bois

Originally published with the title "The Black Faith of W. E. B. Du Bois: Sociocultural and Political Dimensions of Black Religion," *Southern Quarterly* 23, no. 1 (Spring 1985): 15–33.

1. W. E. B. Du Bois, "Immortality," in Sydney Strong, ed., *We Believe in Immortality* (New York: Coward-McCann, 1929), p. 18. Despite the title of the book that includes his essay, Du Bois observed, "My thought on personal immortality is easily explained, I do not know."

2. W. E. B. Du Bois, *The Autobiography of W. E. B. Du Bois: A Soliloquy on Viewing My Life from the Last Decade of Its First Century* (New York: International Publishers, 1968), p. 124.

3. W. E. B. Du Bois, As the Crow Flies, *Amsterdam News*, October 24, 1941.

4. Du Bois, *Autobiography*, p. 57.

5. "Great Barrington News" and "From the Berkshire Hills," *New York Globe*, September 29, 1883; December 29, 1883; and November 22, 1884.

6. W. E. B. Du Bois, Introduction to Milton Rogovin, "Store Front Churches," *Aperture* 10, no. 2 (1962).

7. W. E. B. Du Bois, *Dusk of Dawn: An Essay Toward an Autobiography of a Race Concept* (New York: Schocken, 1968), pp. 107–8; and Du Bois, *Autobiography*, pp. 67, 81–82. Writing at the age of ninety, Du Bois added: "I never did, and indeed, so strong was the expression of her wishes that never in my life since have I felt at ease drinking at a bar. . . . When the Murphy crusade for total abstinence swept the valley, I as a boy was one of the first to don the blue ribbon. I kept the pledge until I went as a student to Germany."

8. Du Bois, *Autobiography*, pp. 83, 88. For a time, Du Bois and his mother lived "next to the horsesheds of the Congregational church." Du Bois's family was Episcopalian, but he and his mother joined the church, becoming its only "colored communicants."

9. Ibid., pp. 82, 89–90.

10. Ibid., p. 103; Du Bois, *Dusk of Dawn*, p. 22; and W. E. B. Du Bois, *The Correspondence of W. E. B. Du Bois*, Vol. 1, *Selections, 1877–1934*, ed. Herbert Aptheker (Amherst: University of Massachusetts Press, 1973), p. 5.

11. Du Bois, *Autobiography*, pp. 107, 280.

12. Du Bois, *Correspondence*, 1:5, 18–19.

13. Du Bois, *Autobiography*, pp. 110–11, 127.

14. Ibid., pp. 114, 115–16.

15. "My journey was done, and behind me lay hill and dale and Life and Death. How shall man measure Progress there where the dark-faced Josie lies? How many heartfuls of sorrow shall balance a bushel of wheat? . . . And all this life and love and strife and failure,—is it the twilight of nightfall or the flush of some faint-dawning day?" (W. E. B. Du Bois, *The Souls of Black Folk: Essays and Sketches* [Greenwich: Fawcett, 1961], p. 64).

16. Du Bois, *Autobiography*, pp. 118–20, 280.

17. Ibid., pp. 114, 119–20.

18. Du Bois, *The Souls of Black Folk*, pp. 141–42.

19. Ibid., pp. 141–43, 187–91.

20. Ibid., p. 143.

21. Du Bois, *Autobiography*, pp. 124, 127.

22. Ibid., p. 133.

23. Francis L. Broderick, *W. E. B. Du Bois: Negro Leader in a Time of Crisis* (Stanford, Calif.: Stanford University Press, 1959), pp. 18–19, 23.

24. Du Bois, *Autobiography*, p. 186.

25. Ibid., pp. 187–88.

26. As quoted in Du Bois, *Autobiography*, pp. 209–10.

27. W. E. B. Du Bois, *The Philadelphia Negro: A Social Study* (Philadelphia: Ginn, 1899); Du Bois, *The Negroes of Farmville, Virginia: A Social Study* (Washington, D.C.: Government Printing Office, January 1898); Du Bois, ed., *Some Efforts of American Negroes for Their Own Social Betterment: Report of an Investigation under the Direction of Atlanta University: Together with the Proceedings of the Third Conference for the Study of the Negro Problems, held at Atlanta University, May 25–28, 1898* (Atlanta: Atlanta University Press, 1898).

28. Du Bois, *The Souls of Black Folk*, p. 144.

29. Ibid.

30. As quoted in August Meier, *Negro Thought in America, 1880–1915: Racial Ideologies in the Age of Booker T. Washington* (Ann Arbor: University of Michigan Press, 1963), p. 190.

31. Du Bois, *Correspondence*, 1:131.

32. W. E. B. Du Bois, "Credo," *Independence* 57 (October 6, 1904), p. 787; reprinted in Du Bois, *Darkwater: Voices from Within the Veil*, 1920 (New York: AMS, 1969), pp. 3–4.

33. W. E. B. Du Bois, "Postscript," *Crisis* 34 (July 1927): 167–68.

34. W. E. B. Du Bois, Preface to Reverdy C. Ransom, *The Negro: The Hope or the Despair of Christianity* (Boston: Ruth Hill, 1935).

35. W. E. B. Du Bois, "The Negro and the Church," *Crisis* 6 (October 1913): 291; Du Bois, "Will the Church Remove the Color Line?" *Christian Century* 48 (December 9, 1931): 1554–56.

36. W. E. B. Du Bois, "Christianity," *Horizon* 1 (June 1907): 3–10.

37. W. E. B. Du Bois, "Opinion" and "The Nine New Bishops," *Crisis* 20 (August 1920): 165–66, 182.

38. W. E. B. Du Bois, "The Methodists," *Crisis* 12 (July 1916): 137; "Opinion," *Crisis* 29 (November 1924): 7.

39. W. E. B. Du Bois, "A Chronicle of Race Relations, 1939," *Phylon* 1 (1940): 90–97.

40. Du Bois, *Correspondence*, 1:308–11.

41. W. E. B. Du Bois, "The Church," *Crisis* 11 (April 1916): 302.

42. W. E. B. Du Bois, "Editorial," *Fisk Herald* 5 (January 1888): 8.

43. W. E. B. Du Bois, "Careers Open to College-Bred Negroes. Two Addresses Delivered by Alumni of Fisk University, in Connection with the Anniversary Exercises of Their Alma Mater." (Nashville: Fisk University, 1898), pp. 1–14.

44. W. E. B. Du Bois, "The Religion of the Negro," *New World* 9 (December 1900): 614–25; reprinted as "Of the Faith of the Fathers" in Du Bois, *The Souls of Black Folk*, pp. 140–51.

45. W. E. B. Du Bois, "Postscript," *Crisis* 38 (June 1931): 207.

46. W. E. B. Du Bois, ed., *The Negro Church: Report on a Social Study Made under the Direction of Atlanta University: Together with the Proceedings of the Eighth Conference for the Study of Negro Problems, held at Atlanta University, May 26, 1903* (Atlanta: Atlanta University Press, 1903).

47. W. E. B. Du Bois, "Men of the Month," *Crisis* 12 (May 1916); 18.

48. Meier, *Negro Thought in America*, p. 180, 218–21.

49. Ibid., pp. 186–87. In 1912 Walters was president of the Colored National Democratic League, which campaigned actively for Woodrow Wilson. Walters solicited a statement from the Democratic presidential nominee pledging his commitment to the civil rights of blacks. On the basis of this letter, which Walters later published in his autobiography, Du Bois tendered his resignation from the Socialist Party and publicly supported Wilson. Once elected, Wilson implemented a strict segregation policy throughout the federal government and repudiated his promises to the small black electorate (Alexander Walters, *My Life and Work* [New York: Fleming H. Revell, 1917], p. 126); Du Bois, *Correspondence*, 1:211–13; Du Bois, *Autobiography*, p. 264.

50. W. E. B. Du Bois, "Postscript," *Crisis* 36 (January 1929): 21–22.

51. W. E. B. Du Bois, "Postscript," *Crisis* 39 (July 1932): 234–35; Du Bois, As the Crow Flies; Du Bois, "The Winds of Time," *Chicago Defender*, January 4, 1947.

52. W. E. B. Du Bois, *A Bibliography of Negro Folk Songs* (Atlanta: Atlanta University Press, 1903).

53. W. E. B. Du Bois, "John Work: Martyr and Singer," *Crisis* 32 (May 1926): 32–34; Du Bois, "Postscript," *Crisis* 34 (July 1927): 167; Du Bois, "Men of the Month," *Crisis* 12 (May 1916): 18; and Du Bois, "Men of the Month," *Crisis* 3 (March 1912): 190.

54. W. E. B. Du Bois, "The Black Man Brings His Gifts," *Survey Graphic* 53 (March 1, 1925): 655–57. Handy was quite pleased with Du Bois's comments, and on April 7, 1925, he forwarded an autographed copy of his collection, *Blues: An*

Anthology, to the black leader. Handy noted, "The service you are rendering our Race in particular and the American people in general . . . is incalculable" (Du Bois, *Correspondence*, 1:313).

55. At Fisk University, Du Bois became a member of the Mozart Society. Even late in life he affirmed, "It did great things for my education" (Du Bois, *Autobiography*, p. 123).

56. Du Bois, *Correspondence*, 1:328–29.

57. W. E. B. Du Bois, "Men of the Month," *Crisis* 15 (March 1918): 229–31.

58. W. E. B. Du Bois, "Our Music," *Crisis* 40 (July 1933): 165.

59. W. E. B. Du Bois, Editorial in *Crisis* 7 (December 1913): 80–81; Du Bois, "The Sermon on the Tower," *Crisis* 31 (December 1925): 59; Du Bois, *Darkwater*, pp. 123–33.

60. Du Bois, As the Crow Flies; Du Bois, "John Brown and Christmas," *Crisis* 5 (December 1909): 1–3; Du Bois, "Postscript," *Crisis* 35 (June 1928): 203–4.

61. W. E. B. Du Bois, "Pan-Africa," *People's Voice* [New York] (February 7, 1948); Du Bois, "Shall We Fight for Freedom?" *Chicago Defender*, April 13, 1946. Du Bois occasionally suggested in his writings that Christ should appear again, but only as a Negro (Du Bois, As the Crow Flies).

62. Herbert Aptheker, "The Historian," in Rayford W. Logan, ed., *W. E. B. Du Bois: A Profile*, pp. 249–73 (New York: Hill and Wang, 1971).

63. August Meier and other historians view the contradictory strands of Du Bois's public career as "an ambivalence that is perhaps the central motif in his ideological biography." The duality they describe is fundamental to the political, social, and psychological behavior of most blacks who live and work in an institutionally racist society. Du Bois's theoretical achievement is his dialectical unity of opposites, the ability to create sound political programs on the quicksand of racist violence and segregation (Meier, *Negro Thought in America*, p. 190).

64. W. E. B. Du Bois, "St. Francis of Assisi," *Voice of the Negro* 4 (October 1906): 419–26.

6. The Pan-Africanism of W. E. B. Du Bois

Originally published in Bernard Bell, Emily Grosholz, and James Stewart, eds., *W. E. B. Du Bois on Race and Culture: Philosophy, Politics and Poetics*, pp. 193–218 (New York and London: Routledge, 1996).

1. C. L. R. James, *The Future in the Present: Selected Writings* (Westport, Conn.: Lawrence Hill, 1990), pp. 202, 208.

2. Kwame Nkrumah, *Revolutionary Path* (New York: International Publishers, 1973), pp. 42–43; Kwame Nkrumah, *Africa Must Unite* (New York: International Publishers, 1970), pp. 122–33, 135.

3. Harold R. Isaacs, "Pan-Africanism as 'Romantic Racism,'" in Rayford W. Logan, ed., *W. E. B. Du Bois: A Profile*, pp. 213, 240, 242 (New York: Hill and Wang, 1971).

4. Francis L. Broderick, *W. E. B. Du Bois: Negro Leader in a Time of Crisis* (Stanford: Stanford University Press, 1959), pp. 130, 135–36, 228.

5. Herbert Aptheker, "The Historian," in Logan, *W. E. B. Du Bois*, pp. 258–60.

6. W. E. B. du Bois, *Dusk of Dawn: An Essay Toward An Autobiography of a Race Concept* (New York: Schocken, 1968), pp. 115–16.

7. Ibid., p. 116.

8. Ibid., p. 111.

9. Isaacs, "Pan-Africanism as 'Romantic Racism,'" p. 223.

10. Broderick, *W. E. B. Du Bois*, p. 16.

11. Ibid., p. 20.

12. Not until the publication of Ron T. Takaki's book *A Pro-Slavery Crusade: The Agitation to Re-open the African Slave Trade* (New York: Free Press, 1970) was there another examination of this issue in any substantial manner.

13. Review by Stephen B. Weeks, *American Historical Review* 2 (April 1897): 555–59.

14. William Claypole and John Robottom, *Caribbean Story*, Book 2, *The Inheritors* (London: Longman, 1981), pp. 79–80.

15. Manning Marable, "Booker T. Washington and African Nationalism," *Phylon* 25 (December 1974): 398. Also see Louis R. Harlan, "Booker T. Washington and the White Man's Burden," *American Historical Review* 71 (January 1966): 441–67.

16. Claypole and Robottom, *Caribbean Story*, p. 80; and W. E. B. Du Bois, *The World and Africa: An Inquiry Into the Part Which Africa Has Played in World History* (New York: International Publishers, 1965), pp. 7–8.

17. Robert A. Hill, ed., *The Marcus Garvey and Universal Negro Improvement Association Papers* (Berkeley: University of California Press, 1983), 1:534.

18. Review in *Political Science Quarterly* 18 (December 1903): 695–97.

19. Review in *The Nation* 111 (September 25, 1920): 350–52.

20. W. E. B. Du Bois, "The Black Soldier," *Crisis* 16 (June 1918): 2.

21. Isaacs, "Pan-Africanism as 'Romantic Racism,'" p. 238.

22. W. E. B. Du Bois, "Migration," *Crisis* 7 (February 1914): 190; Du Bois, "The Latest Craze," *Crisis* 11 (January 1916): 133–34, On Chief Alfred Sam, see William E. Bittle and Gilbert Geis, *The Longest Way Home: Chief Alfred C. Sam's Back-to-Africa Movement* (Detroit: Wayne State University Press, 1964); J. Ayo Langley, "Chief Sam's African Movement and Race Consciousness in West Africa," *Phylon* 32 (Summer 1971): 164–78; and "Chief Alfred Sam," in Hill, *The Marcus Garvey and Universal Negro Improvement Association Papers*, 1:536–47.

23. For example, "Germany," *Crisis* 11 (February 1916): 184.

24. W. E. B. Du Bois, "The African Roots of the War," *Atlantic Monthly* 115 (May 1915): 707–14.

25. Broderick, *W. E. B. Du Bois*, p. 129.

26. J. P. Tumulty to W. E. B. Du Bois, November 29, 1918, W. E. B. Du Bois, *The Correspondence of W. E. B. Du Bois*, Vol. 1, *Selections, 1877–1934*, ed. Herbert Aptheker (Amherst: University of Massachusetts Press, 1973), pp. 231—32.

27. Du Bois, *Dusk of Dawn*, p. 260.

28. Ibid., p. 261. Moton was probably distressed to learn that the preeminent opponent of the "Tuskegee philosophy" was to be his roommate aboard the *Orizaba*.

29. "The Future of Africa," *Advocate of Peace* 81 (January 1919): 12–13; and "Letters from Dr. Du Bois," December 8 and 14, 1918, in *Crisis* 17 (February 1919): 161–62.

30. F. P. Schoonmaker, Major, General Staff, to Intelligence Officers, Secret Memo, January 1, 1919, Du Bois, *Correspondence*, 1:232. Du Bois soon obtained a copy of the secret order, which was stamped by division headquarters.

31. W. E. B. Du Bois, "The Pan-African Movement," in Philip S. Foner, ed., *W. E. B. Du Bois Speaks: Speeches and Addresses, 1920–1963*, p. 163 (New York: Pathfinder Press, 1972).

32. Du Bois, *Dusk of Dawn*, p. 261.

33. George Padmore, *Pan-Africanism or Communism* (Garden City, N.Y.: Pathfinder Press, 1972), p. 98.

34. James, *The Future in the Present*, p. 207.

35. Of the heroic conduct among French West African troops during the war, Du Bois wrote: "Against the banked artillery of the magnificent German Army were sent untrained and poorly armed Senegalese. They marched at command in unwavering ranks, raising the war cry in a dozen different Sudanese tongues. When the artillery belched they shivered, but never faltered. They marched straight into death; the war cries became fainter and fainter and dropped into silence as not a single black man was left living on that field" (*The World and Africa*, p. 7).

36. Padmore, *Pan-Africanism or Communism*, pp. 98–99.

37. Du Bois, *The World and Africa*, p. 10.

38. Du Bois, *Dusk of Dawn*, p. 262.

39. Du Bois, *The World and Africa*, p. 10. Padmore notes that "the American officials in President Wilson's entourage were afraid that the Congress might discuss, among other things, the lynching of Negroes in the United States and the treatment of Afro-American troops in France. The American statesmen had good reason to be alarmed, for apart from maintaining racial segregation between black and white troops serving under the Stars and Stripes, the US Army authorities in France tried to impose their racial prejudices on the French people" (Padmore, *Pan-Africanism or Communism*, pp. 99–100). Also see "The Denial of Passports," *Crisis* 17 (March 1919): 237–38; and "Negro Passports Refused," *Messenger* 2 (March 1919): 4.

40. Du Bois, *The World and Africa*, p. 10.

41. James, *The Future in the Present*, p. 207.

42. Du Bois, *The World and Africa*, pp. 11–12.

43. Nkrumah, *Africa Must Unite*, p. 133.

44. Padmore, *Pan-Africanism or Communism*, p. 103.

45. Ibid., pp. 104–5. In his capacity as Pan-African Conference secretary, Du Bois also notified U.S. Secretary of State Charles Evans Hughes and Sir Auckland

Geddes, British ambassador to the United States, that a second meeting would be held. He emphasized to Hughes that it "has nothing to do with the so-called Garvey movement and contemplates neither force nor revolution in its program." See Du Bois to Hughes, June 23, 1921, and Hughes to Du Bois, July 8, 1921, Du Bois, *Correspondence*, 1:250–51.

46. Du Bois, "The Pan-African Movement," in Foner, *W. E. B. Du Bois Speaks*, pp. 169–71.

47. Du Bois, *The World and Africa*, pp. 240–41; Padmore, *Pan-Africanism or Communism*, p. 112.

48. Du Bois, *The World and Africa*, p. 240.

49. Padmore, *Pan-Africanism or Communism*, pp. 110–11.

50. Du Bois, *Dusk of Dawn*, pp. 277–78.

51. Hill, *The Marcus Garvey and Universal Negro Improvement Association Papers*, 1:cxv–cxvii.

52. Extracts from Garvey speech, Baltimore, December 18, 1918, in ibid., p. 332.

53. The other delegates selected were the black socialist journalist Asa Philip Randolph and anti-lynching activist Ida B. Wells Barnett (D. Davidson, "Bureau of Investigation Reports," December 5, 1918, in ibid., pp. 377–81).

54. Garvey scholar Robert A. Hill suggests that Garvey himself wrote these speeches. Garvey, Editorial, *Negro World*, March 1, 1919, in ibid., pp. 377–81.

55. Cadet's charges against Du Bois had been sent on either March 22 or 23, 1919, but Du Bois had left France on March 22. Cadet quickly tired of pursuing the UNIA's agenda at the peace conference and for most of the remainder of the year worked in Paris as an auto mechanic. He returned to Haiti in late 1919 and eventually "became a vodun high priest of the cult of Damballah (the serpent god)" (ibid., pp. 308, 393).

56. "Addresses Denouncing W. E. B. Du Bois," *Negro World*, April 5, 1919, in ibid., pp. 395–96.

57. Ibid., p. 399.

58. W. E. B. Du Bois, "Marcus Garvey," *Crisis* 21 (December 1920): 58–60, and 21 (January 1921): 112–15.

59. Padmore, *Pan-Africanism or Communism*, p. 106.

60. Ibid., pp. 106–7.

61. Theodore G. Vincent, *Black Power and the Garvey Movement* (San Francisco: Ramparts Press, 1972), p. 58.

62. John Henrik Clarke, ed., *Marcus Garvey and the Vision of Africa* (New York: Vintage Books, 1974), p. 97. As Clarks writes, Garvey and Du Bois were both "Pan-Africanists and both of them had as their objectives the freedom and redemption of African people everywhere. Yet, there was no meeting of minds on the methods of reaching these desirable goals" (p. 97).

63. Du Bois, *The World and Africa*, p. 241.

64. Ibid., p. 242; Padmore, *Pan-Africanism or Communism*, pp. 117–20.

65. Nkrumah, *Africa Must Unite*, p. 133. Also see W. E. B. Du Bois, "Pan-Africa in Portugal," *Crisis* 27 (February 1924): 170.

66. W. E. B. Du Bois, "Opinion," *Crisis* 32 (October 1926): 283.

67. Du Bois, *The World and Africa*, p. 242.

68. Du Bois, "Opinion," *Crisis* 32 (October 1926): 283.

69. Padmore, *Pan-Africanism or Communism*, p. 121.

70. Du Bois, *The World and Africa*, p. 243.

71. "The Pan-African Congresses," *Crisis* 34 (October 1927): 263–64. Marx's statement on race and class oppression is "Labor with a white skin cannot emancipate itself where labor with a black skin is branded." In 1914 Du Bois stated the same concept: "So long as black laborers are slaves, white laborers cannot be free." See Manning Marable, "Why Black Americans Are Not Socialists," in Phyllis and Julius Jacobson, eds., *Socialist Perspectives*, pp. 63–95 (New York: Karz-Cohl, 1983).

72. Du Bois, *The World and Africa*, p. 243.

73. Du Bois, "Postscript," *Crisis* 36 (December 1929): 423–24.

74. Du Bois, "The Winds of Time," *Chicago Defender*, September 29, 1945. Historians disagree as to the actual relationship between Williams and Padmore. Padmore himself claimed kinship to Williams in a personal letter to Du Bois, but Padmore biographer James R. Hooker confirms that the two men were not related. See James R. Hooker, *Black Revolutionary: George Padmore's Path from Communism to Pan-Africanism* (New York: Praeger, 1967).

75. Azinna Nwafor, "The Revolutionary as Historian: Padmore and Pan-Africanism," in Padmore, *Pan-Africanism or Communism*, p. xxv.

76. Padmore, *Pan-Africanism or Communism*, pp. 111, 117.

77. Robert A. Hill, "C. L. R. James in England, 1932–1938," *Urgent Tasks*, no. 12 (Summer 1981): 19–27.

78. Padmore, *Pan-Africanism or Communism*, p. 123.

79. W. E. B. Du Bois, *The Autobiography of W. E. B. Du Bois: A Soliloquy on Viewing My Life from the Last Decade of Its First Century* (New York: International Publishers, 1968), pp. 344–45.

80. W. E. B. Du Bois, As the Crow Flies, *Amsterdam News*, June 22, 1940; As the Crow Flies, *Amsterdam News*, December 26, 1942.

81. W. E. B. Du Bois to George A. Finch, February 11, 1941, W. E. B. Du Bois, *The Correspondence of W. E. B. Du Bois*, Vol. 2, *Selections, 1934–1944*, ed. Herbert Aptheker (Amherst: University of Massachusetts Press, 1976), p. 277.

82. W. E. B. Du Bois to Amy Jacques Garvey, February 9, 1944; Garvey to Du Bois, April 4, 1944; Garvey to Du Bois, April 5, 1944; Du Bois to Paul Robeson, April 7, 1944; Du Bois to Harold Moody, April 7, 1944; Du Bois to Garvey, April 8, 1944; Garvey to Du Bois, April 24, 1944; Garvey to Du Bois, April 26, 1944, in ibid., pp. 375–83.

83. Du Bois, *Autobiography*, p. 326.

84. James became the leading black theoretician of the Workers Party during the early 1940s. But he and his faction, the "Johnson-Forest tendency," feuded with

the orthodox Trotskyists over the nature of the Soviet Union and other issues related to race, class, and social change in the Third World and in advanced capitalist societies. James's other associates of the period who became Marxist theorists of note include Grace Lee (now Grace Lee Boggs) and Ray Dunayevskaya. See Paul Buhle, "Marxism in the USA," and James and Grace Lee Boggs, "A Critical Reminiscence," *Urgent Tasks*, no. 12 (Summer 1981): 28–38, 86–87; C. L. R. James, *Modern Politics: Selected Writings* (Westport, Conn.: Lawrence Hill, 1980); and C. L. R. James, *Nkrumah and the Ghana Revolution* (Westport, Conn.: Lawrence Hill, 1977).

85. C. L. R. James, "Kwame Nkrumah: Founder of African Emancipation," *Black World* 21 (July 1972): 4–10.

86. Padmore, *Pan-Africanism or Communism*, pp. 132–33.

87. W. E. B. Du Bois to J. B. Danquah, September 12, 1944; Du Bois to Norman W. Manley, October 10, 1944, in W. E. B. Du Bois, *The Correspondence of W. E. B. Du Bois*, Vol. 3, *Selections, 1944–1963*, ed. Herbert Aptheker (Amherst: University of Massachusetts Press, 1978), pp. 1–3.

88. Du Bois had learned about the proposed meeting from a press release published in the March 17, 1945, issue of the *Chicago Defender*. It is curious why Padmore chose not to inform Du Bois directly. Aptheker suggests that "while Du Bois and Padmore knew each other before, during the work that led to this congress they became friends, though significant disagreements marked their relationships" (Du Bois to Padmore, March 22, 1945, in ibid., pp. 56–57).

89. Du Bois to Padmore, April 11, 1945; Padmore to Du Bois, April 12, 1945; Du Bois to Padmore, July 9, 1945; Du Bois to Padmore, July 20, 1945; Padmore to Du Bois, August 17, 1945, in ibid., pp. 60–61.

90. Padmore, *Pan-Africanism or Communism*, pp. 139–48.

91. Ibid., p. 139.

92. Ibid., pp. 141–42.

93. Ibid., p. 115.

94. Du Bois, *The World and Africa*, pp. 258–59.

7. Political Intellectuals in the African Diaspora

1. Antonio Gramsci, *Selections from the Prison Notebooks*, ed. Quinton Hoare and G. Nowell Smith (London: International Publishers, 1971), p. 3.

2. Ibid., p. 12.

3. Ibid., p. 10.

4. Tony Martin, *Literary Garveyism: Garvey, Black Arts, and the Harlem Renaissance* (Dover, Mass.: Majority Press, 1983), p. 92.

5. Ibid., p. 15.

6. Claude McKay, *The Negroes in America*, ed. Alan L. McLeod (Port Washington, N.Y.: Kennikat Press, 1970), p. 73.

7. Reprinted in Addison Gayle, Jr., ed., *The Black Aesthetic* (Garden City, N.Y.: Anchor Books, 1972), p. 167.

8. Martin, *Literary Garveyism*, p. 8.

9. Ibid., pp. 31–32, 39–49, 64, 77.

10. P. Olisanwuche Esedebe, *Pan-Africanism: The Idea and Movement, 1776–1963* (Washington, D.C.: Howard University Press. 1982), pp. 95–96, 100, 104.

11. Ibid., pp. 105–6.

8. Peace and Black Liberation: The Contributions of W. E. B. Du Bois

Originally published in *Science and Society* 47 (Winter 1983–1984): 15–33.

1. See Mark Sapir, "Jobs with Peace: Extending the Peace Movement," *WIN* (February 1983): 8–10; Special Issue, "Directions for Disarmament," *WIN* (November 1982); Employment Research Associates, *The Price of the Pentagon: The Industrial and Commercial Impact of the 1981 Military Budget* (Lansing, Mich., 1982).

2. Melvin B. Tolson, "A Legend of Versailles," in Dudley Randall, ed., *The Black Poets* (New York, 1971), p. 118.

3. Ibid., p. 82.

4. Andrew Young, "Tribute to Paul Robeson," in *Paul Robeson: Tributes, Selected Writings* (New York: International Publishers, 1976), p. 27.

5. This is *not*, by any means, to minimize the many decisive contributions of Paul Robeson to the legacy of the American peace movements. The point here is that Robeson and Du Bois played different roles in the same struggle. Robeson was much more influential than Du Bois as a cultural and political symbol of resistance.

6. W. E. B. Du Bois, "Credo," *Independent* 57 (October 15, 1904): 787.

7. W. E. B. Du Bois, "Books," *Horizon* 1 (June 1907): 10. This is not to say that Du Bois was ever really a pacifist. As he noted in his autobiography, "I revered life. I have never killed a bird nor shot a rabbit. . . . Nearly all of my schoolmates in the South carried pistols. I never owned one. I could never conceive of myself killing a human being. But in 1906 I rushed from Alabama to Atlanta where my wife and six-year-old child were living. A mob had raged for days killing Negroes. I bought a Winchester double-barreled shotgun and two dozen rounds of shells filled with buckshot. If a white mob had stepped on the campus where I lived I would without hesitation have sprayed their guts over the grass" (Du Bois, *The Autobiography of W. E. B. Du Bois: A Soliloquy on Viewing My Life from the Last Decade of Its First Century* (New York: International Publishers, 1968), p. 286.

8. W. E. B. Du Bois, *Brownies' Book* 2 (September 1921): 271–72.

9. *New York Times*, October 27, 1931.

10. W. E. B. Du Bois, "Peace, Freedom's Road for Oppressed Peoples," *Worker*, April 17, 1949, p. 8.

11. W. E. B. Du Bois, "The World Peace Movement," *New World Review* (May 1955): 9–14.

12. W. E. B. Du Bois, "The African Roots of War," *Atlantic Monthly* 115 (May 1915): 707–14.

13. W. E. B. Du Bois, "Peace," *Crisis* 10 (May 1915): 27.

14. Robert C. Tucker, ed., *The Lenin Anthology* (New York: Norton, 1975), pp. 261, 266–67.

15. W. E. B. Du Bois, "Opinion," *Crisis* 26 (October 1923): 248. It seems evident that Du Bois did not actually begin to study Lenin's imperialism until the Cold War, when he was in his eighties. On December 21, 1954, he asked Marxist historian Herbert Aptheker for "the best logical follow-up" to Lenin's study. "It leaves me a little dissatisfied, or perhaps I would better say, a little at sea in my own thinking." See Du Bois to Aptheker, December 21, 1954; Aptheker to Du Bois, December 24, 1954, in Du Bois, *The Correspondence of W. E. B. Du Bois*, Vol. 3, *Selections 1944–1963*, ed. Herbert Aptheker (Amherst: University of Massachusetts Press, 1978), p. 378.

16. W. E. B. Du Bois, "The Winds of Time," *Chicago Defender*, January 11, 1947.

17. W. E. B. Du Bois, "Opinion," *Crisis* 31 (March 1926): 215.

18. W. E. B. Du Bois, "The Union of Colour," *Aryan Path (Bombay)* 7 (October 1936): 483–84.

19. W. E. B. Du Bois, As the Crow Flies, *Amsterdam News*, February 14, 1942; February 21, 1942; May 9, 1942.

20. W. E. B. Du Bois, As the Crow Flies, *Amsterdam News*, March 8, 1947.

21. W. E. B. Du Bois, Review of *Crusader Without Nonviolence*, by L. D. Reddick, *National Guardian*, November 9, 1959. In other essays, of course, Du Bois was very positive in his opinion of King and his version of Gandhi's *satyagraha*. See Du Bois, "Gandhi and the American Negroes," *Gandhi Marg* 1 (July 1957): 1–4; and "Portrait of a Scholar," *Pittsburgh Courier*, August 24, 1957, p. 6.

22. W. E. B. Du Bois, "Peace," *Crisis* 6 (May 1913): 26.

23. W. E. B. Du Bois, "The Realities in Africa: European Profit or Negro Development," *Foreign Affairs* 21 (July 1943): 721–32.

24. W. E. B. Du Bois, "A Chronicle of Race Relations," *Phylon* 5 (1944): 68–69.

25. W. E. B. Du Bois, "Imperialism, United Nations, and Colonial People," *New Leader*, December 30, 1944: 5. Max Gordon, a prominent Communist Party writer, attacked this essay in the January 5, 1945, issue of the *Daily Worker*. Significantly, James W. Ford, a founder of the American Negro Labor Congress and the Communist Party's vice presidential candidate in 1932, 1936, and 1940, privately apologized to Du Bois for Gordon's remarks. "I had hoped to make some comment on some of your views on the Colonial question with which I do not agree." He added, "Nevertheless, I want you to know that I disagree entirely with . . . the *Daily Worker* article by Max Gordon, who incidentally expressed his own individual opinion." See Ford to Du Bois, January 8, 1945, Du Bois to Ford, January 17, 1945, in Du Bois, *Correspondence*, 3:28.

26. W. E. B. Du Bois, "The Rape of Africa," *American Negro* 1 (February 1956): 6–13; and Du Bois, "Africa and World Peace," *Bulletin of the World Peace Council* (June 1960): 16. During these years Du Bois wrote dozens of articles on the African liberation movements and the relationships between the end of Euro-

pean colonialism and the realization of world peace. See, for example, Du Bois, "Pan Africa," *People's Choice*, April 12 and 26, 1947, May 3, 1947, and various other issues through March 6, 1948. Also see Du Bois, "Colonial Peoples and the Fight for Peace," *New Africa* (April 1949); Du Bois, "To Save the World—Save Africa!" *New Africa* (May 1949); and Du Bois, "Repression Madness Rules South Africa," *New Africa* (May–June 1950).

27. Kwame Nkrumah to Du Bois, November 4, 1946, Du Bois, *Correspondence*, 3:158–59.

28. Du Bois, "The Winds of Time," *Chicago Defender*, June 23, 1945.

29. The council had been formed almost a decade before by Max Hergan, a black activist in the YMCA, and Robeson. Du Bois had been interested in working with the council for some time but was rebuffed by the politically conservative Yergan. As Du Bois informed Pan-Africanist leader George Padmore in 1946, the council "has a constituency and is doing good work. It is charged that the Council is financed by the Communists, which is probably true. I wanted their cooperation but was not able to ask them officially because of the hesitation of the NAACP." Finally, with Yergan's departure from the council and Du Bois's firing from the NAACP, joint work was possible. See Du Bois to Padmore, July 12, 1946, Du Bois, *Correspondence*, 3:141–44.

30. Du Bois, *Autobiography*, p. 345.

31. Ibid., p. 350.

32. Ibid., pp. 350–55.

33. Ibid., pp. 358–59.

34. Ibid., pp. 361–62.

35. Du Bois to Du Bois Williams (his granddaughter), October 27, 1950, and December 4, 1950; Du Bois to Arthur Shutzer, January 24, 1952; Shutzer to Du Bois, January 28, 1952; Du Bois, *Correspondence*, 3:296–99, 331–32.

36. William E. Foley, Chief, Foreign Agents Registration Section, to Peace Information Center, August 11, 1950; Du Bois to McGrath, undated; Du Bois to Foley, January 1951, Du Bois, *Correspondence*, 3:306–9.

37. Du Bois, *Autobiography*, p. 369.

38. Ibid., pp. 350–55.

39. The NAACP's repudiation of Du Bois hurt him deeply. In his private correspondence to Judge Hubert T. Delany, he admitted, "I have heretofore refrained from any attack upon the NAACP, since it is, in part, my child. But since this indictment the executive officers of the NAACP have warned and frightened their branches from helping in my defense, and on the very day of the verdict, Walter White was telling persons at a meeting in Milwaukee that my guilt was proven by irrefutable evidence in the hands of the Department of Justice" (Du Bois to Delany, December 21, 1951, Du Bois, *Correspondence*, 3:322–23).

40. George Padmore to Du Bois, March 21, 1951; Du Bois to Padmore, April 11, 1951, ibid., pp. 311–13.

41. Frederic Joliot-Curie to Du Bois, November 28, 1951, ibid., p. 320.

42. Du Bois, *Autobiography*, p. 374.

43. Reverdy C. Ransom to the National Council of the Arts, Sciences, and Professions, October 26, 1951, Du Bois, *Correspondence*, 3:317–18.

44. Du Bois to Albert Einstein, November 29, 1951; Hubert T. Delany to Du Bois, November 27, 1951, Du Bois, *Correspondence*, 3:320–21.

45. Du Bois, *Autobiography*, pp. 394–95. Only when Du Bois reached the age of ninety did the NAACP give evidence of some relaxation of its hostility. Hesitantly and somewhat belatedly, it expressed willingness to pay tribute on the occasion of the impressive ninetieth birthday celebration organized, in the main, by left-wing political groups and friends.

46. R. B. Shipley to Du Bois, February 12, 1952, Du Bois, *Correspondence*, 3:332.

47. Du Bois, *Autobiography*, pp. 394–95.

48. W. E. B. Du Bois, "Negroes and the Crisis of Capitalism," *Monthly Review* 4 (April 1953): 478–85.

49. "Du Bois Charges Nixon Trying to Lead Us to War," *Los Angeles Tribune*, June 4, 1954.

50. W. E. B. Du Bois, "Formosa and Peace," *Jewish Life* 9 (March 1955): 20.

51. W. E. B. Du Bois, "Colonialism and the Russian Revolution," *New World Review* (November 1956): 18–22.

52. George Padmore to Du Bois, December 3, 1954; Du Bois to Padmore, December 10, 1954; Du Bois to Padmore, January 27, 1955; Carlton B. Goodlett to Du Bois, June 26, 1957; Du Bois to Goodlett, July 6, 1957; Du Bois to W. A. Domingo, June 11, 1957; Domingo to Du Bois, August 11, 1957, Du Bois, *Correspondence*, 3:373–75, 408–12.

53. Du Bois to Gus Hall, October 1, 1961, Du Bois, *Correspondence*, 3:439–40.

54. Francis L. Broderick, *W. E. B. Du Bois: Negro Leader in a Time of Crisis* (Stanford, Calif.: Stanford University Press, 1959), pp. 228–29.

55. David L. Lewis, *King: A Critical Biography* (New York: Praeger, 1970), p. 376.

9. Harold Washington's Chicago: Race, Class Conflict, and Political Change

Originally published in *Research in Urban Sociology* 1 (1989): 81–105.

1. See Abdul Alkalimat and Doug Gills, "Black Political Protest and the Mayoral Victory of Harold Washington: Chicago Politics, 1983," *Radical America* 17 (October 1983): 11–127; Florence Levinson, *Harold Washington: A Political Biography* (Chicago: Chicago Review Press, 1983); Paul Kleppner, *Chicago Divided: The Making of a Black Mayor* (De Kalb: Northern Illinois University Press, 1985); and Manning Marable, *Black American Politics: From the Washington Marches to Jesse Jackson* (London: Verso, 1985), especially ch. 4, pp. 191–246.

2. Marable, *Black American Politics*, p. 229.

3. "Worst Racial Fears Put to Rest,"in *Mayor Washington's Chicago: A Critical Examination* (Special reprint of a series in the *Chicago Sun-Times*), October 12, 1986.

4. "How Poor Fare with Mayor," ibid., pp. 20–21.

5. David Moberg, "The Man Who Wants to Break the Mold," *Chicago* 32 (October 1983): 171.

6. John Schrag and Diane Reis, "Other Governments Push MBE Programs," *Chicago Reporter* 16 (January 1987): 4. The city's record for equal opportunity for blacks, women, Hispanics, and other minorities improved under Washington, but progress was slow. According to researchers Gregory D. Squires and Wendy Wintermute: "The current structure for implementing contract compliance in the city of Chicago is a kaleidoscope of shifting responsibilities, programs and statistics. Any contract compliance efforts undertaken by the city (and these appear to be few) are at present dispersed throughout the departments with unclear lines of authority. . . . Monitoring is, in fact, impossible, since the necessary information is not systematically collected or reviewed. No information regarding minority employment by city contractors—indeed, no information of any kind regarding city contracts—is readily available for monitoring purposes" (p. 20). See Gregory D. Squires and Wendy Wintermute, *Equal Opportunity in City Contracts: An Examination in Chicago's Contract Compliance Program* (Chicago: Chicago Urban League, 1984).

7. Fred Marc Biddle, "City's Hispanic Businesses Need Help, Study Shows," *Chicago Tribune*, October 6, 1986.

8. Brian Kelly, "The Washington Administration: A Mid-Term Survey," *Chicago* 34 (April 1985): 183; and Harold Washington, "Politics, Plans, and Priorities," *Chicago* 33 (January 1984): 154. Mier is the former director of the Center for Urban Economic Development at the University of Illinois at Chicago.

9. Moberg, "The Man Who Wants to Break the Mold," p. 176.

10. Kelly, "The Washington Administration," p. 183; and Brian Kelly, "Harold Washington's Balancing Act," *Chicago* 34 (April 1985): 200–201.

11. Statement by Richard Saks in "On the Cutting Edge in Chicago Politics," *Forward Motion* 5 (October–December 1986): 16. An excellent background study on the economic factors influencing the Washington administration's strategy is David Flax-Hatch and Wendy Wintermute, *Structural Changes in Illinois Employment: An Analysis of Growth and Decline Industries* (Chicago: Chicago Urban League, 1985).

12. E. R. Shipp, "Chicago's Mayor Can Act As a Majority of One," *New York Times*, May 4, 1986; E. R. Shipp, "Chicago Mayor's Bloc Has Its Debut," *New York Times*, May 10, 1986; Curtis Black, "Three Years After Winning Office, Mayor Washington Wins Power," *Guardian*, May 14, 1986; E. R. Shipp, "Chicago Mayor Backed on Control of Council," *New York Times*, June 14, 1986; and David Fremon, "Religion/Politics: New Mix Makes Hispanic History," *Chicago Reporter* 15 (August 1986): 6–7. Gutierrez consciously "sought relationships with the churches, particularly the evangelical ones" during his successful aldermanic race in 1986. He held prayer vigils, initiated public rallies with prayers, and held breakfast sessions with

clergy. The churches were instrumental in registering several thousand Hispanic voters, most of whom supported Gutierrez.

13. Steve Neal, "Tax Boost Slices Mayor's Lead," *Chicago Tribune*, October 30, 1986; Curtis Black, "Washington Rolls Over White Machine," *Guardian*, October 15, 1986; and Ann Marie Lipinski and James Strong, "Mayor Holds Ax Over Garbage, Health Agencies," *Chicago Tribune*, September 19, 1986. Without a tax hike, the city would have been forced to dismiss 10,666 employees, shutting down one-third of its public mental care centers and half of its health clinics.

14. Andrew H. Malcolm, "Chicago Expecting a Three-Way Campaign," *New York Times*, December 7, 1986; and Curtis Black, "Get Ready for Another Round of Racist Politics," *Guardian*, December 31, 1986.

15. John Kass, "Daley Revives Mayoral Vote Plan," *Chicago Tribune*, November 24, 1986. A September 1986 poll by the *Chicago Tribune* indicated that almost three-fourths of all white voters favored a nonpartisan election, with 17 percent against. Only 23 percent of all black voters polled favored a nonpartisan race.

16. Manuel Galvan, "Mayor to Fight Ballot Ruling," *Chicago Tribune*, August 22, 1986; "Referendum Plan Invalid," *New York Times*, November 2, 1986; and Black, "Get Ready for Another Round of Racist Politics." In July 1986 Washington's supporters on the city council voted to place three advisory referendums on the February 1987 ballot, which technically voided Daley's referendum from the election. Illinois law states that only three referendums may be placed on the ballot of any single election. Chicago Board of Election commissioners ignored this provision of state law, as well as thousands of gross irregularities and forgeries on the referendum petitions.

17. John Kass and Mitchell Locin, "Court Winds Up As a Final Campaign Stop," *Chicago Tribune*, February 24, 1987; and Andrew H. Malcolm, "Chicago Is Electing Candidates for Mayor Today," *New York Times*, February 24, 1987.

18. Steve Neal, "Mayor's Lead Over Byrne Widens in Poll, *Chicago Tribune*, December 22, 1986. In December 1986 the *Tribune's* poll gave Washington a substantial lead over Byrne, 54 to 38 percent.

19. Steve Neal and Jack Houston, "Vrdolyak to Wage Vote 'War,'" *Chicago Tribune*, November 13, 1986; and John Camper, "Hynes Has a Small But Strong Base," *Chicago Tribune*, December 24, 1986.

20. Mitchell Locin, "For Vrdolyak, Fame Is a Drawback," *Chicago Tribune*, December 24, 1986; Malcolm, "Chicago Expecting a Three-Way Campaign," and Andrew H. Malcolm, "Vrdolyak Closer to a Chicago Race," *New York Times*, November 13, 1986.

21. Steve Neal, "Vrdolyak to Join Mayor's Race," *Chicago Tribune*, November 12, 1986; and Steve Neal, "Vrdolyak Targets the Little Guy," *Chicago Tribune*, November 17, 1986.

22. Comments by Luis Gutierrez, in "On the Cutting Edge in Chicago Politics," pp. 22–23.

23. Moberg, "The Man Who Wants to Break the Mold," p. 175. This is not to

suggest that racism was the "ideological glue" that held Vrdolyak's city council together for three years. Patronage and financial interests were the chief motivating factors behind Vrdolyak, Burke, and others. Racial appeals were a cynical tactic to cement the allegiance of white workers and the poor to a political agenda that was antithetical to their own interests.

24. Chip Berlet, "Klan Inspires Violence During Chicago Rallies," *Monitor* 1 (September 1986): 2; and M. Treloar and Julia Zeta, "Stamping Out Racism, Homophobia in Chicago," *Guardian*, July 23, 1986.

25. Black, "Washington Rolls Over White Machine."

26. John Camper, Cheryl Devall, and John Kass, "The Road to City Hall: A Half-Century of Black Political Evolution," *Chicago Tribune*, November 16, 1986.

27. Luis Gutierrez and Robert Starks in "On the Cutting Edge in Chicago Politics," pp. 8, 28.

28. Black, "Get Ready for Another Round of Racist Politics." In November 1986 allies of both Jesse Jackson and Washington sponsored a resolution before the Democratic National Committee (DNC) that would have censured the attempts to create a white united front candidate against the incumbent. The resolution was defeated. Later, DNC chairman Paul Kirk declared that the national party "would support whoever won the Democratic primary."

29. Richard Saks in "On the Cutting Edge in Chicago Politics," p. 18.

30. Neal, "Mayor's Lead Over Byrne Widens in Poll"; and Black, "Get Ready for Another Round of Racist Politics."

31. "Keeping Current," *Chicago Reporter* 16 (March 1987): 10; and John Schrag, "Competing Demands for 'Our Fair Share' Strain Ties That Bind Tenuous Alliance," *Chicago Reporter* 16 (July 1987): 7.

32. Michael Kiefer, "New Faces, Old Dreams," *Chicago* 33 (March 1984): 127–30; Jorge Casuso and Eduardo Camacho, "The Puerto Ricans," *Chicago Reporter* 13 (December 1984): 1–4; Jorge Casuso and Eduardo Camacho, "Hispanics in Chicago: Conclusion," *Chicago Reporter* 14 (April 1985): 1–4. According to the 1980 Census, Cubans clearly represent an elite socioeconomic stratum within the Hispanic community, while Puerto Ricans remain the most oppressed major group, in terms of unemployment, residential discrimination, vocational discrimination, substandard health care, and other criteria. Cubans are disproportionately represented among Chicago's managers and professional class (17.2 percent of all Cubans versus 8.6 percent of Puerto Ricans and 6.4 percent of Mexican Americans), and a large percentage of Cuban families earned more than $30,000 annually in 1980 (29.8 percent versus 16.8 percent for Mexican Americans and 9.2 percent for Puerto Ricans).

33. Schrag, "Competing Demands for 'Our Fair Share,'" pp. 1, 7–8; and David Fremon, "Religion/Politics: New Mix Makes Hispanic History," *Chicago Reporter* 15 (August 1986): 6–7.

34. Kiefer, "New Faces, Old Dreams," pp. 127, 130–33.

35. Schrag, "Competing Demands for 'Our Fair Share,'" p. 8.

36. Kevin B. Blackstone, "Chicago's Arab-Americans Fight Ethnic Stereotypes," *Chicago Reporter* 15 (April 1986): 1–5.

37. Schrag, "Competing Demands for 'Our Fair Share,'" p. 9; and Treloar and Zeta, "Stamping Out Racism, Homophobia in Chicago."

38. Kelly, "Harold Washington's Balancing Act," p. 200; and Curtis Black, "Reelected Mayor to Push 'Action Agenda,'" *Guardian*, April 22, 1987. Jean Mayer, a leader of the Southwest Parish and Neighborhood Federation, states that Washington received a poor reception at the white ethnic convention in 1984: "[He] listened to us say some not very nice things about him [but] showed a lot of guts and took it like a man."

39. Kelly, "Harold Washington's Balancing Act," pp. 182–83. Of blacks in the eleven largest metropolitan areas in the United States, blacks in Chicago ranked lowest overall in a number of social indicators. The disparity between white and black median family incomes was greatest ($25,644 versus $12,716 in 1980 income); the percentage of blacks below the poverty level was highest (34.5 percent); the difference in labor force participation rates between whites and blacks was greatest (66.3 percent for whites versus 56.6 percent for blacks). See Chicago Urban League, Research and Planning Department, *A Perspective on the Socio-Economic Status of Chicago-Area Blacks* (Chicago: Chicago Urban League, 1983).

40. Schrag, "Competing Demands for 'Our Fair Share,'" p. 7.

41. Julio Ojeda, "Analysis of Hispanic Precincts Shows Mexican/Puerto Rican Split," *Chicago Reporter* 16 (April 1987): 4; and Raymond Davis and Manuel Galvan, "Washington Wins at Wire," *Chicago Tribune*, February 25, 1987.

42. Sheila Jones, a member of the ultra right-wing political cult of Lyndon La Rouche, sought the Democratic mayoral nomination and received fewer than three thousand votes. See R. Bruce Dodd and Mitchell Locin, "Second Wave of Opponents Hits Mayor," *Chicago Tribune*, February 26, 1987.

43. Ojeda, "Analysis of Hispanic Precincts," pp. 3–4; and "Mayoral Vote 1983 and 1987," *Chicago Reporter* 16 (May 1987): 8.

44. Schrag, "Competing Demands for 'Our Fair Share,'" pp. 8–9.

45. Curtis Black, "Washington Out Front as Rivals Self-Destruct," *Guardian*, April 1, 1987.

46. Editorial, "Harold Washington for Mayor," *Chicago Tribune*, April 7, 1987; R. Bruce Dodd and John Camper, "Hynes Quits Race for Mayor," *Chicago Tribune*, April 6, 1987; and Mitchell Locin, "Candidacy Lacked Fire, Effective Plan," *Chicago Tribune*, April 6, 1987. Throughout the mayoral campaign, public-opinion polls consistently indicated that Vrdolyak was generally perceived as being "unfit to be mayor." In late March, 49 percent of registered voters polled stated that they were "absolutely opposed" to Vrdolyak. Thirty-six percent of all Hynes's supporters polled were also "absolutely opposed to Vrdolyak as mayor." Forty-four percent of all white voters had an "unfavorable" opinion of him. See R. Bruce Dodd, "Voters Reject Vrdolyak Pitch," *Chicago Tribune*, March 23, 1987.

47. Manuel Galvan, "Washington Stumps for Votes Right Up Until the End," *Chicago Tribune*, April 8, 1987; Mark Eissman and James Strong, "Mayor's Race Ends in Spring," *Chicago Tribune*, April 7, 1987; Schrag, "Washington Mutes Opposition But Gains Few New Supporters," *Chicago Tribune*, April 9, 1987; and Mitchell Locin and Manuel Galvan, "Mayor Grips Council's Reins," *Chicago Tribune*, April 9, 1987.

48. Data collected from exit polls by the Midwest Voter Registration Education Project showed that Mexican Americans supported Washington by 49.3 percent in the Democratic primary and by 76.1 percent in the general election. See "Hispanic Vote Analysis Faulty," *Chicago Reporter* 16 (July 1987): 11. Also see Julio Ojeda, "Hispanic Vote Split Again," *Chicago Reporter* 16 (May 1987): 9; and Schrag, "Washington Mutes Opposition But Gains Few New Supporters." The *Chicago Tribune* also estimated Washington's support within the four predominantly Hispanic wards at 62 percent in the general election.

49. Robert Davis and Terry Wilson, "Mayor Seen Keeping Control of City Council," *Chicago Tribune*, April 8, 1987; Dean Baquet and Ann Marie Lipinski, "Lucky 13 Are Council's Class of '87," *Chicago Tribune*, April 9, 1987; Dirk Johnson, "Washington, Victorious in Chicago, Is in Control," *New York Times*, April 9, 1987; and Dirk Johnson, "Chicago Mayor Gains Power in Party," *New York Times*, June 26, 1987.

50. Curtis Black, "Re-Elected Mayor to Push 'Action Agenda,'" *Guardian*, April 22, 1987.

51. Abdul Alkalimat, "Mayor Washington's Bid for Re-Election: Will the Democratic Party Survive?" *Black Scholar* 17 (November–December 1986): 7, 12–13; and Curtis Black, "How Should Left Relate to Washington?" *Guardian*, June 24, 1987.

10. The Rhetoric of Racial Harmony

Originally published in *Sojourners* 19, no. 7 (August–September 1990): 14–18.

11. Black Fundamentalism: Louis Farrakhan and the Politics of Conservative Black Nationalism

1. Peter Drier, "What Farrakhan Left Out: Labor Solidarity or Racial Separatism?" *Commonweal* 122, no. 22 (December 15, 1995): 10–11. For general interpretation of the Million Man March and its political aftermath inside black America, see Manning Marable, *Speaking Truth to Power: Essays on Race, Resistance, and Radicalism* (Boulder: Westview, 1996), pp. 139–45.

2. See Edwin S. Redkey, *The Flowering of Black Nationalism: Henry McNeal Turner and Marcus Garvey* (New York: Vintage, 1974), pp. 236–41; and Alphonso Pinkney, *Red, Black, and Green: Black Nationalism in the United States* (New York: Cambridge University Press, 1976).

3. E. Franklin Frazier, "Garvey: A Mass Leader," in John Henrik Clarke, ed., *Marcus Garvey and the Vision of Africa* (New York: Vintage, 1974), pp. 236—41.

4. Doug Gutknecht, "The Importance of Symbolic and Cultural Politics in the Marcus Garvey Movement," *Mid-American Review of Sociology* 7, no. 1 (1982): 87–107.

5. Mattias Gardell, *In the Name of Elijah Muhammad: Louis Farrakhan and the Nation of Islam* (Durham: Duke University Press, 1996), p. 272.

6. Quoted in Thomas Spence Smith, "The Release of the Romantic Impulse: Charisma and Its Transformations," *Current Perspectives in Social Theory* 10 (1990): 31–62.

7. Ibid., pp. 31–62.

8. There is a substantial body of sociological literature on the politics of charisma and charismatic leadership. Some references include K. Miyahara, "Charisma: From Weber to Contemporary Sociology," *Sociological Inquiry* 53 (1983): 368–88; and C. Camic, "Charisma: Its Varieties, Preconditions, and Consequences," *Sociological Inquiry* 50 (1980): 5–23.

9. Elijah Muhammad held a private meeting with Martin Luther King Jr. in Chicago on February 23, 1966. The meeting did little to improve the relations between the two leaders. See Claude Andrew Clegg III, *An Original Man: The Life and Times of Elijah Muhammad* (New York: St. Martin's Press, 1997), pp. 131, 195–96, 237–38.

10. Ibid., p. 253.

11. Elijah Muhammad was deeply hostile to communism. See ibid., p. 156.

12. Ibid., pp. 272–73.

13. Gardell, *In the Name of Elijah Muhammad*, p. 273.

14. Ibid., p. 274.

15. Ibid., pp. 321, 335–37.

16. Ibid., pp. 275–77.

17. See Dennis King, *Lyndon La Rouche and the New American Fascism* (New York: Doubleday, 1989).

18. "Lyndon La Rouche: Beyond the Fringe," *Newsweek*, April 7, 1986.

19. See James Ridgeway, "Lyndon La Rouche in the Can: Where the Wild Things Are," *Village Voice* 34, no. 8 (February 21, 1989).

20. Eugene H. Methvin, "Lyndon La Rouche's Raid on Democracy," *Reader's Digest* 129, no. 772 (August 1986): 90–94.

21. William Bastone, "Roy: No Pride and Joy," *Village Voice* 33, no. 28 (July 12, 1988).

22. A. Philip Randolph Institute, "La Rouche Fringe Really Anti-Black?" *Atlanta Voice*, April 12–18, 1986.

23. Benjamin F. Chavis, "La Rouche Invades Black Community," *New York Voice*, August 2, 1986.

24. "Day of Resistance Against Neo-Nazis," *New Solidarity*, March 5, 1985.

25. "Leaders of 1960s Civil Rights Movement Endorse La Rouche–Bevel," *New Federalist*, October 26, 1992.

26. Gardell, *In the Name of Elijah Muhammad*, p. 278.

27. Charisse Jones, "Thousands Rally at United Nations on 'Day of Atonement,'" *New York Times*, October 17, 1996; and James L. Bevel, "World's Day of Atonement Was God Breaking In," *New Federalist*, October 28, 1986.

12. Black Leadership and Organized Labor: From Workplace to Community

Originally published in Steven Fraser and Joshua A. Freeman, ed., *Audacious Democracy: Labor, Intellectuals, and the Social Reconstruction of America*, pp. 199–212 (Boston: Houghton Mifflin, 1997).

1. Peter Drier, "What Farrakhan Left Out: Labor Solidarity or Racial Separatism?" *Commonweal* 122, no. 22 (December 15, 1995): 10–11.

2. William H. Harris, "The Black Labor Movement and the Fight for Social Advance," *Monthly Labor Review* 110, no. 8 (August 1987): 37–39.

3. Louis Uchitelle, "Union Goal of Equality Fails the Test of Time," *New York Times*, July 9, 1995.

4. James P. Smith, "Affirmative Action and the Racial Wage Gap," *American Economic Review* 83, no. 2 (Spring 1986): 14–27.

5. Norman Hill, "Blacks and the Unions: Progress Made, Problems Ahead," *Dissent* (Fall 1989): 496–500; Larry T. Adams, "Union Membership of Wage and Salary Employees in 1987," *Current Wage Developments* 40 (February 1988): 8; and Uchitelle, "Union Goal of Equality Fails the Test of Time."

6. Lori G. Kletzer, "Job Displacement, 1979–86: How Blacks Fared Relative to Whites," *Monthly Labor Review* 114, no. 7 (July 1991): 17–25.

7. Ibid., pp. 23–24.

8. Lou Ferleger and Jay R. Mandle, "Whose Common Destiny? African Americans and the US Economy," *Socialist Review* 20, no. 1 (January–March 1990): 151–57.

9. Gregory Defreitas, "Unionization Among Racial and Ethnic Minorities," *Industrial and Labor Relations Review* 46, no. 2 (January 1993): 284–301. Also see Opinion Research Service, *American Public Opinion Data* (Boston: Opinion Research Service, 1990); and Thomas A. Kochan, "How American Workers View Labor Unions," *Monthly Labor Review* 102, no. 4 (April 1979): 23–31.

10. Hill, "Blacks and the Unions," p. 497.

11. Bureau of Labor Statistics, "Union Members in 1995," Internet Homepage, February 16, 1996.

12. Douglas C. Lyons, "The Growing Clout of Black Labor Leaders," *Ebony* 44, no. 8 (June 1989): 40–46.

13. Drier, "What Farrakhan Left Out," p. 11.

14. Howard N. Fullerton Jr., "Labor Force Projections: The Baby Boom Moves On," *Monthly Labor Review* 114, no. 11 (November 1991): 31–44.

15. Ferleger and Mandle, "Whose Common Destiny?" p. 156.

16. Harris, "The Black Labor Movement and the Fight for Social Advance," p. 38.